The Economic Analysis of Universities

The Economic Analysis of Universities

Strategic Groups and Positioning

Susanne Warning

University of Trier and IAAEG, Germany

Edward Elgar
Cheltenham, UK • Northampton, MA, USA

Published by
Edward Elgar Publishing Limited
Glensanda House
Montpellier Parade
Cheltenham
Glos GL50 1UA
UK

Edward Elgar Publishing, Inc.
William Pratt House
9 Dewey Court
Northampton
Massachusetts 01060
USA

A catalogue record for this book is available from the British Library

Library of Congress Cataloguing in Publication Data

Warning, Susanne, 1975-
  The economic analysis of universities : strategic groups and positioning / Susanne Warning.
      p. cm.
  Includes bibliographical references and index.
  1. Public universities and colleges–Germany–Finance. 2. College costs–Germany–Econometric methods. I. Title.
  LB2342.2.G4W37 2007
  378.050943–dc22

                                                              2007000720

ISBN 978 1 84542 833 4

Printed and bound in Great Britain by MPG Books Ltd, Bodmin, Cornwall

Contents

Abbreviations

After WWII	Foundation after Second World War
AHI	Arts and Humanities Index
ApplU	University of Applied Sciences
ard	absolute research dominance
atd	absolute teaching dominance
av4	average over four years
av5	average over five years
BCC	Banker-Charnes-Cooper
CA	Cluster Analysis
cont.	continued
Corr	Correlation
Coun.	Country
crd	comparative research dominance
CRS	Constant Returns to Scale
ctd	comparative teaching dominance
DEA	Data Envelopment Analysis
Dep.	Department
DFG	Deutsche Forschungsgemeinschaft, German Research Foundation
e.g.	exemplum gratum
ECTS	European Credit Transfer System
FTE	Full Time Equivalents
GDP	Gross domestic product
GLS	Generalized Least Squares
I-O	Input-Orientation
i.e.	id est
ibid.	ibidem
IO	Industrial Organization
ISI	Institute for Scientific Information
MBA	Master of Business Administration
na	not available
no.	number of
O-O	Output-Orientation
OECD	Organisation for Economic Co-operation and Development
R	Research

R&D	Research and Development
ResearchQ	Research Quality
RQ	Research Quality
SCI	Science Citation Index
SciU	Scientific University
SCP	Structure Conduct Performance
SFA	Stochastic Frontier Analysis
SSCI	Social Science Citation Index
T	Teaching
T&R	Teaching and Research
TeachingQ	Teaching Quality
TQ	Teaching Quality
UK	United Kingdom
Univ.	Universities
US	United States
VRS	Variable Returns to Scale
ZA	Zivot-Andrews

Preface

When I began to work on the topic of university positioning in the year 2000, education, and higher education in particular, was on the verge of substantial changes and reforms in many countries. Discussions about performance and competition in the education sector, especially in the higher education sector, had started and intensified rapidly. University rankings became increasingly popular, even in Germany where universities previously had been considered on a par and the results of the PISA study directed attention to the education sector in general. As more and more rankings appeared in academic journals and in magazines, and proposals for reforms were put forward, education and especially higher education moved to the centre of interest for policy makers and the general public. Increased competition, manifest in a higher mobility of students and researchers as well as in higher awareness of performance and accountability, brought positioning of higher education institutions in this new competitive environment into the centre of discussion.

This book provides a theoretical and empirical analysis of strategic positioning of public universities, the type of institution to which the new competitive environment poses the greatest challenge. It will be shown that publicly funded universities are able to position themselves and have been positioning themselves for many years. Teaching and research quality serve as the two main strategic variables of universities, even in the absence of direct monetary incentives for providing high quality. The choice of quality levels in these two attributes determines a university's position in a national higher education sector. There are of course, other factors beyond the immediate control of university management that influence the university's position. Data from German public universities will be used to empirically test the theoretical reasoning.

After giving basic information on German higher education as an example of a university sector dominated by public institutions and presenting a selective survey of the literature on differences in universities' choices, i.e., heterogeneity, the book develops two theoretical approaches for the analysis of public universities. The first one, the concept of strategic groups, originates from management theory. It implies that due to different returns on investment, for the two dimensions teaching quality and research quality, there will be heterogeneity in the university sector. The second, a three-stage duopoly game of competition between universities, is motivated by the industrial economics literature. Universities in this model position themselves in terms of teaching quality and research quality in order to attract students. In equilibrium universities choose to be different from each other to enjoy a strategic effect. They differentiate maximally in one dimension and minimally in the other.

Using data for German publicly funded universities, the empirical tests apply Data Envelopment Analysis and econometric methods. Empirical evidence suggests that the strategic variables, teaching quality and research quality, affect productivity heterogeneously in the sense that their influence is significantly higher for the top universities than for the other institutions. There is heterogeneity across German universities that on closer inspection leads to the idea of a group structure based on performance. While the empirical analysis is based on German data, the theory and the empirical results offer important insights for all countries with a sector of higher education where publicly funded universities play a role.

Like every author of a book, I owe much to many people. This is the time and opportunity to express my deep gratitude to those who accompanied, inspired and guided me on this long journey.

The book originates from work done for my dissertation at the department of economics at the University of Konstanz, Germany, which I completed in spring 2005. During these years at Konstanz I had the privilege to enjoy the extremely stimulating atmosphere at the department and to grow familiar with a competitive research-oriented environment. In Konstanz I benefited especially from intensive and inspiring discussions with Professor Oliver Fabel. As my supervisor he directed my attention to the higher education sector and gave me the freedom to pursue my own way. I am very grateful to Oliver Fabel for the atmosphere in his research group, for the motivation to participate in conferences and establish first contacts in the scientific community and for his outstanding and continuing support. His influence was much stronger than he may have realized at that time.

I am also very grateful to Professor Dieter Sadowski who was on my dissertation committee. He provided me with a great work environment at the Institute for Labour Law and Industrial Relations in the European Union at the University of Trier, Germany, during the final stages of the project. His critical comments and questions undoubtedly helped to improve the book.

Over time, I have enjoyed very helpful discussions with former and current colleagues. At the University of Konstanz I am grateful to Bodo Hilgers, Gerald Eisenkopf, Erik Lueders, Dirk Schindler and Ulrich Wacker. To Erik E. Lehmann I am especially grateful for many very helpful discussions at the early stages of the project and for our close cooperation during our time at Konstanz. At the Institute for Labour Law and Industrial Relations in the European Union I am grateful to Catharina Leilich, Mihai Paunescu and Martin Schneider. For technical support, especially in the final stage of the book, I want to thank Helena Frick. For proofreading I am very grateful to Douglas Bice and Adam M.

Lederer who read different versions of the manuscript very carefully.

Parts of the research for this book were undertaken while I was a visiting researcher at the Institute for Developing Strategies at Indiana University's School of Public and Environmental Affairs in Bloomington, USA, in 2003. I benefited greatly from discussions with David B. Audretsch on various issues related to universities. I am grateful for his hospitality and his benevolence and encouragement, which have outlasted the dissertation project. Furthermore, I am grateful to Rui Baptista and Adam M. Lederer for numerous discussions on higher education systems.

I also want to thank Mikulas Luptacik for the hospitality at the Institute for Quantitative Economics at the Vienna University of Economics and Business Administration, Austria. He provided me with the opportunity to become familiar with Data Envelopment Analysis. For many discussions I am also grateful to Dieter Gstach.

I am very grateful to John J. Siegfried for constructive comments on a main paper and to participants of the International Industrial Organization Conference 2003 in Boston, USA, who motivated and encouraged me to continue working on this topic. Comments and suggestions from participants of the conferences of the Allied Social Sciences Association, the European Economic Association, the European Association for Research in Industrial Economics, the European Association of Labour Economists, the German Economic Association and the German Economic Association for Business Administration and a number of workshops also helped to improve this book.

Three anonymous referees from Edward Elgar provided extremely detailed and helpful comments. I want to express my deep gratitude to those colleagues whose suggestions helped to improve my analysis and to make my line of reasoning more compelling. I am also grateful for the support and advice from Francine O'Sullivan and Jo Betteridge at Edward Elgar who steered my book project with benevolence and efficiency.

Vera E. Troeger proved to be a dear and reliable friend and a competent and supportive colleague especially in discussions on methodological issues. To her I want to express my deep gratitude, as I do to Thomas Plümper and Peter Welzel for their unfailing support and willingness to discuss ends, sometimes loose, and to serve as sounding boards for ideas, sometimes callow. During this project they gave me encouragement, assured me of the worthiness of my efforts and told me about the new challenges awaiting me.

For financial support I am grateful to the Universitätsgesellschaft Konstanz which awarded me with the Promotionsförderpreis in 2002 and thus supported my stay at Indiana University. To EADS, Friedrichshafen, I am very grateful for the Dornier Forschungspreis 2006.

The usual qualifying remark applies; none of the above mentioned is to be held responsible for the final contents of this work or for any error contained within it.

1 Introduction

Higher education, especially when it is publicly funded, receives increased scrutiny from politicians and the public as competition in this sector increases. This book contributes to the examination of higher education, using examples drawn from Germany. Section 1.1 motivates and introduces the line of the argument of this book. To illustrate its logic and intuition, Section 1.2 presents the organization of the study.

1.1 MOTIVATION

Higher education is a service sector moving towards a more competitive environment both nationally and internationally. Governments in a number of countries have recently taken steps to reform and strengthen their university systems. These reforms may be particularly relevant where publicly funded universities play a dominant role, as, for example, in Germany. There are a number of interesting questions that arise when we look at public universities in a competitive environment: If government provides financial means primarily on the basis of an institution's size, do they compete in quality? What is the role of research quality and teaching quality in such competition? Will these public universities turn out to be homogeneous or will they differ as a result of competition? When we look at the literature, we find that there is a lack of both theoretical and empirical research on public universities of the type found in Europe. This book helps to fill the gap in the economics of universities literature by showing theoretically and empirically how such institutions position themselves in competition. While the empirical analysis is based on German data, the results offer important insights for all countries where publicly funded universities play an important role in providing higher education.

If we take Germany as an example, we observe that international comparisons of universities have gained more and more attention during recent years. In worldwide rankings of higher education institutions, performance of German universities is rather weak. Universities from the United States, such as Harvard, Berkeley, Stanford and MIT, or from Britain, such as Cambridge and Oxford, typically hold the top ranks in international comparisons. According to the most reliable of these global rankings, only one German institution – the Technical University of Munich – is placed among the top 50 universities in the world (Ranking of World Universities 2004).

Public institutions of higher education in Germany neither choose quality-related tuition as a price signal, nor do they systematically build up reputation by hiring outstanding researchers. Scholars working at American academic institutions have won about ten times more Nobel Prizes than the scholars from all German academic institutions together. Among politicians, prospective students and the general public, awareness of the quality of higher education in Germany has risen considerably. Against this background, German politicians have recently begun a discussion on how to improve the performance of German universities. As yet, their best idea seems to be a quality contest among German universities for excellence programs, in which the winners will receive higher funding.

At first sight, this does not look like a remarkable policy turnaround; however for Germany this change is not a trivial move, since in the past German policy always aimed to guarantee equal conditions in the German higher education sector. The concept of special financial support for 'elite universities' is therefore a new one. Traditionally, German universities of a similar size receive approximately equivalent transfers from the state governments, regardless of the quality they provide in teaching or in research. In addition, universities had only very limited freedom to select their students until very recently. Students in general are free to decide on the subject of study, on the length of study and on the university they want to attend. Most of these characteristics are more or less in a process of reform.

A closer look at German universities reveals that despite the politicians' preoccupation with equality there is dispersion in the performance of these institutions. No doubt German universities are more homogeneous than their US counterparts, still there is considerable variation in quality. In short: there is heterogeneity among German universities. This immediately raises important research questions with policy implications: Where does this observed heterogeneity come from in a system of public funding for universities, designed to establish institutions of equal quality? In which dimensions do universities actually differ?

This study provides new insights into the competitive behavior of public universities in general and the structure and conduct in German higher education in particular. Two theoretical approaches – one from management theory, the other from industrial organization – will be transferred and adapted to the sector of higher education in Germany. Applying the theoretical concepts, while taking into account important institutional factors such as public funding of universities or the absence of tuition and fees, provides new insights into the behavior of German universities and the structure evolving in German higher education. Results show that it makes sense for universities to be heterogeneous with respect to teaching quality or research quality. These are the two strategic variables that drive the theoretical part of this study. In the empirical part of this study, another aspect is highlighted: Universities differ in their overall performance. Clusters or groups of high-ranked and low-ranked universities can be identified and the strategic variables teaching quality and research quality, supplemented by variables beyond the short- or medium-term control of university management, such as the competitive environment, regional factors and university characteristics like size or composition of fields, explain group membership. The empirical analysis in this study tests three hypotheses on heterogeneity and the role of teaching quality and research quality. It provides empirical tests for the theoretical approaches and confirms the relevance of the theoretical insights as the hypotheses cannot be rejected.

Teaching and research quality serve as the two main strategic variables of universities, even in the absence of direct monetary incentives for providing high quality levels. Influencing quality levels in these attributes determines, jointly with other factors beyond the immediate control of university management, a university's position in the national higher education sector. These two strategic variables have an impact on the performance of universities, which will be measured in the empirical analysis by a Data Envelopment Analysis score of overall efficiency. Both in the theoretical and in the empirical part of the study, strategic variables are found to influence the structure of the university sector.

The concept of strategic groups, which is the first of the two theoretical approaches applied to German universities in this study, originates from management theory. In its original version it explains why firms in an industry form a group structure with homogeneous performance within the group and heterogeneous performance between groups. This can immediately be transferred to the university sector. Specific investments act as barriers to mobility between groups and play a prominent role in this concept. Heterogeneity in the sector is the result of different returns to investment in research quality and investments in teaching quality. Universities investing in high research quality – by hiring top researchers or by improving research conditions – improve their reputation, resulting in a relatively long-lasting comparative advantage. The concept of strategic groups describes how these specific investments work like barriers to mobility. If a university wants to enter the group of high-ranked universities, it has to undertake research-related investments even though the returns of these investments will be apparent only later.

Furthermore, the impact on performance of teaching quality and research quality differs between high-ranked and low-ranked universities. This holds especially for research quality as the empirical analysis confirms. Quality has a higher impact for high-ranked universities than for low-ranked universities. Non-linear returns on investments explain these different effects on the two groups of universities. Neither potential employers nor students observe a university's small improvements in research. Only if a university ranks among the very best universities in a specific discipline, does quality become known to the public. Whether a department performs poorly or is just average is hardly known to the public. As a consequence, improving research quality at higher ranked universities has a stronger impact on productivity than it has at low-ranked universities. Thus, different returns to investments in teaching quality and research quality lead universities to choose different positions in these two dimensions, as increasing quality for the low-ranked group promises less success than for the high-ranked group. Taken together, universities become more heterogeneous and a group structure evolves.

The second of the two theoretical approaches applied is a duopoly model of a three-stage game where universities position themselves in terms of teaching quality and research quality in order to attract students whose preferences are heterogeneous. In the first stage, universities choose teaching and research quality. Then they decide on the support level they want to provide to their students. Finally, students choose a university on the basis of teaching quality, research quality and the support level the university offers. These support levels capture the fact that German students do not have to pay tuition and fees and at the same time enjoy several infrastructure benefits from their university. In equilibrium universities choose to be different from each other to enjoy a strategic effect. They differentiate maximally in one dimension and only minimally in the other. The analysis shows that maximum differentiation prevails in the dimension where the interval of quality levels is larger. At this point an insight from the first theoretical approach, the concept of strategic groups, can be used to identify the dimension with maximum differentiation. The concept of strategic groups implies that heterogeneity in research is greater than in teaching, which is confirmed by the empirical analysis. Therefore, the equilibrium with maximum differentiation in research quality and minimum differentiation in teaching quality is the most plausible outcome from the industrial economics model of university positioning. As a result, research should have a higher impact on the probability of being in the high-ranked or low-ranked group of universities. Again, the empirical analysis confirms this insight.

Empirical evidence suggests that the strategic variables, teaching quality and research quality, have a productivity-increasing impact in German universities. However this impact is not the same for all universities, which causes the formation of groups in the sector. As claimed earlier, teaching quality and research quality affect productivity heterogeneously in the sense that their influence is significantly higher for the top universities than for the other institutions. In addition, the influence for being among the high-ranked universities based on productivity in Germany is higher from research quality than from teaching quality. Both empirical findings suggest heterogeneity across German universities, which on closer inspection leads to the idea of a group structure based on performance.

Combining two theoretical explanations for heterogeneity in higher education

– strategic groups and the formal equilibrium model – this study contributes to the literature on the strategic positioning of public universities in an environment without market prices for higher education. To test both theoretical approaches and the hypotheses derived from them empirically, a new dataset for German public universities was created. While there is a strong focus on the strategic variables of teaching quality and research quality, a considerable number of other variables had to be collected in order to control for effects from outside the university. There can be no doubt that more detailed and systematic data would have facilitated the empirical analysis. Data limitations, however, are an almost ubiquitous problem in research. Given the need to combine theory with empirical tests, this study is a first and useful attempt to shed some light on heterogeneity in the German university system and to explain heterogeneity as the result of university decisions in a system politically designed to create and sustain homogeneity.

1.2 ORGANIZATION OF THE BOOK

The study is structured as follows: Chapter 2 provides information on the institutional background of German higher education and presents some stylized facts. Chapter 3 then surveys theoretical as well as empirical contributions found in the literature on university positioning and briefly introduces general explanations of heterogeneity in an industry. Chapters 4 and 5 develop two theoretical approaches to examine and explain positioning of German universities, taking into account the characteristics of a publicly financed university system. The theoretically derived hypotheses are tested in Chapters 6 and 7 using non-parametric and parametric empirical methods. To illustrate the relation of the chapters and their logical positions in the argument, Figure 1.2 displays these relations among the different parts of the book.

Chapter 2 presents some stylized facts and institutional information on German higher education that is overseen by the federal states. Coordinating institutions and the role of the federal government are briefly mentioned. Using a production-theoretic framework, I provide data on the main output factors, teaching and research, as well as on the main input factors, scientific staff and capital. Compared to other countries, German higher education shows a rather low rate of new entrants into the university system. Altogether, the findings suggest that universities position themselves not only internationally but also nationally.

Next, Chapter 3 reviews the literature on positioning of universities, focusing on the two main attributes of universities, teaching and research. There are theoretical explanations for how universities allocate resources to teaching and research. While literature provides few explanations for heterogeneity of universities, general theoretical approaches for firms in for-profit industries offer

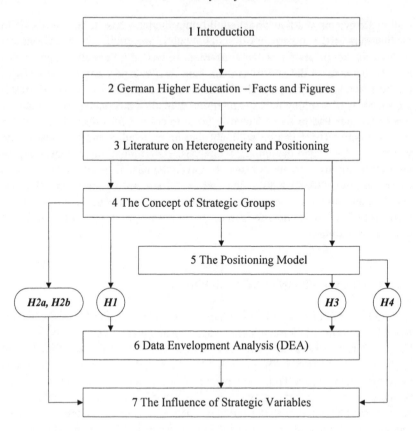

Figure 1.1   Relation of the Chapters

a variety of explanations for heterogeneity and different positioning of firms within a sector. The two approaches examined more in detail are the concept of strategic groups from management theory and the differentiation models from industrial organization. There are, however, empirical studies on higher education that put forward heterogeneity in teaching and in research, mapped by performance in these two dimensions. Also, studies on overall performance of universities are widespread and provide clues for the existence for heterogeneity.

Chapters 4 and 5 develop theoretical approaches for explaining heterogeneity in higher education. One-dimensional indicators in German higher education and overwhelming empirical evidence for heterogeneity beg for an explanation. Both approaches offered in Chapters 4 and 5 deal with positioning of universities in a higher education sector. Chapter 4 transfers the concept of strategic groups from business firms to universities, focusing on performance differences by examining teaching and research quality as strategic variables that influence a university's position. Different returns to teaching quality and research quality lead to a group structure in the sector of higher education. The hypotheses claim that heterogeneity is greater in research than in teaching (*H1*) and that the impact of teaching quality and of research quality is greater for the group of high-ranked universities than for the group of low-ranked universities (*H2a, H2b*). An explanation in the tradition of industrial organization in Chapter 5 supplements this explanation for heterogeneity originating from business administration.

Chapter 5 develops a two-dimensional formal differentiation model to reveal positioning of universities in equilibrium. Taking into account the stylized facts of German higher education, especially public financing and students paying no tuition and fees, the model concentrates on teaching and research as separate tasks of universities and predict equilibrium with maximum differentiation in one dimension and minimum differentiation in the other dimension. It hypothesizes that universities attach greater weights to teaching than to research (*H3*). Taking findings from the concept of strategic groups into account, I argue that maximum differentiation occurs in research, while minimum differentiation occurs in teaching. The hypothesis claims that the probability of being a high-ranked university depends more on research quality than on teaching quality (*H4*).

Based on data from 1997 through 2000, Chapters 6 and 7 test the hypotheses derived from the theory of strategic groups and the positioning model for German universities. Applying the non-parametric method of Data Envelopment Analysis, Chapter 6 empirically reveals not only heterogeneity in teaching and research (*H1*), but also overall performance differences across institutions of higher education in Germany. Chapter 7 examines these performance differences with econometric methods by considering teaching quality and research quality as strategic variables, controlling for given university characteristics, competitive factors and environmental variables which are not under the control of university management. Taken together, the results lend support to the hypothesis of strategic groups. They confirm the existence of a heterogeneous impact of research quality (and, respectively, teaching quality) on performance (*H2a, H2b*). Finding differences in the influence of the two strategic variables on membership of the high-ranked university group supports the positioning model (*H4*). To sum up, Chapters 6 and 7 provide empirical evidence for heterogeneity across German universities which results in a group structure suggested by the theoretical approaches in Chapters 4 and 5. Finally, Chapter 8 summarizes the results.

2 German Higher Education – Facts and Figures

There is strong evidence that investments in education, particularly in higher education, influence labor productivity and economic growth positively. As a result of low growth rates in Germany, compared to other OECD countries, politicians, firms and the media are to discussing the capability of German higher education to perform sufficiently well to serve the country in an increasingly competitive environment.

The purpose of this chapter is to review German higher education in general and also to reveal stylized facts. Within a production-theoretic framework it is assumed that institutions of higher education can be seen as modern production units that use capital and labor as input factors producing at least two outputs, teaching and research. Within this general framework the underlying chapter describes and analyzes the main factors of higher education institutions in Germany.

In recent years there have been a number of changes of lesser and greater importance that affect the way German higher education institutions are financed and run. These changes have taken place after the time period covered by my data. I will describe the most important ones briefly in this chapter and in the recent development section in the final chapter and will use the concluding remarks to comment on how the results of my analysis lend support to these new elements of higher education policy.

After some general remarks about the background of German higher education in Section 2.1, Sections 2.2 and 2.3 illustrate the two main outputs, teaching and research of universities, focusing on institutions that conduct both teaching and research to a substantial degree. Section 2.4 portrays the basic inputs of institutions of higher education: staff and expenditure. After that, Section 2.5 conducts an international comparison for selected countries again presenting teaching, research and expenditure related numbers in higher education.

All these sections are descriptive and do not focus on productivity or efficiency measures. Most sections concentrate on data from publications by the Federal Ministry of Education and Research as well as by the Federal Statistical Office ('Statistisches Bundesamt'). The international perspective uses data provided by OECD publications.

2.1   INSTITUTIONAL BACKGROUND OF GERMAN HIGHER EDUCATION

In 2003, the German higher education sector consisted of 373 institutions, cate-gorized into two groups: Scientific Universities ('Universitäten') and Universi-ties of Applied Sciences ('Fachhhochschulen') (Statistisches Bundesamt 2003a). This section discusses both types of higher education institutions, however Uni-versities of Applied Sciences (ApplUs) are excluded from the proceeding anal-ysis as they differ substantially in providing teaching and research, the main focus of the book. Nevertheless, they are an important part of German higher education so that this general institutional section includes them. According to the OECD definition both kinds count as higher education institutions. After discussing the main characteristics of these two types of higher education insti-tutions, we present briefly the role of state and federal government in German higher education.

The group of Scientific Universities (SciUs) includes all classical full uni-versities, Colleges of Theology, Colleges of Education and Colleges of Arts and Music which amount to 178 institutions together. Full universities – called 'universities' in the following – also include specialized institutions such as universities of medicine or sport and the former comprehensive universities ('Gesamthochschulen'). All six Colleges of Education are located in the state of Baden-Württemberg and specialize in providing training of teachers. Other training of teachers is integrated into the full universities. There are 17 Colleges of Theology consisting of independent institutions run by the Church as well as those state-owned Colleges of Philosophy and Theology. Finally, there are 52 Colleges of Arts and Music in Germany that provide education in visual arts, design, music, film and television. In contrast to other SciUs, applicants to these Colleges are expected to demonstrate special skills in these fields in order to enroll.

Scientific Universities are shaped by the 'Humboldtian' idea of unity of teach-ing and research implying that all professors are to engage in both teaching and research; this unity was introduced by 'Wilhelm von Humboldt' (1767–1835). In contrast to most other countries, there is no division between researchers and lecturers as the basic idea of Humboldt was to transfer research results to students and to guarantee that the education is research-related. The 195 Uni-versities of Applied Sciences focus primarily on teaching. They were mostly founded in the late 1970s as a result of the increasing demand for higher edu-cation and the increasing number of high-school graduates. In general, ApplUs are not expected to conduct research to the extent of SciUs. A special type of ApplUs, the Colleges of Public Administration, offers the education necessary for a career in the middle-level non-technical public sector.

Universities of Applied Sciences offer practically oriented education and fo-cus on the application of scientific methods. Courses are highly structured and classes are much smaller than those at SciUs. Furthermore, ApplUs, which are often well-connected to regional firms, educate students for specific jobs. As a consequence of their mostly applied focus, students typically enroll in the fields of business administration, engineering, social studies, agriculture and design. Transferring theoretical concepts into practice is the major concern of the ApplUs. Therefore, professors at ApplUs are expected to have at least two years working experience outside higher education institutions in addition to a doctoral degree. Table 2.1 summarizes the distribution of institutions of higher education in Germany by type in 2003.

Table 2.1   Types of Higher Education Institutions in Germany in 2003

Type of Institution	Number	Labelling
Universities	103	
Colleges of Education	6	Scientific Universities
Colleges of Theology	17	178
Colleges of Arts and Music	52	
Universities of Applied Sciences	164	Universities of
(without Colleges of Public Administration)		Applied Sciences
Colleges of Public Administration	31	195
Total	373	

Source: Data from Statistisches Bundesamt (2003a), p. 9.

The total number of higher education institutions has increased by 17 percent from 1992 to 2003. While the number of ApplUs has risen by 28 percent, the growth of the number of SciUs was smaller at about 8 percent (Statistisches Bundesamt 2003a). The larger expansion of ApplUs is a result of new private institutions emerging. SciUs and ApplUs, the two groups of institutions, do not only differ in their aims and scope, but also in size.

While 52.3 percent of the institutions of higher education in Germany are ApplUs, they matriculated 26.6 percent of the students. At the 178 SciUs, which comprise 47.7 percent of all higher education institutions, the total number of students captures 73.4 percent of the nation-wide enrollment. The average number of students at an ApplU is 2,467, while it is 7,993 at SciUs. The total students enrolled have been increasing almost continuously since the 1970s. Figure 2.1 presents the development of the number of students at SciUs and ApplUs.

In 2002, there were 1,422,688 students at SciUs and 516,123 students at ApplUs, of which 11.7 percent were foreign students (Statistisches Bundesamt 2003a). It is an increase of overall enrollment by 105 percent at SciUs and by 256 percent at ApplUs, since 1975. This enormous increase in students' enrollment has induced major changes in the higher education system in Germany. While the number of students was decreasing after the peak in 1993 (reunification of Germany in 1990) it reached new levels in 2002 at SciUs as well as at ApplUs. The ratio of new entrants – the number of new entrants into institutions of higher education as percentage of the population within a comparable age group – in SciUs has increased from 14 percent in 1975 to 23.8 percent in 1998. During the same time period the number of new entrants to ApplUs has more than doubled from 5 percent to 10.7 percent (KMK 1998, p. 26).

In comparison to other countries, in Germany new entrants to higher education (and also graduates) are relatively old. They start studying just after finishing high school (and often after an apprenticeship) at the age of 22.5 years at ApplUs and 21.0 years at universities. While the rate of new entrants in both SciUs and ApplUs approximately doubled from 1975 to 2000, the graduation rate at SciUs remained nearly constant, implying that the total increase from 13.4 to 16.6 is a result of the increasing ratio attending ApplUs (KMK 1998 and Statistisches Bundesamt 2003a). The graduation rate increase at ApplUs at 47.5 percent was much larger than for SciUs which only had an increase of 29.8 percent from 1975 to 2000. As a whole in Germany 35.1 percent of the reference group have graduated from institutions of higher education.

In contrast to most other policy areas in Germany the federal states have cultural autonomy and therefore they are mainly responsible for all aspects of education. For higher education there is a general framework given by the federal government, to ensure relatively homogenous standards. The law providing guidelines for higher education ('Hochschulrahmengesetz') regulates general issues of organization and administration, of research and study and of

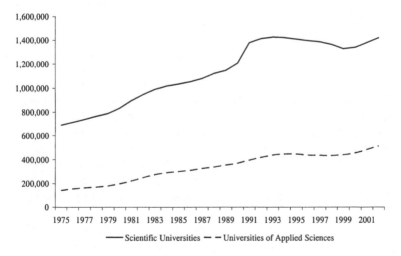

Source: Data from KMK (1998) and Statistisches Bundesamt (2003a)

Figure 2.1 Number of Students in Germany, 1975–2002

staffing. However within this framework the single states are free to regulate the details individually. To provide coordination between the different states and the federal government, a number of organizations have been created over the last decades ('Bund-Länder-Kommission für Bildungsplanung und Forschungs-förderung', 'Hochschulrektorenkonferenz', 'Kultusministerkonferenz', 'Wissenschaftsrat'). All these organizations serve the purpose of ensuring a similar quality of teaching and research across institutions and across states.

German higher education institutions are publicly funded and students were not charged tuition and fees until very recently. Even if there has not been a legal decision on tuition and fees, state presidents agreed on not charging students since 1970.[1] After some political discussion on the federal and state level from 1998 to 2002, the federation passed a law that free access to higher education for one qualified degree to each person. However the Constitutional Court rejected this law because it is not in the jurisdiction of the federation to decide on tuition and fees of public universities. Therefore, the single states plan individual models for charging tuition and fees. A number of states has decided to introduce tuition of 1000 Euros per year for all students at a university in the state. However there are also states that have decided not to introduce tuition and fees at that point. But up to now, most states charge tuition and fees (around 1000 Euros per year) to those students that study for longer than five to six years or exceed the age of 60 (confirmed by court). All in all, the system is in an evolutionary state and things are changing very rapidly.

All students who are qualified have access to public higher education. The required appropriate qualification for SciUs is the 'Abitur' (regularly after 13 years schooling), for ApplUs the qualification required is the 'Abitur' or the 'Fachhochschulreife' (regularly 12 years of schooling plus 6 months practical experience). Application at ApplUs is also possible after certain types of further education.

Private institutions only play a minor rule. Mostly they offer only a limited number of fields, often concentrated on social sciences. Although, the number of privately run universities increased from 19 in 1992 to 62 in 2003 (Statistisches Bundesamt 2003a, p. 10), this increase of institutions is mostly based on new ApplUs. In 2000, only ten out of 96 full universities were privately funded and 51 out of 154 ApplUs were private institutions (BMBF 2002, p. 151). In 2002, around 14 percent of institutions of higher education were run privately, but they enrolled only 1.7 percent of all students and are rather small with an average size of 652 students.

Public institutions of higher education play an important role in German higher education.[2] The following analysis concentrates only on Scientific Universities: first, they enroll the largest number of students. Second, SciUs (in contrast to ApplUs) conduct two tasks, teaching and research, simultaneously. As there are no market prices of teaching or research, the distribution of resources and evaluation of tasks may be difficult and is examined more closely.

2.2   TEACHING AT GERMAN UNIVERSITIES

After presenting the main institutional features of the German higher education system, this section focuses on teaching at SciUs. Although some institutions have started student evaluations of teaching and faculty reviews, there is no generally accepted, standardized evaluation procedure in Germany yet.

SciUs differ in size, measured by number of students, with universities being the largest type of institution. On average, full universities have 13,601 students. While the largest institution of higher education in 2001 had an enrollment of 61,292 students, there were also 12 universities with fewer than 500 students (Statistisches Bundesamt 2003b). With an enrollment of 1,346,500 students in 2001 universities are the largest group of SciUs, followed by the Colleges of Arts and Music with 29,883 students. Even though there are only six Colleges of Education, they are third in number of students with 16,432 students. In 2001, the 17 Colleges of Theology had only 2,284 students combined (Statistisches Bundesamt 2003b).

Durations of study until the first degree (diploma, master; not bachelor) vary across institutions and even more across fields of study. Most students exceed the anticipated study time by two or more years. Based on data from 2000 it appears to take 6.7 years of study at a university to receive a first degree. The average age of a student is 28 years at completion. Average study duration at Colleges of Education was 5.0 years (average age 26.6 years), at Colleges of Theology 7.5 years (average age 30.0 years), at the Colleges of Arts and Music 6.6 years (average age 28.1 years). The average duration of study in 2000 was 6.1 years and the average age at passing the first examination was 28.2 years varying across institutions (Federal Ministry of Education and Research 2002, p. 114).

Another important characteristic of German students is a considerable immobility. Only 31 percent of new entrants choose to study in a state different from the one where they gained their entry qualification. Among the mobile students, 18.3 percent start studying in a neighboring state. This observation does not differ significantly across fields (KMK 2002). Economics students – who can safely be assumed to be at least as rational as other students – do not choose their location to study based on objective criteria of the university, such as quality. They tend to start studying at places with a pleasant environment (Fabel et al. 2002).

The structure of studies is different from most other higher education systems. Undergraduate and graduate degrees are not common in German higher education. This, however, will change in the near future due to the 'Bologna Process'. In fact, some universities/departments have recently introduced bachelor and master degrees. The traditional German Diploma (or 'Staatsexamen' for teachers and graduates in law and medicine) consists of two phases that are completed with an intermediate exam, the 'Vordiplom' and the Diploma. However the 'Vordiplom' does not count as an academic degree as the Bachelor does. Basically, there are two types of degrees in the German system: the diploma and the teaching qualification that is required to become teacher.

Students receiving a diploma composed the largest group of graduates. In 2000, about 95,000 students graduated with a diploma and about 27,000 students graduated with a teaching qualification. Figure 2.2 shows the number of diplomas and teaching qualifications conferred in the different fields of study at German SciUs in 2000.

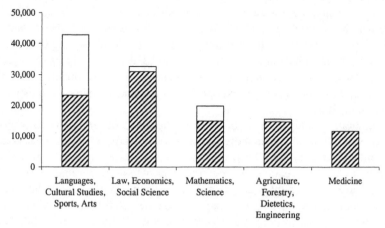

☑ Diploma ☐ Teaching Qualifications

Source: Data from Federal Ministry of Education and Research (2002)

Figure 2.2   Diploma and Teaching Qualifications Awarded in 2000

Graduates receiving diplomas in law, economics and social sciences (31,000) are the largest group, followed by the graduates from languages, cultural studies, sports and arts (23,000). Graduates from mathematics and natural sciences are in third place in number of diplomas awarded (14,900), with engineering, agriculture, forestry and dietetics a close fourth (14,700). About 11,600 students in 2000 graduated in medicine. Dominant fields include languages, cultural studies, sports and arts. With 19,500 graduates they are not only dominant among the teaching qualifications, but also account for almost half of the total graduates. The dominance of this field is due to the importance of languages at schools. In mathematics and science about 4,900 teaching qualifications were earned.

With the ongoing 'Bologna-Process' universities must start offering or introducing internationally comparable bachelor and master degrees. However out of 208,606 examinations in 2002, there were only 985 bachelors' and 2,150 masters' degrees (Statistisches Bundesamt 2003a, p. 18).

In summary, German students enter higher education relatively late in their life. The two main degrees awarded by SciUs vary across fields. Teaching qualifications comprise the majority in languages, cultural studies, sports and arts, while the majority of diplomas are awarded in law, economics and social science.

2.3 RESEARCH AT GERMAN UNIVERSITIES

Within a production-theoretic framework, the second output of German universities is research. Although, research institutes, for example the Max-Planck Institutes and industry, play an important role in conducting research, SciUs also have a significant role in conducting research and designing innovations. In 2001, higher education institutions spent 8,524 million Euros on research and development, while the federal government and private nonprofit spent 2,146 million Euros. Both sums are small relative to firms, which spent 36,350 million Euros (Statistisches Bundesamt 2003b). While firms usually concentrate on applied research, universities can conduct basic research as they do not have the pressure to use the results immediately. Consequently, they can take greater risks.

Research can be measured in various ways. Generally accepted research performance indicators are the number of publications in refereed journals (Dusansky and Vernon 1998), the number of citations (Laband 1985), the number of presentations at reviewed conferences (Hinshaw and Siegfried 1994; Kirman and Dahl 1994) and the value of external research grants (Thursby 2000). While in the US system the number of PhDs awarded measures research quality (Siegfried 1972; Thursby 2000), employing this measure in the German system is not appropriate. As the number of doctoral students might result from a large number of external students, this number is not necessarily correlated with research quality. Instead, the number of habilitations can be applied as a performance indicator for research. This formal qualification to become a professor at a SciU requires conducting research successfully (Welsch and Ehrenheim 1999). Therefore, a high number of habilitations suggests a high research output at an institution.

Measuring research of SciUs in German higher education puts the three indicators in the following sequence: the number of publications, the amount of research grants and the number of habilitations. As in most fields scholars publish new research results in journals in order to present them to other researchers and to the interested public, we utilize the number of publications in scientific journals to measure research. Considering only refereed journals captures the quality as well as the quantity of academic research. Publications in reviewed journals exhibit a certain quality standard and in this way they serve as an external quality signal for the SciU. The number of publications accounts for the quantity dimension. Research grants also represent an external evaluation, as successfully applying for grants requires either a profound theoretical research agenda or it requires applied research in which industry or firms are interested. Grants from industry and public institutions are based on an external evaluation and thus present a research quality indicator for the university. Finally, the habilitation is still the dominant formal qualification for a tenured professorship at German SciUs. In contrast to publications and grants, the number of habilitations of a SciU is based on internal evaluations.

While there is significant data related to teaching, research-related data for German universities are rare, especially with respect to publications. No overall research performance ranking of institutions based on publication data is available. Empirical studies reviewing research performance of German universities are very scarce and mostly deal with economics or business administration departments. Based on publications, Bommer and Ursprung (1998) evaluate economics departments in Austria, Germany and Switzerland. Fabel and Heße (1999) present a ranking of German-speaking business departments and find only a low correlation with public media rankings. An extended study was recently published by the Science Council (Wissenschaftsrat 2002a) that presents a bibliometric analysis of German economics and business administration departments and gives recommendations to improve research. Finally, there is the research ranking of the 'Centrum für Hochschulforschung', which mainly produces field-specific rankings based on criteria that are collected from various field-specific databases (Berghoff et al. 2005).

To provide an overall picture of research performance based on publications of German higher education institutions, the Citation Indexes from the Institute for Scientific Information (ISI) were searched. This database consists of selected high quality journals separated by the fields of social sciences, natural sciences and arts and humanities. The number of publications by authors with German affiliations in the ISI Citation Indexes was examined for 1990 to 2000 to describe the development in Germany in terms of publications and exhibit differences across fields.

In absolute numbers the publications in the Science Citation Index (SCI) are highest for Germany. For German institutions of higher education, there were 30,093 publications in 1990. In 2000, publications numbered 52,816, an increase of 15.5 percent. The second largest group is the publications in the Social Science Citation Index (SSCI) that numbered 2,033 in 1990 and increased by 91.1 percent to 3,885 in 2000. Different publication strategies and lengths of publications may explain the difference between these disciplines. With 1,552 publications the Arts and Humanities Index (AHI) shows the smallest number of publications in 2000, an increase of only 28.3 percent since 1990. Figure 2.3 shows the fraction of publications for 1990 to 2000 published by authors affiliated with German institutions of higher education in relation to the total number of publication in the citation indexes.

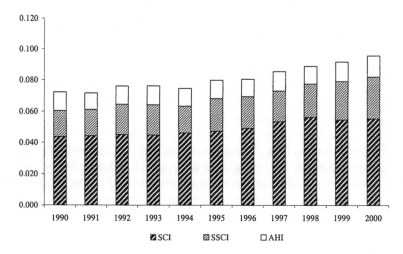

Source: Evaluation of data in the Social Science Citation Index (SSCI), the Science Citation Index (SCI) and the Arts and Humanities Index (AHI) by ISI.

Figure 2.3 Proportion of Publications of German Universities

Figure 2.3 shows that not only the absolute number of publications by Germans has increased over time, but also the German share of the total number of publications in the citation indexes. The distribution of publications by field within Germany remained relatively stable. Consequently, the relative presence of publications of German affiliated researchers has increased to almost 10 percent in 2000.

In addition to publications as a direct research output, externally provided grants also serve as an indicator of research of SciUs. In Germany various institutions offer external grants to institutions of higher education. Financing institutions vary across fields and the kind of research supported. There are funding institutions with special foci like the 'Alexander von Humboldt Stiftung' which mainly supports international contacts between researchers not focused on special disciplines. Otherwise, the 'Deutsche Forschungsgemeinschaft' (DFG, German Science Foundation) offers grants to almost all disciplines. Public organizations dedicate about two-thirds of external grants to higher education institutions. The share of industry grants is approximately 25 percent. Within the public sector, funding from the German Science Foundation (DFG) has the highest share (and reputation) (35 percent of all grants), followed by projects financed by the federal government (23 percent of all grants) (Wissenschaftsrat 2000a, p. 61).

As a third research measure for SciUs the number of habilitations – the formal qualification to teach in a tenured position at a SciU – is evaluated. This number demonstrates the human capital output in research. Young researchers, especially those who want to complete the habilitation, are very active researchers, as passing the habilitation requires significant research activity. Furthermore, universities do not have an incentive to approve the habilitation of young researchers if there is not a reasonable opportunity for employment as a professor. And, if universities do not limit habilitations just to promising candidates, the candidates themselves will select those universities or departments which offer good research conditions.

Although the information is of limited value in Germany, the number of doctoral degrees awarded (Welsch and Ehrenheim 1999; Ursprung 2003), Figure 2.4 displays the number of habilitations and doctoral degrees given by fields in 2000. One reason to consider this measure is that at least one federal state applies these numbers for performance-based resource allocation (Fandel and Gal 2001).

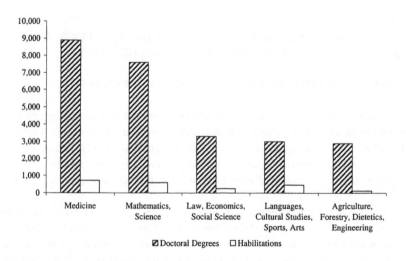

Source: Data from BMBF (2002), p. 220.

Figure 2.4   Absolute Number of Habilitations and Doctoral Degrees in 2000

Apparently, the absolute number of habilitations and doctoral degrees correlates closely across fields. Almost one third of the doctoral degrees in 2000 were conferred in medicine. This totaled 8,900 degrees. In mathematics and natural sciences the number of doctoral degrees came close to that level. Looking at habilitations, for all disciplines, medicine holds the largest share. This distribution is similar to the one for the number of doctoral degrees. One explanation for this observation might be the value a habilitation holds also outside the university system in medicine as well as in mathematics and the natural sciences. Presumably, the habilitation confers reputation and/or prestige and enhances promotion and employment opportunities. There were 714 habilitations in medicine, 587 in mathematics and science, 253 in law, economics and social science, 453 in languages, cultural studies, sports and arts, but only 121 in agriculture, forestry, dietetics and engineering in 2000.

Summarizing the results for research in German SciUs, the impact of German researchers across fields has increased in recent years. Close to 10 percent of publications in the Citation Indexes are from researchers with German affiliations. The number of habilitations in medicine and the natural sciences exceeds the number in the social sciences and other areas.

2.4   FINANCING AND STAFF IN GERMAN HIGHER EDUCATION

The German higher education system is mostly publicly funded and as a result of the federal structure, the federal and the single states governments finance higher education. As a consequence of the states being principally responsible for higher education, they provide the major part of financing for the public institutions. The federation contributes to financing buildings and to offering specific programmes for higher education. Apart from this basic financing, higher education institutions, additionally, apply for grants for teaching and research at public and private organizations ('Drittmittel'). However universities also offer services that are 'sold'. Medical departments and associated university hospitals, provide the major part of this income ('Einnahmen'). Together with other income, such as that provided by sponsorships and the sale of assets, they constitute administrative income ('Verwaltungseinnahmen').

While in 2000 the federal government spent about €2.4 billion for higher education, the 16 states collectively spent €16.28 billion. More precisely, federal government funds one half of buildings and large equipment and states finance the other half. As several hospitals belong to departments of medicine, a large share of universities' budgets is financed by private households and health insurance in an indirect way (€9.8 billion) (Statistisches Bundesamt 2003c).

To provide some more information on financing of German higher education, the three components of income and spending of higher education institutions as well as the so-called basic financing amount, is discussed. In 2001, German higher education institutions spent about €29.8 billion (€12.12 billion for Scientific Universities, excluding medical departments). As German universities follow the principle of 'unity of teaching and research' (see Section 2.1), it is difficult to decompose this total into funds for teaching and funds for research. However it can be stated that about €17.5 billion are spent on personnel (€8.14 billion for SciUs), €8 billion on ongoing costs of materials, €3.2 billion on investments, and the remaining €2.2 billion on pension and insurance for civil servants and further spending. Expenditure varies across types of higher education institutions. The major part, 46.3 percent (which is €13.3 billion) goes to medical organizations of universities, including hospitals. Excluding medical services, about 43.3 percent (€12.6 billion) is spent on SciUs. Income of higher education institutions split up into administrative income ('Verwaltungseinnahmen') of €9.0 billion and external grants ('Drittmittel'), which amount to €3.1 billion. Medical services generate the majority of administrative income (94.3 percent). External research grants are mainly acquired by Scientific universities (70.3 percent, excluding medical organizations). Basic financing ('Grundmittel'), the third component of the financing system of German higher education institutions, basically fills the gap between spending and income on a rolling basis. It has the highest value for Scientific universities. The Federal Statistical Office (Statistisches Bundesamt 2003c) provides a detailed documentation on the financial situation of German higher education institutions.

In recent years autonomy in financing has been strengthened in several states, leading to more flexibility of higher education institutions and also allowing institutions to pursue different strategies in a more and more competitive market. Models for financing vary across states: some condition the amount of basic financing on performance indicators, such as the amount of grants received by the institution, and others negotiate with their institutions of higher education on concrete goals, e.g., the number of graduates or the number of dissertations, for a given basic financing amount.[3] Internal resource allocation follows a similar mechanism: universities or departments distribute parts of the funds on the basis of performance indicators, such as the number of graduates or the number of PhDs awarded, but the process differs widely across institutions.

With €943 million the most important organization in providing grants is the German Research Foundation ('Deutsche Forschungsgemeinschaft', DFG), followed by private firms and the federation (€831.7 and €735.4 million) (Statistisches Bundesamt 2003c). The share of external research grants in 2001 is at about 31 percent (Statistisches Bundesamt 2003c, p. 25). Since the majority of external research grants come from public institutions this combination indicates an almost exclusively publicly funded higher education system.

Now consider the two basic inputs, capital and labor, in more detail. Labor comprises scientific and creative staff as well as administrative staff and varies as well as the importance of capital across fields. The distribution of staff and expenditure for different fields shows this statement quite convincingly (see Table 2.2). In 2002, there were more than 500,000 people employed at higher education institutions in Germany. Almost half belong to the category of scientific staff while the other half are administrative and technical support staff. Professors amount to approximately 7.5 percent of total staff (Statistisches Bundesamt 2003c). When we take a closer look at the personnel resources of SciUs, Table 2.2 shows clear differences in the number of scientific staff across the fields represented at German SciUs in 2000.

In medicine, mathematics and science, labor input is highest, which can be explained by small teaching classes due to teaching in laboratories and due to

Table 2.2 Basic Financing and Number of Scientific Staff per Field

	Scientific staff per student	Basic financing per student	Number of students
Languages, Cultural Studies, Sports	0.048	2,981	417,883
Mathematics, Sciences	0.092	7,682	360,007
Law, Economics, Social Sciences	0.047	2,035	264,485
Engineering	0.149	8,144	125,370
Medicine	0.401	27,007	101,256
Arts	0.072	5,642	63,495
Agriculture, Forestry, Dietetics	0.153	10,500	21,706

Source: Statistisches Bundesamt (2003b) for basic financing and number of students; BMBF (2002) for number of scientific staff.

the reliance on practical elements as part of the university education. The high number of staff in medicine can also be explained by medicine departments operating in hospitals and having a different personnel structure. Financing per students (excluding expenditure on staff) across different fields, shows similar differences. Here medicine also ranks first, followed by agriculture, forestry, dietetics and engineering. Low expenditures for students in languages, cultural studies, sport, law, economics and social science reflect larger classes and smaller laboratory needs to be provided by a university for teaching and research.

2.5 GERMAN HIGHER EDUCATION IN THE INTERNATIONAL CONTEXT

Increased demand for high-skilled labor and increased mobility foster international competition for students as well as for researchers. Consequently, having discussed some stylized facts of German higher education, the position of Germany's higher education system in the international context needs to be examined. Following the same structure as for the stylized facts of the German system, this section presents data based on the OECD's 'Education at a Glance' (OECD 2003) within a production-theoretic framework. Indicators connected to the main outputs of an institution of higher education, teaching and research, are displayed, followed by figures describing the input factors of selected OECD countries for higher education.

2.5.1 Teaching

For a developed country, human capital is an important source of economic growth. Therefore, the attractiveness of higher education serves as important growth factor for countries. However potential students evaluate the individual benefits and costs, especially opportunity costs, as well as the attractiveness of higher education. Consequently, the accessibility and attractiveness of higher education as well as distribution of graduates by field are presented here. The quota of new entrants is defined as persons of a given age interval who enter an institution of higher education as share of all persons in this age group and indicates accessibility to higher education in a country.

Referring to tertiary education type A in OECD terminology, the following quota includes rates for Germany Universities, Colleges of Education, Colleges of Theology, Colleges of Art and Music and Universities of Applied Sciences but excludes Colleges of Public Administration. In the OECD classification the latter ones belong to higher education type B. Figure 2.5 displays these entry ratios for selected OECD countries.

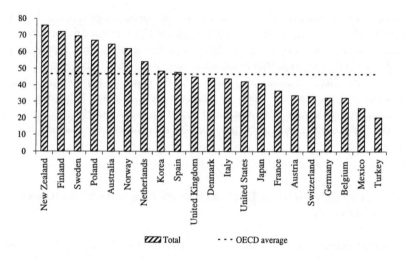

Source: Data from OECD (2003), p. 268.

Figure 2.5   Entry Rates to Tertiary Education Type A (OECD countries)

Germany, with a ratio of new entrants into higher education type A of about 32.4 percent is below the OECD average of 47.9 percent. Despite continuous increase in the recent past, German higher education ranks still very low in the international statistics. Even if some geographically close and culturally similar countries like Austria (34 percent) and Switzerland (33 percent) have low entry rates too, Poland (67 percent) and the Netherlands (54 percent) have much higher rates. The quota of new entrants is very high in New Zealand (76 percent), Finland (72 percent) and Sweden (69 percent), whereas European countries like Belgium (32 percent) and Turkey (20 percent) show the lowest entry rates.

However relatively low entry rates into the higher education type A sector may be compensated by higher rates in type B, which in Germany includes Colleges of Public Administration, Health Sector Schools for Assistants and Nurses, Specialized Academies, and Trade and Technical Schools. Furthermore, Germany offers its traditional apprenticeship system, which includes practical training and schooling ('Duales System') that is an alternative to attending higher education institutions. This system is not available in most other countries.

The attractiveness of the German higher education institutions is relatively high for foreign students as measured by the proportion of foreign students in tertiary education in Germany. About 10 percent of all students enrolled in 2001 were foreign students (OECD 2003, p. 281). This figure is greater than the OECD mean of 5 percent. Germany ranks sixth in the OECD statistics on the ratio of foreign to total students. Students from Turkey (1.3 percent; second generation), Poland (0.5 percent), China (0.4 percent) and the Russian Federation (0.4 percent) are the largest groups (ibid., p. 282). However German students leave their country to study either for a limited time or for a full degree program. The number of German students in tertiary education studying abroad is measured by the number of German students enrolled at institutions of higher education in other countries as percentage of students enrolled in the Germany. In 2001, 3 percent of the German students studied abroad. The favorite countries were the United Kingdom (0.6 percent), the United States (0.4 percent) as well as Austria (0.3 percent) and Switzerland (0.3 percent) (ibid., p. 284).

Perfectly in line with the low ratio of new entrants in Germany we observe that the quota of graduates is far below the OECD average (31 percent). Leading nations in terms of successful graduation are Australia (42 percent), Finland (41 percent) and New Zealand (40 percent). Germany attempts to increase the number of entrants, for example by allowing practically qualified persons to start studying. Not only are entry rates and the graduation rates different across countries, but also the distribution of graduates across fields. While Hungary and the United States have a large number of graduates in the social sciences, Germany, Finland and Sweden have a higher percentage of graduates in the natural sciences (ibid., p. 60).

2.5.2   Research

While the OECD provides information on teaching-related measures in the international context in detail, publications on university research are very rare. For the field of economics there is a publication ranking in economics sponsored by the European Economic Association. Kalaitzidakis et al. (2003) conduct a ranking of European economics institutions based on publications in a set of ten economics core journals from 1991 to 1996. They measure the research performance of institutions by American Economic Review standardized pages and reveal that only one German institution ranks among the top 50 economics institutions. Four are among the top 100 and Germany as a whole ranks 10th out of 24. As Kalaitzidakis et al. (2003) applied four further publication indexes with similar results, the rankings reported here are robust. Combes and Linnemer (2003), Coupé (2003) and Lubrano et al. (2003) support these findings.

To present the research performance in all main areas and compare it across different countries, the most important Citation Indexes were searched for universities and various countries. The Social Science Citation Index (SSCI), the Science Citations Index (SCI) and the Arts and Humanities Index (AHI) were used for the year 2000. Table 2.3 displays the share of publications in the citation indices for selected countries.

Table 2.3 Proportion of Publications for Selected Countries in 2000

Country	Total	SCI	SSCI	AHI
United States	0.307	0.306	0.401	0.193
England	0.060	0.055	0.090	0.060
Germany	0.048	0.055	0.027	0.014
Canada	0.034	0.034	0.043	0.026
France	0.026	0.030	0.010	0.013
Netherlands	0.017	0.019	0.018	0.004
Spain	0.017	0.020	0.008	0.004

Source: Own search in the ISI Citation Indexes.

The United States show the largest number of publications in journals included in the citation indexes. In all three citation indexes the share of publications is 4.8 percent for Germany. Covering 30.7 percent of publications in the indices of the total number of publications the dominate country is the United States. While Germany holds a second place, jointly with England, in the SCI, its publication shares in the SSCI and the AHI are rather low.

2.5.3 Financing

Education systems must not just be effective, but also efficient. Therefore, the applied input factors used have to be taken into account. Annual expenditure on educational institutions per student in US dollars in 2000 varied considerably across OECD countries. The average expenditure in the OECD countries for higher education in 2000 was $9,571. Germany, with a total expenditure per student in 2000 of $10,898 is slightly above the average (data from OECD (2003), p. 197).

Not only does spending on higher education differ across countries, but there is also variation in the source of resources for higher education. Differences in public and private financing are especially striking. In the international context, the percentage of gross domestic product (GDP) measures the expenditure for higher education of a country. Figure 2.6 presents the expenditure on tertiary education in institutions from public and private sources.

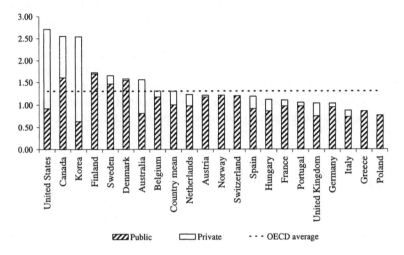

Figure 2.6　Expenditure on Tertiary Education (Percentage of GDP)

The mean percentage of GDP spent for tertiary education in the OECD countries is 1.3 percent, with 1.0 percent from public and 0.3 percent from private sources. While the share of GDP from public resources in Germany (0.95 percent) and the United States (0.90 percent) are almost the same, the United States spent the largest share of the OECD countries on higher education, a total of 2.7 percent of GDP. Private financing is high in the United States (1.8 percent of the GDP), while in Germany the share of private resources remains very low at 0.08 percent of GDP. It seems apparent that private funding in German higher education is not very important. The percentage of private resources is about 8 percent and far below the OECD average of 21 percent. Variance in the relative importance of private financing is considerable. While in the USA, Korea and Japan the percentage of private financing in higher education is far above 50 percent, in other countries like Norway, Switzerland or Denmark private funding is almost non-existent.

To sum up, there is not only variance in teaching and research across German universities but also in higher education systems across countries. They differ in teaching measures as well as in research measures. However the role of international positioning is still minor. One reason might have been low mobility of students, another is that universities in different countries get financing from different organizations.

For Germany, nevertheless, the question of positioning in a European or even in an international stage has been almost irrelevant. For the years covered by this study and for the vast majority of German universities, positioning in the international market for higher education can be ignored. Internationalization in higher education is limited to a small number of programs, in particular MBA programs.

Consequently, the degree of competition between universities as whole institutions in an international context is low. Due to this minor importance of international positioning the following chapters concentrate on the positioning of universities in teaching and research within Germany. In the final chapter of this book I will comment on future development and if and how this might change.

NOTES

1 BVerfG, 2BvF 1/03, date: January 26, 2005; www.bverfg.de I, (3).
2 For further organizational characteristics of German higher education see Backes-Gellner and Sadowski (1991).
3 Leszczensky and Orr (2004) discuss various models for eleven German states in details.

3 A Review of the Literature

Universities differ not only across but also within countries. Differences can be found in size, admission standards, financing structure, performance, teaching quality and research quality among others. Until now, little attention has been paid to how universities position themselves with regard to teaching and research. This chapter reviews theoretical arguments and empirical evidence concerning the degree of heterogeneity across universities in these two tasks.

Section 3.1 presents theoretical results from the positioning of universities in a competitive framework especially focused on teaching and research which are outputs from the production process of universities. Therefore, performance differences between universities in providing these two tasks also reveal different positions in teaching and research themselves. Following the production theoretic perspective introduced in Chapter 2, Section 3.2 reviews studies from performance measurement of teaching, research and both teaching and research simultaneously. In this way the degree of homogeneity in teaching and research, as well as in overall performance, is revealed.

As theoretical explanations for heterogeneity and positioning across universities are rare, Section 3.3 suggests two general explanations for heterogeneity within an industry: the concept of strategic groups and product differentiation. Section 3.4 summarizes the insights from university literature and other general approaches on heterogeneity within an industry.

3.1 TEACHING AND RESEARCH POSITIONING

Considering the number of mainly publicly financed university systems, there are surprisingly few theoretical studies. University positioning and the resulting structure of higher education have received little attention. Del Rey (2001, 2003) and De Fraja and Iossa (2001) are the only works analyzing both teaching and research positioning of public universities.

Focusing on university allocation of funds to teaching and research, Del Rey (2001) models duopolisitic competition between publicly funded universities explicitly. She assumes a two-stage game with two identical universities. In the first stage universities simultaneously choose the quality of teaching. This quality will be provided to every student attending the institution. Considering information about teaching quality, students apply to the universities. Universities there allocate resources between teaching and research as a means of increasing the productivity of students. Based on average student quality in the second stage universities decide on the number of students they will admit. Del Rey (2001) postulates the students choose the university they apply to in the framework of a spatial competition model. As universities are interested in teaching and research, they compete for students characterized by their ability. Resources needed to provide the announced level of teaching quality are smaller for high-ability students. Universities are publicly funded by a lump sum and by a per-student transfer from government, and the educational production function depends on students' average ability as well as on the resources devoted to teaching.

The resulting equilibrium from the two-stage game is unique and symmetric. It depends on the universities' preferences for research, the technology of the education production and the relative weight of the components of the finance scheme. Depending on the parameter relations, there exist four types of equilibria: full-time teaching, full-time research, selective teaching and research, and mass teaching and research. In full-time teaching universities do not carry out any research, but allocate all resources to teaching. If institutions concentrate on research (full-time research), total demand is shared equally and no resources are allocated to teaching. Under another parameter combination an equilibrium with selective teaching and research universities occurs. Here universities only admit some applicants and conduct research. Finally, if the equilibrium results in mass teaching and research, universities concentrate on teaching and therefore allocate most resources to teaching. The market of students is equally shared among the universities, and all applicants will be admitted to study at either university. Recall that universities are assumed to be identical and consequently pursue the same strategy. Therefore, the different positions of the institutions in either teaching or in research result by assumption.

Dropping the assumption of student mobility, Del Rey (2003) is a variant of Del Rey (2001). In this modified setup, universities devote all resources either to teaching or to research. The mixed equilibrium types from Del Rey (2001) do not occur in this version of the model. However universities still choose identical teaching levels and identical research levels; homogeneity within the sector is maintained.

In contrast to the aforementioned studies which show identical strategies in teaching and research across universities. From their symmetry assumptions, there is also theoretical evidence for heterogeneity. Most studies focus on heterogeneity in teaching in terms of admission standards. The framework of De Fraja and Iossa (2002) is similar to Del Rey (2001). They assume two competing universities that also decide about the allocation of resources between teaching and research. Another strategic option of the universities is admission standards. Universities set an admission standard and those students who fulfill these standards decide whether or not to enroll. A student's decision to apply depends upon the cost to move to the university.

In contrast to Del Rey (2001), De Fraja and Iossa (2002) allow the cost of mobility for students to differ. Nevertheless, this leads to a symmetric equilibrium for high mobility costs, where both universities set the same admission standard, allocate the same amount of resources to research, and admit the same number of students. If students face low mobility costs the only existing equilibrium is asymmetric, meaning that universities pursue different strategies. While one university admits only the best students, the other institution competes by having a lower admission standard. Universities do not show explicit differences in the research levels.

Other studies explaining university behavior mainly focus on teaching related characteristics like admission standard or curriculum choice and do not explicitly take research into account. Focusing on teaching, Gary-Bobo and Trannoy (2002), in line with DeFraja and Iossa (2002), analyze the allocation of public subsidies in public higher education, suggesting a discrete choice model. They show that an optimal subsidy scheme is given if public subsidies are increasingly dependent on the additional wage graduates receive from a university's degree. Under monopolistic competition, tuition levels converge to the optimal positive value. Using two specific objective functions for the different organizational forms Gary-Bobo and Trannoy (2004) contrast financing schemes of universities, both public and private funding. They assume that universities want to maximize social surplus, which is compatible with a publicly funded university system. Additionally, they model universities as profit maximizers, which represents a system of private universities. In this framework universities have four strategic variables to manipulate: tuition and fees, admission standard, quality and total enrollment.

The model has four principal results. First, with a perfect capital market and complete information students select themselves to the 'correct' institution. It is optimal for universities to set positive tuition levels that may exceed marginal costs. Admission standards do not play any role in this case. Second, if information about students' abilities is asymmetric, non-profit universities use both instruments, tuition and admission standards. Tuition can either be positive and below the marginal costs or negative as direct support/subsidy to students. Third, profit maximizing universities tend to set tuition too high and admission standards too low. Finally, under capital market imperfections universities again use both instruments, tuition below marginal costs and low admission standards.

Also focusing only on teaching Eisenkopf (2004) analyzes the curriculum choice of universities and predicts heterogeneity of universities in educational products and prices of higher education if tuition and fees are not regulated. Closely related is the work of Kemnitz (2006) examining the reform of university funding and its impact on teaching quality. He contributes to the discussion by offering three main results. First, uniform tuition does not lead to the welfare optimum; second, a graduate tax with differentiated tuition by government ensures the optimum; and third, university autonomy hinders the efficacy of funding reforms.

In summary, theoretical approaches show heterogeneity across institutions of higher education in teaching but not in research. However depending on the theoretical framework teaching is usually stated to be homogenous across universities. Looking at the relationship of teaching and research there is discussion at the individual level but none on an institutional level. In a meta analysis of 58 studies Hattie and Marsh (1996) reveal evidence for both a direct relation between teaching and research and an inverse relation between teaching and research. Additionally, they report that some evidence suggests that teaching and research are not systematically related. Consequently, the literature provides evidence for teaching and research as substitutes as well as a complementary relation.

Discussing the topic of stratification in higher education institutions, some studies point at changes over time in US higher education. While Geiger (2004, 2005) describes various changes in US higher education – focusing on university costs, undergraduates and academics – he develops the consequences of increasing competition. The expression 'Research Universities and the Paradox of the Marketplace', is both the insight into his work and the subtitle of his book. He argues that on the one hand a higher degree of competition leads to greater resources in the universities and to better students. However, on the other hand, it leads to a higher of inequality in wealth. Gumport (2005) reviews the interdependence between graduate education and research. Owen-Smith (2003) considers the changing relation between different research dimensions. He looks at the interdependence between commercial and academic systems and its influence on competition between universities. Based on panel data of 89 US Research One universities after passage of the Bayh-Dole Act, which allows universities to market research results, he shows that academic and commercial science has integrated over time. Implicitly, two groups of universities arise, those that succeed in establishing the complementary relation and those that do not.

There are numerous other contributions in the literature that focus on other aspects of higher education. However they do not focus on teaching and research as strategic parameters of universities. These studies deal with the economics of higher education in general, with specialized topics not directly related to positioning or public universities. For example, Wilson (2002) finds that centralized budgeting of universities is superior to a decentralized budgeting process in which university units compete for students. Winston (1999) discusses the special conditions under which universities are run in comparison to 'normal' for-profit firms.

Rothschild and White (1995) introduce 'customer-input technology' to higher education: Students serve as customers and at the same time they are important inputs to the production function of universities. They argue that student ability may have an effect on the tuition charged and human capital received. In this way the marginal productivity, student mix and technology of universities may differ. In a theoretical framework they state productivity differences, which suggest heterogeneity across universities. Winston (1999) highlights the peer effects that accompany customer-input technology. Following this argument, high quality education results from student interactions in that they 'educate both themselves and each other' (ibid., p. 17). In this way students' quality apart from other inputs plays a major role in influencing institutional quality, which has also been shown empirically. Winston argues that peer quality is an important input to a university's production function that should be brought from the same university's customers. Selectivity helps universities in the composition of the student body.

In addition to these theoretical papers there exists a body of empirical work focussing on other aspects of higher education. Getz and Siegfried (2004) examine the sensitivity of capital use to price in higher education. Kwoka and Snyder (2004) present the dynamic adjustment of the US higher education sector.

3.2 HETEROGENEITY IN HIGHER EDUCATION AND PERFORMANCE

Theoretical studies suggest heterogeneity in teaching across universities, but little attention is given to research. Therefore, this section examines the empirical evidence on teaching and research performance separately and simultaneously to find empirical evidence for the degree of heterogeneity in teaching, research and overall performance. If universities are relatively homogenous in teaching and research, performance differences should be small. However common performance criteria – such as profit, return on assets or return on investments – cannot be used to evaluate university performance.

In contrast to for-profit firms there are no market prices for university inputs and outputs. As universities compete not just with other universities but also with other public institutions and expenses, another performance measure is needed. An appropriate performance measure is how well an institution transforms input into outputs. Economically, this relationship is captured by productivity or efficiency. To measure university performance appropriately, Subsection 3.2.1 introduces four methods for performance measurement in higher education. Then, Subsection 3.2.2 presents modeling and results of the most common method for performance measurement in higher education, Data Envelopment Analysis (DEA). Finally to detect heterogeneity in teaching and research as well as heterogeneity in overall performance, Subsection 3.2.3 summarizes the results on performance measurement.

3.2.1 Performance Measurement Methodology

Performance measurement in a predominantly publicly funded university system is difficult. From a production-theoretic view universities consume multiple inputs to produce multiple outputs. Teaching and research capture various output dimensions. The number of graduates in different fields is widely accepted as outputs of a university in the area of teaching while the number of publications and the number and value of research grants measure the research output. Universities usually use staff as the labor input factor and expenditure on library or infrastructure as the capital input factor.

Determining the degree of heterogeneity in teaching, research and overall performance, performance levels across higher education institutions are calculated by evaluating the production process. Coelli et al. (1998) propose dividing the main methods into four groups: least squares econometric production models, productivity indices, Stochastic Frontier Analysis (SFA) and Data Envelopment Analysis (DEA).

First, there are the estimation of cost and production functions using econometric methods, typically least square estimation. These studies assume input and output quantities and a specified functional form of the transformation process, for example a Cobb-Douglas function. Multi-product cost functions for universities are estimated for the USA (Cohn et al. 1989; DeGroot et al. 1991; Nelson and Hevert 1992; Dundar and Lewis 1995; Koshal and Koshal 1999, 2000; Koshal et al. 2001), for the UK (Johnes 1996, 1997; Glass et al. 1997, 1998), for Turkey (Lewis and Dundar 1995) and for Japan (Hashimoto and Cohn 1997). These studies consider stochastic influences as well as the functional form of the production process, and mainly focus on technical change and scale economies.

Second, there are productivity indices measuring changes in economic variables based on quantities and prices. Examples of applying the concept of productivity index are available for regional colleges in Norway (Forsund and Kalhagen 1999), for UK accounting departments (Glass et al. 1997) and for university institutions in the UK (Glass et al. 1998). They compute the Malmquist Index and identify efficiency increases in all cases.

The third method, stochastic frontier analysis, estimates frontier production functions and thus provides an efficiency measure based on econometric methods. Thereby the SFA is based on an 'a priori' parametric specification of the production function. Aigner et al. (1977) and Meussen and van den Broek (1977) developed the method by adding two error terms to the frontier production function: one random variable represents 'technical inefficiency', the other error term captures measurement errors and other random factors. Izadi and Johnes (1997) apply this method to UK institutions of higher education.

Fourth, Data Envelopment Analysis uses an output to input ratio to measure the efficiency of each institution. Extending the one-input–one-output case to multiple dimensions and identifying a best-practice production function DEA neither specifies the functional form of the production function nor assumes information about the efficiency term. Accounting for measuring efficiency in the presence of multiple inputs and multiple outputs, DEA appears to be the most appropriate method. As there is no generally accepted functional form for the production process of universities, it determines the production frontier in a non-parametric way and does not assume a predetermined form of the production function. This characteristic of DEA assures flexibility in modelling. Furthermore, it considers the multiple inputs and outputs of the university simultaneously and thus not only reveals if a university is efficient or not, it even provides a score indicating the degree of efficiency for each unit relative to other universities. For a more detailed review of the DEA approach see Section 6.1.

While the other approaches implicitly assume technically efficient units, SFA and DEA measure directly the degree of relative efficiency in the underlying sample. Typically, DEA has been applied in non-profit sectors where market prices for inputs and outputs are not available, which is the case in a publicly financed university system.

3.2.2 Data Envelopment Analysis

Data Envelopment Analysis (DEA) is the most appropriate and commonly used method for evaluating teaching and research in higher education institutions and provides a productivity measure for each institution that considers the multiple input and multiple outputs associated with higher education. Consequently, comparing each institutions productivity scores leads to empirical evidence on the degree of heterogeneity in all three dimensions. Therefore, this section reviews the results of efficiency measurement focusing on each of the different dimensions: teaching efficiency, research efficiency and overall efficiency. Studies vary in the options of the DEA model and for different countries.

Subsection 3.2.2.1 surveys the different DEA models in higher education. Then, Subsection 3.2.2.2 analyzes the results from performance measurement in teaching and research separately, focusing on the degree of heterogeneity in teaching and research across institutions of higher education. Finally, Subsection 3.2.2.3 presents the overall performance of university institutions, again concentrating on differences across institutions.

3.2.2.1 Modeling the 'Production Process'
Three elements characterize a DEA model: the input-output specification, the assumption about returns to scale and the orientation of the model. Most analyses focus on universities or on specific departments. To start with this review of the input-output specifications of the DEA models I describe the inputs and outputs of higher education institutions. Teaching and research staff comprise most of the labor input. Capital is mainly expenditure on library, computers,

buildings or on personnel. Following Rothschild and White (1995) new entering students are an input for universities. Employing these inputs or a set of them, universities produce at least two outputs: teaching and research. Different kinds of publications, like journal articles, books, or contributions to edited books measure the research output. Additionally, research grants won capture a research output of a university or a department. The number of undergraduates or postgraduates typically covers the teaching output.

Input Factors   Library expenditure can be viewed as a high quality input for research as well as for teaching (for example Rhodes and Southwick 1993; Arcelus and Coleman 1997; Thursby 2000; Lehmann and Warning 2002). The availability of recently published academic journal articles and textbooks has a positive impact on the performance of students as well as on the performance of teachers and researchers. It serves as a proxy variable for the general infrastructure quality of a university or a department.

A number of studies also model the infrastructure explicitly, taking into account expenditures on computing or operating expenditures separately. Ahn et al. (1989), Arcelus and Coleman (1997) and Forsund and Kalhagen (1999) include operating expenditure, Beasley (1990, 1995) and Moreno and Tadepalli (2002) use equipment expenditure. Breu and Raab (1994) as well as Athanassoupoulos and Shale (1997) consider this kind of infrastructure spending as general expenditures. Furthermore, some treat research income as capital input, although more treat it as research output. But technically, research income serves as additional capital input for a university. Athanassopoulos and Shale (1997) as well as Beasley (1990, 1995) and Johnes and Johnes (1995), for example, use research grants as an input factor.

Formally, expenditure for faculty and or number of staff is also a capital input of the university production process (Sinuany-Stern et al. 1994; Beasley 1995; Moreno and Tadapelli 2002). Nevertheless, salary for staff also describes the labor input of a university for all staff, often divided into teaching staff (Arcelus and Coleman 1997), research staff (Johnes and Johnes 1995, Ng and Li 2000) and administrative staff (Arcelus and Coleman 1997). Further distinctions are academic staff (Johnes 1995) and non-academic staff (Avkiran 2001; Abbott and Doucouliagos 2003). Sometimes building space (Forsund and Kalhagen 1999; Moreno and Tadapalli 2002) or simple ratios, such as faculty to student, work as input factors (Colbert et al. 2000).

Students comprise an important input factor for higher education institutions, that differs significantly from traditional production theory. The ability of a university's students determines the quality of this input. Either number of undergraduates (Athanassopoulos and Shale 1997) or scores on a standardized exam can be used to measure this input. Colbert et al. (2000) used average GMAT of incoming students and Breu and Raab (1994) used average SAT score.

Teaching Output Factors   Teaching outputs also have direct and indirect characters. While direct teaching output measures the students still enrolled at the university, indirect teaching output examines the success of graduates on the labor market. Studies focusing on teaching more often employ direct outputs than indirect outputs due to data availability. Most frequently, teaching output measures are the number of undergraduate students (Arcelus and Coleman 1997; MacMillan and Datta 1998; Abbott and Doucouliagos 2003) and graduate students (receiving a degree in a given year) (Beasley 1990, 1995; Arcelus and Coleman 1997; MacMillan and Datta 1998). Further direct teaching outputs are the student retention rates (Breu and Raab 1994; Avkiran 2001) and the graduation rates (Breu and Raab 1994; Lehmann and Warning 2002).

Indirect teaching output measures include scores on teaching evaluation (Sarrico and Dyson 2000) and the success of students on the labor market. Along these lines Avkiran (2001) as well as Sarrico and Dyson (2000) incorporate the employment rate of students as a teaching output. The more students who find employment after graduation, the greater the quality of teaching at the university from which they graduated can be assumed. Colbert et al. (2000), in an extensive study, calculate five models evaluating teaching efficiency of 24 US Master of Business Administration (MBA) programs. They look at student satisfaction as well as at recruiter satisfaction separately and in various combinations. Generally, measuring teaching output is more difficult than research output because student evaluations of teaching quality are neither reliable nor valid. However data on indirect teaching outputs is infrequently available.

Research Output Factors   Research is the other principal output of universities and departments. It has both a direct or indirect nature. Direct research output measures include publications, articles and books (Johnes and Johnes 1993, 1995; Luptacik 2003) or even the numbers of citations by other researchers (Thursby 2000). Johnes and Johnes (1995) as well as Korhonen et al. (2001) discuss various publication types.

Indirect research outputs are those factors that result from other research dimensions. Winning a project competition, for example, leads to research grants (MacMillan and Datta 1998; Post and Spronk 1999; Abbott and Doucouliagos 2003). On the one hand previous good research results may help to win a grant, while on the other hand success is based on the potential for future research results. Moreover, evaluations in the US also use the number of PhDs awarded as indirect indicator for research quality (Thursby 2000; Korhonen et al. 2001). Thursby and Kemp (2002) use patent applications and licenses executed as measures of research output and in this way they emphasize applied research.

In addition to the input-output specification of DEA models its orientation distinguishes input- and output-orientation. Under output-orientation, universities face a set amount of inputs and must improve outputs as much as possible. The reverse holds for input-orientation (for a formal description see Section 6.1). Twenty-one of the 42 studies assume an output-oriented DEA model. The modelling option, input orientation or output-orientation, depends on the center of the analysis. For focusing on cost reduction, input-orientation turns out to be appropriate. However assuming government sets fixed inputs and universities try to increase their output, then output-orientation is the appropriate model option.

Returns to scale are the third element of the production process in higher education. Returns to scale capture size effects. Seventeen studies assume the standard DEA model with constant returns to scale which delivers efficiency scores for each unit supposing universities or departments working at the optimal scale size. About ten studies ran a model with variable returns to scale, seven studies ran both options.

Evaluation of departments usually focuses on departments of economics or business economics. Due to available data, most studies examine higher education in the UK or in the US. For Germany there are four studies evaluating institutions of higher education. Backes-Gellner (1992) and Backes-Gellner and Zanders (1989) study economics and business economics departments in Germany focusing on research, while Meyer et al. (1995) evaluate units within a department of a university with respect to teaching. Warning (2004) focuses on German universities as complete entities.

Table A.4 in the Appendix summarizes the three elements of a DEA model for higher education: the input-output specification, the assumption about returns to scale and the orientation. Contributions are ordered by focal point: teaching, research and both teaching and research; taking four levels of examination into account: universities as entities, departments in the same or similar fields from different universities, departments within the same university, implying different fields and entire countries.

3.2.2.2 Performance in Teaching and Research

To inspect productivity differences in teaching, research or in both, we analyze all DEA efficiency scores of the 42 studies containing 159 DEA models. As most studies report several DEA model variants, in total 159 DEA models are examined. For each model all efficiency scores were collected from the original articles to compute descriptive statistics. The sample covers 45 models examining teaching, 53 models focusing on research, and 61 simultaneously evaluating teaching and research. Table 3.1 summarizes the distribution of studies by country, considering the focus in teaching, research or the combination of teaching and research.

Table 3.1   Composition of the Sample of DEA Models (Countries)

	Teaching&Research	Research	Teaching	All
UK	0.111	0.396	0.328	0.289
Europe (without UK)	0.467	0.226	0.098	0.245
USA	0.178	0.057	0.115	0.113
Other Countries	0.244	0.321	0.459	0.353

The majority of higher education DEA models are calculated for institutions in the UK. About 29 percent of all models scrutinize the efficiency of higher education in Britain; in research the fraction is almost 40 percent. The remaining European countries cover only 24 percent of DEA models to evaluate efficiency. DEA models calculated for higher education in the US capture 11 percent, and all other countries exhibit a market share of 26 percent. Comparisons over complete countries are only carried out in research and in teaching and research simultaneously and cover about 9 percent of DEA models.

Apart from the country being analyzed, the level of examination influences the efficiency results. Most DEA models are run at the departmental level (43 percent) followed by models of the university level (41 percent). DEA within an institution of higher education and DEA across OECD countries are rare. Table 3.2 displays the distribution of the DEA studies by study focus.

Table 3.2   Composition of the Sample of DEA Models (Examination Level)

	Teaching	Research	Teaching &Research	All
Country	0	8	6	14
University	15	14	36	65
Department	26	31	11	68
Within University	4	0	8	12
Total	45	53	61	159

Most studies that analyze efficiency in teaching and research simultaneously, are conducted on the university level. Based on this dataset for each DEA model, descriptive statistics are calculated for the average DEA scores of each model. Summarizing these average results from the different studies leads to average efficiency values in teaching, research and in teaching and research. Table 3.3 displays the descriptive statistics on performance measurement in teaching compared to research and both.

Mean efficiency across all DEA teaching models is 0.666, with a standard deviation of 0.272. The model with the lowest average score in teaching at all reveals a degree of efficiency of 0.180; the model with the highest average score achieves 0.993. For research, the averages of the models are similar. As an additional measure of performance Table 3.3 displays the number of efficient units, which supports the finding that average performance in teaching and research tends to be similar. Both dimensions show an average of 8 efficient units, while the average number of units in the analysis in teaching is 39; in research it is 41. However dispersion tends to be greater in research than in teaching. While the standard deviation of the number of efficient units in teaching is only 8.599, it amounts to 11.088 in research. To support this observation of higher dispersion in research, we look at the maximum and minimum numbers of efficient units where the spread of research is again greater.

Table 3.3   Results from Performance Measurement with DEA

		Teaching	Research	Teaching & Research	All
	Mean	0.666	0.623	0.826	0.713
Average	Std. Dev.	0.272	0.198	0.123	0.218
Efficiency	Min	0.180	0.225	0.460	0.180
	Max	0.993	0.948	0.998	0.998
	Mean	8 (of 39)	8 (of 41)	14 (of 42)	10 (of 41)
Efficient	Std. Dev.	8.599	11.888	10.797	10.920
Units	Min	1.000	1.000	1.000	1.000
	Max	47	69	56	69

While the preceding table analyzes the results of average performance levels, further information about the distribution of the scores in the teaching and research models is now provided. Average performance over the DEA models seems to be similar in the separate teaching and research models. To explore the dispersion over these two dimensions, teaching and research, of the DEA models more in detail, Table A.1 in the Appendix lists efficiency results of 13 DEA studies examining teaching efficiency. It shows for each study some structural characteristics: country of examination, institution type, number of observations and the year of the data. Additionally, it displays two indicators mapping the dispersion of teaching across the units: the minimum efficiency score and the standard deviation of the scores in the DEA models. As the maximum value of efficiency is always 1, low values of the minimum efficiency score suggest a high degree of heterogeneity, i.e., a low dispersion. A high standard deviation of efficiency scores in a study also suggests a high degree of heterogeneity.

The teaching studies tend to have very low dispersion in efficiency scores going along with high minimum efficiency values (for example Colbert et al. 2000) and standard deviations that range from 0.01 to 0.03. But there are also studies centering on teaching that find a much higher standard deviation. For example Alfonso and Santos (2004) find values standard deviation from 0.20 to 0.36. Consequently, the empirical evidence of the degree of teaching heterogeneity is mixed. However most of the evidence in teaching efficiency across universities suggests a great deal of homogeneity across universities.

Interpreting the results of DEA efficiency analysis across different studies, it is important to consider that results also depend on the number of observations, the number of inputs, the number of and outputs used. Furthermore, assumptions about the orientation and returns to scale also influence the results. However, over a sufficiently large number of studies these effects should cancel out across teaching and research models.

To examine the degree of heterogeneity in research efficiency, Table A.2 in the Appendix displays information for the DEA research models. Again, the minimum efficiency score and the standard deviation of the DEA scores serve to indicate the degree of heterogeneity. Studies of research output exhibit a tendency to higher dispersion of DEA scores. Johnes (1995) for example, shows standard deviations between 0.18 and 0.25 estimated over nine models. Although Thursby (2000) only reveals a standard deviation of 0.10 the majority of research models displays higher dispersion (for example Kocher et al. 2006; Martinez Cabrera 2000). Minimum efficiency scores also tend to be small and thus indicate high dispersion of research across universities. Therefore, DEA studies suggest a relatively high degree of heterogeneity in research performance across institutions.

3.2.2.3 Overall Performance
Evaluation of the overall performance of higher education institutions concerns teaching and research simultaneously. Average efficiency estimates across all studies is significantly greater than in the separate models for teaching and research (see Table 3.3). Furthermore, in contrast to the separate analyses, the results in the simultaneous teaching and research models tend to reveal lower dispersion of the average efficiency scores. To measure teaching and research efficiency simultaneously, most studies focus at the university level (see Table 3.2).

Table A.3 in the Appendix displays studies focusing on overall performance. Apart from structural information of the study, it also shows the minimum efficiency score of all models as well as the standard deviation. Among the overall performance studies, the minimum efficiency value ranges around 0.01 (e.g., Madden et al. 1997). But most studies show minimum efficiency ratings between 0.4 and 0.6. Again, the standard deviation is the measure for the degree of heterogeneity in overall performance at universities. Abbott and Doucouliagos (2003) as well as MacMillan and Datta (1998) reveal small values, below 0.10, and thus suggest a high degree of homogeneity in the DEA scores. However others, e.g., Sinuany-Stern et al. (1994) as well as Tomkins and Green (1988), show much larger dispersions of 0.2 and 0.8. Evidence of the degree of heterogeneity seems to be mixed. Some studies reveal a low degree of heterogeneity in overall performance, while others show a considerably higher degree of heterogeneity.

Only a small number of studies explain heterogeneity in the performance of universities. Most of them utilize DEA to describe efficiency across units. However some studies also detect factors that influence differences in efficiency of universities. In a two stage approach these studies explain DEA inefficiency scores in a regression model by university-related and environmental factors, following the idea of Lovell (1993).

For 45 Canadian universities MacMillan and Datta (1998) find that university characteristics, such as the fraction of science of faculty and university size, always have significant impact on the inefficiency. They also report a number of variables that do not impact inefficiency. Class size, the fraction of part time students, the percentage change in total enrollment, and the percentage change in total revenue do not exhibit any significant influence on inefficiency. Indicators denoting the specializations on undergraduates and the ratio of undergraduates to the number of undergraduate degrees awarded are only significant in some specifications.

Rhodes and Southwick (1993) compare the relative efficiency of 180 public and private universities in the US during 1979/1980. In the first stage, they run a DEA model. Then, in a second stage they relate the level of inefficiency to various aspects by applying tobit regressions and reporting that competition, as measured by the number of universities in a state, decreases inefficiency as well as university size.

Lehmann and Warning (2002) analyze UK universities and reveal that university-related variables are the primary determinants of inefficiency. Examining 112 UK universities it appears that universities are more efficient at providing teaching than at providing research. Furthermore, the variation of efficiency is greater in research than in teaching. Finally, factors characterizing the district where the university is located do not affect the degree of inefficiency significantly. Thus, the variation of the efficiency of universities seems to be under the control of the university administration. The student admission policy appears to be an area university administrators control that influences efficiency significantly.

For German universities, Warning (2004) endogenizes the DEA efficiency score, employing quantile regression incorporating not just university related but also industry and environmental variables. Differences appear between the social and natural sciences as well as differences between teaching and research.

3.2.3   Summary of Performance in Higher Education

DEA models are characterized by three elements. First, input-output specifications for teaching efficiency, research efficiency, or the simultaneous teaching and research efficiency are specified. Staff and operating expenditures are the prominent input factors in the empirical studies. Publications and grants are the principal output factors for research, while the number of graduates is the usual teaching output factor. Input-orientation as well as output-orientation are common assumptions in modeling the university production process. There are a variety of assumptions regarding the orientation and returns to scale in modeling the production process of institutions of higher education.

Based on 159 DEA models from 42 different studies, descriptive results reveal some interesting features of DEA studies. The majority of DEA studies are conducted for the UK, particularly in research. Studies about UK research are numerous because there is systematic evaluation of all universities in the form of the Research Assessment Exercise. Hence, not just economic and business departments are evaluated; one can find studies of physics and chemistry departments, for example. For Germany there are only four studies evaluating university units applying DEA: two examine economics and business departments across universities (Backes-Gellner and Zanders 1989; Backes-Gellner 1992), one evaluates business economics chairs within one university (Meyer et al. 1995) and one examines universities as a whole (Warning 2004).

With respect to the examination level of the studies for other countries, it turns out that models calculated at the departmental level usually analyze teaching and research separately. At the university level most studies analyze both teaching and research simultaneously. Efficiency scores between different teaching and research DEA models are very similar, measured in average efficiency as well as in number of efficient units. However there seems to be a tendency to higher standard deviation of average values in research. A detailed description of standard deviations by focal point as measure of dispersion supports this finding. Heterogeneity across efficiency scores in research seems to be greater than in teaching. However evidence is mixed. The same holds true for overall efficiency.

In summary, empirical evidence on the degree of heterogeneity in performance – teaching, research and overall – points in various directions. Some studies reveal a low degree of heterogeneity, while others find significant differences in efficiency scores across institutions. Studies with theoretically founded determinants to explain these differences, also considering competitive and environmental factors, are difficult to find and will be carried out in the underlying chapters.

3.3 GENERAL EXPLANATIONS FOR HETEROGENEITY AND POSITIONING

Empirical evidence of university performance suggests heterogeneity in teaching, research and in overall performance. However theoretical explanations focused on heterogeneity in teaching and research across universities are unusual. Therefore, this section provides two general explanations from the literature for heterogeneity within an industry. Subsection 3.3.1 introduces the concept of strategic groups that focuses on explaining performance differences across firms within an industry and Subsection 3.3.2 presents product differentiation as a theoretical explanation for heterogeneity within an industry. While the concept of strategic group focuses on performance differences, the product differentiation approach concentrates on the strategic choice of product characteristics.

3.3.1 The Concept of Strategic Groups

The concept of strategic groups states that there are subgroups within an industry characterized by similar performance levels and similar strategies. Across the industry, however, groups are heterogenous. Subsection 3.3.1.1 introduces the general idea and the elements of the concept of strategic groups. Subsection 3.3.1.2 provides some empirical evidence for different fields in the literature. Finally, Subsection 3.3.1.3 discusses theoretical explanations for the existence of subgroups within one branch.

3.3.1.1 The Basic Idea

Caves and Porter (1977) introduced the concept of strategic groups, which provides an explanation for heterogeneity of firms within an industry. Firms within an industry differ in performance because they pursue different strategies due to varying asset configurations or different willingness to take risks. As some firms choose similar strategies, firm clusters emerge that are characterized by similar strategies resulting in similar performance. Firms pursuing similar strategies are called 'strategic groups' (Porter 1979, p. 215). Thus, an industry consists of several strategic groups. While firms within a group pursue similar strategies, firms across groups differ significantly.

Modifying the traditional SCP paradigm from industrial organization (Scherer and Ross 1990; Martin 2002) leads to the concept of strategic groups. SCP stands for 'structure conduct performance' and implies that the industry structure influences firms' strategic behavior, and strategic behavior influences firm performance within that industry. Under complete competition (structure) for example, firms set prices (strategies) equal to marginal costs that results in zero profits (performance). Caves and Porter (1977), however, argue that the strategic behavior of firms affects performance as well as the structure of the industry. Strategic groups in an industry mirror the structural effect, resulting in high- and low-performance groups.

Three structural types may occur from firm strategy. If all firms choose different strategies in the main dimensions, then all firms within the industry locate in equal distance to each other with respect to the key variables. Then each firm builds its own strategic group. If all firms choose to pursue identical strategies, then there is only one large group consisting of all firms in the industry. However, if only some firms choose identical strategies, while other firms pursue different strategies, those firms with similar strategies tend to cluster in groups. Strategic groups capture structure below the industry level but above the firm level. Previous theory suggests that market structure implies performance differences of firms.

Following Caves and Porter (1977) and Porter (1979) two factors can explain performance differences across groups: barriers to mobility between groups, and competitive rivalry within and across groups (Porter 1979, p. 215). Barriers to mobility are an extension of the barriers to entry from classical industrial organization theory. However they prevent firms not only from entering into the industry, but they also impede firms from moving easily from one group into another. Barriers to mobility picture strategic variables that separate firms into clusters by choosing different strategies. Barriers to mobility result from strategic decisions of firms. Therefore, firms not only differ in size, but also other attributes like geographical extension, the degree of vertical integration or R&D intensity. The main sources for mobility barriers are economies of scale, product differentiation, large capital requirements, cost advantages and proprietary knowledge.

Based on the existence of barriers to mobility Porter (1979) develops a 'theory of profit determination' (p. 218) which also takes competitive rivalry between firms into account. The degree of competition within a group influences the performance of the group members. More firms in a group increases competition within the cluster and thus reduces performance. Due to economies of scale, larger firms enjoy advantages in performance, even if the firms are all in the same group. Moreover, firms within a group may not only differ in size, but also in the cost for entering the strategic groups. Depending on the time entering a group, the barriers may differ in their height. Finally, Porter states differences between firms in the ability to pursue strategies 'in an operational sense'. In addition, he hypothesizes differences within groups (ibid., p. 210). These four factors on intra-group rivalry, as well as barriers to mobility, influence the performance of firms within an industry and lead firms to form strategic groups. Firms facing similar barriers to mobility and similar competitive rivalry show homogeneity in performance levels. Therefore, they belong to the same a strategic group.

Briefly, within an industry there exist groups based on similar performance levels within groups and different performance levels across groups. In the simplest method of group formation, there are two performance-based groups in an industry, one with high- performance firms and the other with low-performance firms. Consequently, the resulting groups could be called the high-performance group and the low-performance group.

3.3.1.2 Some Empirical Evidence
The concept of strategic groups states that similar strategies characterize the existence of groups within an industry. These groups are said to show different average performance levels due to barriers to mobility. There is a large amount of literature, both in industrial organization and in strategic management. While studies focusing from the IO perspective are primarily interested in the structural effects of strategic groups and the influence on performance of the industry, studies in strategic management evaluate firms' individual behavior. As the empirical literature on strategic groups is extensive, this section provides a survey of selected empirical studies covering selected foci that can be identified in strategic group literature.

Profitability differences across firms motivate most empirical contributions in the area of strategic groups. Consequently, performance measures are the key variable in many studies. Usual performance measures are the return on investment (e.g., Morrison and Roth 1992), market share (e.g., Fiegenbaum and

Thomas 1995) and return on assets (e.g., Mehra 1996; Houthoofd and Heene 1997; Nair and Kotha 2001; Gonzàlez-Fidalgo and Ventura-Victora 2002). But more sophisticated performance measures are also applied to detect significant differences across strategic groups. Ferguson et al. (2000), for example, identify significant differences in reputation across groups and confirm that better reputation goes along with higher performance. To capture the different dimensions of firm performance, some studies incorporate various performance measures sequentially.

Literature on strategic groups falls into three categories. The first one consists of studies examining the existence of groups within an industry and searches for profitability differences across groups (e.g., Houthoofd and Heene 1997; Nath and Gruca 1997; Ferguson et al. 2000). Second, there is a category focusing on the influence of profitability of the branches on group structure (e.g., Porter 1979; Gonzàlez-Fidalgo and Ventura-Victora 2002). And the third category of empirical studies concentrates on group structures and group membership over time (Más Ruís 1998; Nair and Kotha 2001). The majority of empirical studies belong to the first group, dealing with the influence of the structure within an industry on performance.

Identifying strategic groups researchers either start with the complete industry as one group and then splitting it up to several homogenous groups or they start with one firm as the smallest group and merging. Multivariate methods, such as factor analysis, cluster analysis, or variance analysis detect most frequently groups within an industry. Then in the second stage, usually, regression analysis deals with the performance differences across the different groups. Empirical investigations tend to focus on banking, insurance, breweries, hospitals or pharmaceuticals. There seems to be evidence that in many industries heterogeneity within the sector exists and that strategic groups can be identified (e.g., Nair and Kotha 2001 for Japanese steel industry; McNamara et al. 2002 for banks; Gonzàlez-Fidalgo and Ventura-Victora 2002 for manufacturing; McNamara et al. 2002 for top management teams from US banks).

Nevertheless, there are some studies that do not support the existence of strategic groups (Kling and Smith 1995 for airlines; Nath and Gruca 1997 for hospitals). However the investigations of the relation between the structure of an industry and performance are less striking. Some studies reveal significant differences across groups while others do not. Nath and Gruca (1997) as well as Kling and Smith (1995) do not show any performance differences within the industry. But Ferguson et al. (2000), Gonzàlez-Fidalgo and Ventura-Victora (2002), and McNamara et al. (2002) show performance differences across strategic groups.

Applications of strategic groups in higher education are rare. For higher education in Germany, Warning (2004) provides evidence that strategic variables related to social sciences on the one hand, and to natural sciences on the other hand, characterize performance-based groups in German universities. The influence of teaching and research relation as strategic variables seems to be significantly weaker in that sample.

Empirical research of strategic groups considers the main elements of the concept: the strategic variables and their influence on performance. With respect to the two main implications of the concept of strategic groups, the literature reveals two tendencies: First, there seems to be evidence for clusters, i.e., strategic groups, in many industries and second, while the evidence for performance differences across groups is weaker, performance differences are observed.

3.3.1.3 Theoretical Foundations

Apart from barriers to mobility, there are further theoretical explanations for the existence of strategic groups, i.e., heterogeneity within a branch. After Caves and Porter (1977) introduced the concept of strategic groups into the economic and business economic literature, subsequent research was mostly based on empirical studies. Theoretical explanations for the existence of strategic groups started much later. Strategic groups were introduced into the literature after empirically revealing performance differences that did not depend on the structure of the industry. However performance differences were and are observed under identical structural circumstances.

There are four general theoretical approaches for explaining heterogeneity within industries. Tang and Thomas (1992) as well as Thomas and Pollack (1999) survey these theoretical explanations for heterogeneity within an industry. They present spatial competition, management cognition, interorganizational networks and the resource-based view as possible explanations. These theoretical approaches are from different fields and can be taken to explain the existence of strategic groups, and consequently heterogeneity within an industry. While spatial competition originates from traditional industrial organization, management cognition is from psychology and interorganizational networks stem from sociology.

Spatial Competition   Using the traditional Hotelling model of spatial competition, Tang and Thomas (1992) show that firms tend to locate in similar positions. They assume that two firms are competing in a market, called the linear city (Hotelling 1929). Furthermore, customers are equally distributed in this linear city, firms cannot differentiate in price and the cost of relocation is zero. If a firm enters the market and locates anywhere (not in the middle) of the linear line, then the second firm entering positions itself in the middle of the longer free area and receives a higher market share, as customers face linear transportation costs from their home to that firm's location. Therefore, firm 1 has an incentive to move toward the second firm so that it covers the longer portion of the line. In an ongoing relocation process, both firms end up locating in the middle of the linear city. Reinterpretation of the spatial function 'distance' to other dimensions as reliability or availability (Thomas and Pollock 1999) leads to a general result of positioning as firm clusters within an industry based on strategic dimensions.

However varying the above assumptions (e.g., the amount of relocation costs), D'Aspremont et al. (1979) as well as Economides (1986) show that firms tend to move to the edges of the linear line and that firms stay separated. But Tang and Thomas (1992) believe these two extreme positioning strategies, absolute clustering and absolute separation, can be combined. If relocation costs are moderate within an industry, groups of firms are observed, while groups themselves tend to maximize attribute distance from each other. In this way spatial competition provides a theoretical explanation for the barriers to mobility. Apart from the models discussed by Tang and Thomas (1992) or Thomas and Pollack (1999) other variants of product differentiation models are explored to study the construction of mobility barriers. However the literature provides further explanations for firm clustering.

Management Cognition   From a psychological point of view the mental models of managers and other decision-makers cause the existence of structural differences within an industry. In this way, the cognitive view starts at the firm level and composes firms into groups where decision makers share mental models. Sharing these beliefs with other managers leads to a 'cognitive community' (Thomas and Pollack 1999) that can also be interpreted as a strategic group because managers with similar beliefs lead their firms to choose similar strategies, resulting in homogenous performance and, thus, producing the characteristics of a strategic group.

Interorganizational Networks   The network approach from sociology focuses on the relation of firms within an industry by collaboration considering that firms form strategic alliances, joint ventures, research cooperation etc. as formal networks (Thomas and Pollack 1999). Formal networks distribute and share fixed costs. Also firms within an informal network can be assumed to built up barriers to mobility.

Resource-Based View   While the preceding approaches explain groups within an industry, the resource-based view relates compatibly to the concept of strategic groups. It suggests that resources, human capital and physical capital, determine firm strategy. Thus group building is based upon firm resources, in interaction with the environment and explains performance differences across groups. Briefly, not competitive strategies, but rather internal choice and resources determine firm performance and thus group membership (Wernerfeldt 1984).

3.3.2   Product Differentiation

This section discusses various variants of product differentiation as explanations for the heterogeneity of firms within an industry. While differentiation models on the one hand focus explicitly on positions of firms, on the other hand Subsection 3.3.1.1 interprets product differentiation as building up barriers to mobility. In this way they also serve as a theoretical explanation of strategic groups. First, I briefly discuss two types of product differentiation, horizontal and vertical, in the one-dimensional context. The second part presents insights of multi-dimensional product differentiation models; again, considering horizontal and vertical differentiation. Additionally, this section presents the effects of allowing differentiation in the horizontal and vertical dimensions simultaneously.

Horizontal product differentiation is discussed when, for an increase of a product's characteristic, there is a consumer whose utility increases and there exists another consumer whose utility decreases (Phlips and Thisse 1982). There is no explicit ordering of the preferability of the characteristic. Consequently, horizontal differentiation models are also called variety competition models. Vertical product differentiation is present when all consumers benefit from an increase in the level of the product's characteristic in the product space (Phlips and Thisse 1982). While under horizontal differentiation only some consumers prefer more of the characteristic, under vertical differentiation all consumers prefer the characteristic, which leads to an alternative name of quality competition.

The basic structure of differentiation models assume that there are two firms competing in at least one dimension. Consumers pay a price for the product. Furthermore, there is a profit function $\Pi_i = p_i D_i$ of the firm $i = A, B$, given by the product of the price consumers pay and the demand for product A (or equivalently for buying at firm A). Marginal costs are assumed to be constant and equal to zero for all firms. In a two-stage or three-stage game firms choose product characteristic(s) and price. The utility function of the consumers varies with the type of differentiation, horizontal or vertical.

Research on one-dimensional product differentiation is not a recent development. Hotelling (1929) presented a two-stage model in which a product was differentiated horizontally in one dimension along a linear line ('linear city') and established the principle of minimum differentiation, as explored in Subsection 3.3.1.3. Minimum differentiation means that firms choose the same location. Later, D'Asprement et al. (1979) show for horizontal differentiation that there is maximum differentiation equilibrium, assuming quadratic transportation costs for the consumers. Apart from the linear-city model, there are other models of horizontal product differentiation, like the circular-city model by Salop (1979). Under the assumption of firms locating on a circle, he achieves maximum differentiation. However, Gupta et al. (2004) recently extended this standard result of Salop to a circular city model, where agglomeration as well as dispersion occurs in equilibrium. Furthermore, a combination of both positioning strategies is possible. Nonequidistant, multiple or a continuum of equilibria arise.

The basic vertical the differentiation models originate from Mussa and Rosen (1978) as well as from Shaked and Sutton (1982) who identify maximum product differentiation in one-dimensional models. Maximum differentiation is present if firms maximize distance and reduce price competition in this way.

In summary, in the standard framework of one-dimensional product differentiation, the result of maximum differentiation is robust, independent of the kind of differentiation. However most products are characterized by more than one dimension or attribute. Therefore since the 1990s multi-dimensional product differentiation, especially two-dimensional differentiation, has gained interest. This will be more closely examined in the following paragraphs.

The literature on multiple dimensions can be categorized into three groups: first, multiple horizontal differentiation; second, multiple vertical differentiation; and third, differentiation in both horizontal and vertical dimensions. The literature on multi-dimensional product differentiation that explores horizontal differentiation is more extensive than the literature that explores vertical differentiation.

Under two-dimensional horizontal product differentiation, the utility function of the consumers is given by $V_A = S - p_A - w_1 (z_1 - a_1)^2 - w_2 (z_2 - a_2)^2$. Here a consumer receives a utility V_A by purchasing the product from firm A and the constant basic utility S; p_A is the price the consumer has to pay buying the product of firm A. Her 'address' (z_1, z_2) characterizes each consumer. The weights a consumer attaches to the different dimensions of the product are labelled with w_1 and w_2, while a_1 and a_2 represents the location of firm A in dimension 1 and 2.

There are a number of examples of models to study multiple horizontal differentiation (Economides 1986, 1989, 1993; Tabuchi 1994; Ansari et al. 1998; Irmen and Thisse 1998; Braid 1999). Using different assumptions they all finds qualitatively similar results. Economides (1986) examines a two stage location-price game between two firms assuming a family of utility functions and shows that in equilibrium differentiation is meither minimal nor maximal. Tabuchi (1994) models two firms that first decide on location, then on price; finding three results. First, there is max-min differentiation in distances; second, it is better to locate sequentially than simultaneously; finally, the welfare loss in equilibrium compared to the optimum lower.

In a two- and three-dimensional differentiation model, Ansari et al. (1998) show that in a two-stage game firm choices lead to maximum differentiation only in one dimension, but minimum differentiation in (the other) dimensions. Irmen and Thisse (1998) confirm this result by extending the two-dimensional horizontal differentiation model to n dimensions and show that maximum differentiation in one dimension and minimum differentiation in all other dimensions occurs. This result of multiple differentiation models is supported by some empirical evidence. Netz and Taylor (2002) show that gasoline stations in Los Angeles differentiate horizontally in physical space and in space of product attributes.

The utility V_A for buying at firm A and paying price p_A in the standard multi-dimensional vertical differentiation model is $V_A = S - p_A + w_1 a_1 + w_2 a_2$. S is a positive constant, w_1 is the preference parameter for dimension 1, and w_2 is the preference parameter for the second dimension. Vandenbosch and Weinberg (1995) analyze the classic model of vertical product differentiation in two dimensions and find three types of equilibria. Each type reveals maximum differentiation in one dimension, but the degree of differentiation in the other differs and is not always minimal.

There is a another paper dealing with two vertical dimensions. Garella and Lambertini (1999) introduce one dimension as a good and the other dimension as a bad, finding maximum differentiation or minimum differentiation along both dimensions. However Bontems and Réquillart (2001) show that this analysis reduces to a one-dimensional vertical differentiation model. They explain that only an explicit two-dimensional model captures all effects correctly. Therefore, explicit modelling of two dimensions is necessary.

Some authors combine horizontal and vertical product differentiation (Neven and Thisse 1990; Canoy and Peitz 1997; Bester 1998). In a mixed model the standard utility function contains elements of the horizontal differentiation model and the vertical differentiation model. Consumers receive utility V_A from buying at firm A: $V_A = S - p_A - w_1 (z_1 - a_1)^2 + w_2 a_2$.

In the standard model, Neven and Thisse (1990) combine horizontal and vertical product differentiation assuming that not all products fall in either one of the groups. First firms compete in variety (horizontally) and in quality (vertically) simultaneously. Then price competition takes place in the second stage. They find two types of equilibria. There is maximum quality differentiation and minimum variety differentiation, if the quality difference is sufficiently bigger than the interval of varieties. In contrast, maximum differentiation in variety and minimum differentiation in quality exists, if the interval of variety is larger than the quality interval.

To sum up, in the standard mixed model there is minimum differentiation in one dimension and maximum differentiation in the other dimension. There are further extensions assuming that the horizontally and vertically differentiated dimensions are not independent but interact. Degryse (1996), for example, analyzes banking interactions, Degryse and Irmen (2001) examine the incentives to improve quality if there is interaction in variety. However in an experimental analysis Mangani and Patelli (2001) cannot support this min-max result and they do not find differentiation in any dimension.

While the standard result in one-dimensional product differentiation models exhibits maximum differentiation, this tendency is reduced under multiple dimensions. Almost all multi-dimensional differentiation models reveal a common characteristic in equilibrium: firms tend to differentiate maximally in one dimension and minimally in all remaining dimensions. For all except one dimension the principle of minimum differentiation suggested by Hotelling (1929) holds.

3.4 CONCLUSIONS FROM THE LITERATURE

The theoretical literature has done well in identifying the basic trade-off that all universities face: the trade-off between improving teaching and research. This trade-off exists because resources are scarce – the scarcest resource being the time of the faculty members. Time devoted to teaching and self-organization cannot be used for research and vice versa. If universities place too much emphasis on teaching, the quality and/or quantity of research output declines, causing the reputation of the university to suffer. The university eventually might lose students to more prestigious institutions. If, on the other hand, the university overinvests in research, the quality of teaching might decline and student numbers decrease. This strong focus on the number of students is especially warranted if one tries to understand the German university system. In Germany, universities' budgets to a very large extent depend on transfers from the state governments and the size of these transfers usually depends upon the number of students each university has attracted.

However, while the theoretical literature has correctly stressed the importance of the trade-off between research and teaching, it has failed to understand how individual universities strategically behave. Specifically, the theoretical literature has neglected that strategic positioning is not similar across universities. Quite the contrary, universities differ largely in respect to the budget share they direct into research. While some universities primarily try to improve the quality of teaching, other universities go as far as possible, given the German academic system, in the direction of becoming a research university.

Surprisingly, theoretically oriented researchers only rarely developed this argument. Instead, based on Data Envelopment Analysis, empirical research has revealed how diverse all universities are, including German ones. Heterogeneity in performance across universities is significant, but heterogeneity in research seems to be greater than in teaching. These empirical results contradict theoretical studies that have identified heterogeneity in teaching-related dimensions but have ignored heterogeneity in research.

The next chapters blend the contribution of the literature on strategic groups to explain the heterogeneity of universities and develop a game-theoretic model of strategic positioning in both teaching and research in the market for higher education. Although, I will apply this model to the German case, I belief that the model is more general and allows the organization of research on all types of universities. I will solely use this model to derive testable and falsifiable hypotheses on the behavior of universities in the German academic system.

4 Strategic Groups in Higher Education

To explain heterogeneity this chapter transfers the concept of strategic groups from an industrial context to higher education. Section 4.1 examines whether the concept of strategic groups is applicable to higher education in Germany. It then presents strategic variables, performance and industry structure as the main elements of the concept. Having found heterogeneity in teaching and research earlier, Section 4.2 discusses teaching and research as strategic variables of universities. The choices made for these strategic variables determine the structure of the industry – in this case, higher education in Germany – and influence performance. Section 4.3 transfers the two elements of industry structure and performance to higher education and finally, Section 4.4 derives testable hypotheses from the concept of strategic groups in higher education.

4.1 THE MAIN ELEMENTS

Universities differ in various ways, particularly in their focus on teaching or research and in their performance. For German universities such differences can be observed as will be seen later in this chapter. To explain this heterogeneity, the idea of strategic groups can serve as a starting point. The strategic groups concept claims that the existence of heterogeneity within an industry is due to different strategies of the firms in that industry. And this results in a group structure in the sector.

A similar choice of strategies (i.e., strategic variables) that lead to relatively similar performance levels for firms within groups characterizes each firm in a group. Strategies and performance differ between groups. Before discussing the three main elements of the concept – strategic variables, industry structure and performance – evidence from the German university sector that indicates heterogeneity in higher education, and thus supports the relevance of the concept of strategic groups, is presented.

Section 4.1.1 provides some stylized facts on heterogeneity in German higher education focusing on teaching and research. Then Section 4.1.2 applies the concept of strategic groups to higher education and presents the elements in the framework of a modified Structure-Conduct-Performance paradigm.

4.1.1   Stylized Facts and Heterogeneity

Examining descriptive statistics for teaching and research at German universities suggests a considerable degree of heterogeneity. The graduate-per-student ratio reflects teaching quality and the value of grants per professor reflects research quality. The terms 'teaching quality' and 'teaching' will be used interchangeably throughout this chapter; the same is true for 'research' and 'research quality'.

Of course, neither teaching quality nor research quality can be measured or observed directly. Therefore, appropriate indicators – selected to consider the specifics of German universities – measure the quality dimension. Discussing the elements and characteristics of both measures shows why they are especially appropriate in this framework.

As the number of graduates does not necessarily provide information on a university's commitment to either teaching in general or teaching quality in particular, the ratio of the number of graduates to the total number of students is used as a proxy. The justification is that universities with a stronger teaching focus will have fewer students dropping out prior to graduation. Applying the graduate-to-student ratio as a measure for teaching quality confounds two performance indicators, the completion rate and the time taken to complete studies. In contrast to other countries, e.g. the UK, the graduate-to-student ratio in Germany captures teaching quality quite well, since German universities have significant dropout rates and give students freedom to determine the length of their studies.

In the mid-1990s, the dropout rate – including those students who enrolled and left a scientific university without any degree – amounted to 26 percent and thus was remarkably high. The percentage of students graduating in the field they have started studying is only about 40 percent across all areas (Heublein et al. 2005, p. 26). Higher dropout rates, i.e. low completion rates, might go along with lower teaching quality. A high graduate fraction of students hints at a small time taken to complete studies. In fact the duration of studies varies not only across fields, where we observe mean values below 9.3 semesters (e.g., law, pharmaceutical) and above 12 semesters (e.g., computer science, geology, medicine) (Wissenschaftsrat 2005, pp. 27-28), but also within a field. In 2003 the duration of study varied substantially, in business administration at publicly financed universities, for example, the median ranges from 9.3 and 13.3 semesters (ibid., p. 32), in economics it ranges from 9.1 to 13.7 semester (ibid., p. 76). Taking both performance indicators, dropout rate and time taken to graduate, into consideration hints at taking the graduate-to-student ratio as an appropriate indicator for teaching quality at German universities.

Figure 4.1 presents the ratio of graduates to the total number of students in 2001. Universities are ordered by the success rate, from the highest on the left to the lowest on the right. The larger the number of graduates as a share of all students, the more successful a university is at teaching. Note that demographic factors, such as an unusually strong cohort entering the university system, may distort the graduate-to-student ratios. However, since I am not interested in levels but in the existence of differences between universities, this does not affect my conclusion on heterogeneity.

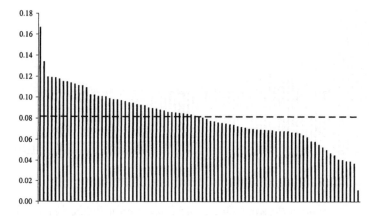

Source: Calculations using Statistisches Bundesamt (2003b) data.

Figure 4.1   Graduate-to-Student Ratio for Public Universities

With respect to teaching activities Figure 4.1 indicates considerable heterogeneity among German universities. In 2001 the ratio of graduates to students varied between 0.17 and 0.01 for the 83 included universities. The dotted line in the diagram is the average for all universities, implying that a mean of 8 percent of the enrolled students graduated in 2001.

Consider next some stylized facts about the heterogeneity of universities in research. External research grants reflect research activities in both applied and theoretical fields. Therefore, the value of research grants per professor captures the diversity of German universities in this area. Applying the value of research grants per professor as a measure for research activity can be justified by noting that applications for research grants have to be prepared carefully as they are evaluated carefully. Earlier work by the grant applicant serves as one criterion in the decision process on grants. A good reputation might also help to acquire research grants. Furthermore, the prospect of generating further grants in the future provides a strong incentive for the grant recipient to maintain quality. To normalize for size, the total amount of grants is divided by the number of professors at a university. For public universities in 2001 Figure 4.2 depicts grant values in thousands of Euro per professor.

In 2001 the value of external research grants per professor at public universities varied between 366,700 Euros and 13,470 Euros with an average of 114,600 Euros as the dotted line indicates. There is a correlation of 0.96 between all

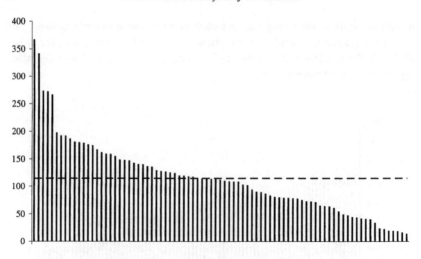

Source: Calculations using Statistisches Bundesamt (2003b) data.

Figure 4.2   Value of Research Grants per Professor for Public Universities

research grants and grants from DFG (*Deutsche Forschungsgemeinschaft*, the German Research Foundation), which are considered the most prestigious in the German scientific community (DFG 2003, p. 36). Given this high correlation coefficient, it is safe to conclude that a high volume of external grants relates with a high quality research. The DFG reports a correlation between DFG research grants and international publications of 0.86 (ibid., p. 119), which strengthens the case for using this measure. There are two conclusions: first, research grants are a good indicator of research activity and the quality of research. Second, there is considerable heterogeneity in research across German public universities.

Data from 2001 depicted in Figures 4.1 and 4.2 not only suggest heterogeneity in teaching and research among German public universities, but additionally, the descriptive statistics in Table 4.1 complement information on the distributions of teaching and research quality and thus point at different degrees of heterogeneity.

At first sight the distributions of the teaching and the research variable look almost symmetric. However the relative dispersion, defined as standard deviation divided by the mean (coefficient of variation), which makes dispersion of two differently scaled variables comparable, suggests a significant difference between the two distributions: dispersion in the grants variable is almost twice as large as dispersion in the graduate per student variable. This observation suggests that university strategies vary more in research than in teaching, which suggests that barriers to mobility in research are higher than in teaching.

The two indicators presented hint at the existence of heterogeneity across

Table 4.1 Statistics for Teaching and Research at German Public Universities

	Graduate per student	Grants per professor (in €1000)
Mean	0.082	114.600
Median	0.082	111.640
Std. Dev.	0.025	68.860
Minimum	0.011	13.470
Maximum	0.167	366.700
Relative Dispersion	0.305	0.601

Source: Calculations using Statistisches Bundesamt (2003b) data.

German universities. Institutions showing a high graduate-to-student ratio seem to focus on teaching, while universities characterized by high grant values per professor are likely pursuing a research-oriented strategy. In summary, there seems to be heterogeneity across German universities, which means utilizing the concept of strategic groups is possible in the higher education sector in order to explain its structure.

4.1.2 Transfer and Adaptation of the Concept

Starting with the assumption that there is a systematic structure in the German public university sector, examining whether the concept of strategic groups can be utilized to explain observed performance differences is important. Universities with a high graduation rate seem to be focusing on teaching, consequently, striving to maintain teaching quality. Other universities have a large value of research grants per professor, which suggests that research is important to universities.

When we transfer the concept of strategic groups to universities, the most important point emanating from the theory is the following: universities pursue different strategies resulting in different performance levels. Previously observed heterogeneity is consistent with this statement. More sophisticated empirical methods (see Chapter 7) will demonstrate that there is indeed a well-defined group structure underlying this heterogeneity. The concept of strategic groups offers a rationale for the observation that heterogeneity in research is greater than in teaching which can be explained by the differences in the barriers to mobility between teaching and research. Such barriers to mobility prevent universities in one group from moving to another. If barriers in teaching are lower than in research, universities find it easier to move to a group with high teaching quality compared to a move to a group with high research quality. Thus greater dispersion prevails in research. It is important to remember that barriers to mobility are not the only explanation for different performance levels among German universities. Competitive rivalry within and across groups is another strong force working towards heterogeneity.

Universities can focus on different things. They may differ in the fields they offer, which explain why social sciences dominate some institutions and natural sciences dominate other institutions. Furthermore, they can focus on interdisciplinary or disciplinary studies; concentrate on theoretical or industry-related studies and focus on teaching qualifications or diplomas. Perhaps the most important decision in an education sector providing teaching and research simultaneously is the allocation of resources to these two tasks. Seen from this perspective, one can consider the university sector an industry, consisting of institutions that conduct teaching and research. The concept of strategic groups, as well as other theoretical approaches, suggests that the heterogeneity observed is not random. One would expect universities to behave rationally rather than randomly in how they focus.

To describe the relationship of the two elements from the concept of strategic groups, the Structure-Conduct-Performance (SCP) paradigm from industrial organization is adapted to higher education. The traditional view of the paradigm suggests that basic characteristics of the university sector determine the institutional strategy: the choice of teaching and research quality levels. Teaching quality and research quality then act as principle factors influencing the productivity and efficiency of the university. Figure 4.3 depicts the main elements of the concept of strategic groups in higher education in a SCP framework: the strategic variables teaching and research and the relative efficiency (productivity) as performance measure – adapting the general framework of Porter (1981, p. 161).

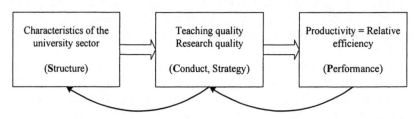

Figure 4.3   Modified SCP–Paradigm Adapted to Universities

By allowing for feedback and reverse effects, the concept of strategic groups implies an extension of this relationship. Performance influences the teaching and research quality levels universities choose, because institutions with high performance levels want to preserve their advantage. Strategy, that is to say, the strategic choices regarding teaching and research quality, affects the structure of the university sector. As opposed to the earliest form of the SCP paradigm in industrial organization, which would imply a simple linear causality from structure within the university sector to university behavior and university performance, the concept of strategic groups implies a more modern view of SCP acknowledging forces working backwards. In this sense, performance also influences strategy, which in turn changes the structure within the university sector.

4.2   TEACHING AND RESEARCH AS STRATEGIC VARIABLES

Strategic variables in higher education do not just determine university performance but also influence structure. This section will discuss teaching and research quality as strategic variables and the associated barriers to mobility. To be eligible to serve as strategic variables of universities, the variables considered need to be under the control of university administration. Teaching quality and research quality fulfill this precondition satisfactorily to an extent for empirical research. While it is not possible to claim that university administrations control these qualities directly, administrators are capable of allocating personnel resources and infrastructure investment to influence teaching and research quality.

Teaching quality and research quality have different impacts on the formation of strategic groups in the university sector. Barriers to mobility appear rather low in teaching when compared to research. To provide high-quality teaching, universities need to allocate classrooms and staff to teaching. Note that teaching staff is a less specialized type of human capital while staff allocated to research usually requires specialized human capital. Therefore, decisions concerning university research involve more specialized investments, which in turn create and explain the higher barriers to mobility in research. Furthermore, researchers in the natural sciences require large and highly specialized laboratories. These requirements for specific capital correlate with the need for large numbers of assistants working on projects due to the skills needed for research in the natural sciences. Undoubtedly, there are also investments with sunk cost characteristics in the social sciences, e.g. for libraries or general infrastructure. However sunk investments play a larger role in the natural sciences and may account for higher barriers to mobility in that part of academia.[1]

As a result of these high barriers to mobility in research, universities that want to differentiate in the two-dimensional space of teaching and research quality will find it difficult to switch from a teaching-intensive to a research-intensive institution. This provides a tentative explanation for the heterogeneity observed in German higher education both within teaching and within research and across teaching and research: similar strategies in research and dispersion in teaching characterize strategic groups and their members. Clearly, there is more than one explanation for these barriers to mobility, such as different foci during the founding years or strategic choices in an environment where competitive spirit becomes more and more relevant.

Teaching quality and research quality serve as the main strategic variables of a university. University administration uses them to steer performance, but teaching quality and research quality also influence the structure of the sector. Improvement along either dimension attracts students. However changing a university's position in research is much more difficult than in teaching. While an increase of teaching quality means graduating more and better students, an increase in research quality requires more and better publications and more success in the competition for research grants, aiming at an improved reputation that will ultimately attract more and/or better students. At the same time, improving research reputation is more costly and takes more time than improving teaching quality. Depending on the differing barriers to mobility, the influence of the two quality variables, in teaching and in research, differs between universities in a higher vs. a lower performance group of the sector.

A main criticism of strategic groups is the lack of theoretical foundations for strategic variables used in empirical research. Here I have shown that university administrators have at least two strategic variables. A formal model in the next chapter will evaluate the role of teaching quality and research quality in a setting where public universities, such as the ones in Germany, compete in a multi-stage game.

4.3   INDUSTRY STRUCTURE AND PERFORMANCE

This section deals with the performance and industry structure of the university sector. To explain the structure of the university sector consider that universities serve multiple interests: students, firms, the public sector, the scientific community and the general public. There are different ways for universities to adjust to varying demand from these markets. In particular, they can alter their efforts at teaching and research quality. Different adjustments by choosing different levels of teaching and research quality result in the structure of the university sector comprising different types of universities, which may cluster in strategic groups. Generally, there are three types of adjustments or reactions.

The first is that all universities react in the same way by choosing the same or very similar combinations of strategic variables that results in a university system where all institutions are alike. Stylized facts of the German university sector presented earlier, seem to contradict this kind of homogeneity. In addition, the theoretical analysis in the next chapter will show that such a strategic parallelism is not a plausible result of competition among public universities. Second, each university in the sector could choose a different strategy in terms of teaching and research, thus leading to the institutions of higher education being almost randomly distributed. They would be equally dispersed and the degree of heterogeneity in the sector would be very high. Descriptive data for German public universities does not reject this possibility, but theory suggests a different solution to the universities' positioning problems. This is that some universities choose to react similarly to changing conditions in the market, while other universities will respond differently, but as a group also homogeneously, by opting for another combination teaching and research qualities. As a consequence, two groups of universities arise. Universities within a given group make similar choices of the strategic variables.

University performance consists of several dimensions. These institutions of higher education produce two main outputs, teaching and research, while using a number of inputs. In contrast to industries outside the public sector, market prices are not available for the outputs of public universities. Consequently, outputs cannot simply be aggregated into a monetary measure like revenue. Therefore performance analysis for public universities takes place in multiple dimensions. To capture all dimensions of inputs and outputs in one performance indicator for universities, the concept of multi-dimensional productivity, also called relative efficiency, will be used. In this way the investigation incorporates several one-dimensional performance indicators simultaneously.

Similar performance levels characterize a strategic group. While performance within groups is homogenous, it is heterogeneous across groups. Therefore, explaining performance differences also contributes to the explanation of strategic groups. Following the reasoning of the preceding section, strategic variables are under the control of a university's administration and have a strong impact on performance. However not only do the strategic variables and barriers to mobility previously discussed determine different performance levels across universities, but also competitive rivalry within and across groups. Therefore, the following paragraphs transfer the 'theory of firm profit determination' of Porter (1979, p. 218) to higher education.

Universities build up barriers to mobility with the main strategic variables, teaching quality and research quality. Given the specificity of investments involved, the height of barriers to mobility differs between teaching and research. The performance measure corresponding to profit is multi-dimensional productivity, that is to say, the relative efficiency of one university in an industry consisting of multiple universities. By preventing universities from moving from one group to the other, barriers to mobility influence the performance of universities. In this way barriers to mobility protect universities in one group from competing with universities of other groups. Nevertheless, there is also competition within strategic groups, so that competitive rivalry within as well as across groups determines the performance of universities.

Porter (1979) discusses three additional factors influencing performance: size of the groups, strategic distance between groups and market interdependence across groups. Thus the degree of competition within the groups of universities clearly influences performance. Larger group size tends to generate more intensive intra-group competition. This is due to the fact that universities sharing similar strategies and belonging to the same group compete for the same students. Furthermore, universities within groups differ in size, measured by the number of students or the number of scientific staff. Due to economies of scale larger institutions enjoy an advantage in performance. Consequently, the size effects of universities have an impact on intra-group rivalry.

Universities differ in costs of mobility to enter a group. The height of mobility barriers universities face depends, among other sources, on the age of the university, which differs considerably across institutions. Older established universities did not face the same barriers to mobility as those founded after World War II where a number of institutions which had built up impediments to move already existed. Clearly barriers to mobility are very similar to barriers to entry. However differences in the composition of fields or subjects of a university influence its capability to move from one group to another. One can also speak of strategic distance or closeness. For example, universities that already have a medical department operating a hospital have assets that make it easier to move to a high-performance group because other universities with a number of natural science departments but without a hospital might want to be allowed to share some facilities of the hospital. Thus, initial assets may help universities to overcome barriers to mobility.

Finally, the ability of a university's administration to pursue and execute strategies also influences the institution's performance. The successful implementation of strategies of universities depends on a number of factors. Within the university, organization plays an important role. However the degree of competition in a region or a state or environmental variables depending on the location of a university, also belong to this category. Reflection on these three factors of the 'theory of firm profit determination' in the light of a sector consisting of public universities, suggests a number of control variables for the empirical investigation to be conducted later. While age, composition of fields and size, which together map intra-group rivalry characterize universities, competitive measures like student concentration and direct regional competition reflect outside competition.

In summary, the concept of strategic groups provides an explanation for heterogeneity in higher education that may result in a high- and a low-ranked group. Universities within a group show similar performance levels, whereas performance across groups differs substantially. The resulting groups within the university sector are principally characterized by the impact of two main strategic variables, which are teaching quality and research quality.

4.4 DERIVATION OF HYPOTHESES

Heterogeneity, according to the theory, is present in the strategic variables of teaching and research, as well as in performance. A high degree of homogeneity in performance characterizes universities within a group, while performance across groups is heterogeneous. This heterogeneity results from differences in the barriers to mobility associated with teaching and research. Pursuing similar strategies, universities cluster into groups: high- and low-ranked. A pairing of teaching quality and research quality, which determines a university's position subject to external factors, characterizes each university. Two hypotheses arise from the concept of strategic groups. The first hypothesis concentrates on the strategic variables, while the second one links performance differences across groups to the strategic variables.

Considering these hypotheses in greater detail and indicating how the analysis of the following chapters will test them empirically will now be discussed. Hypothesis *H1* deals with the relationship between teaching and research across universities. Teaching quality and research quality are the most important strategic variables of universities as they serve as instruments for university administrations to attract students. Increasing the number of students is one objective of universities because the state ministries provide funding on a per student basis in Germany. While higher teaching quality attracts students directly, higher research quality improves the reputation of the institution and in this way helps to attract more and better students.

As discussed in Section 4.2 teaching quality is easier to change for a university than research quality. Building a reputation for high quality research – which is closely related to the general reputation of an institution – takes a longer time and is more costly than producing teaching quality. In terms of the strategic groups concept these specific investments are called barriers to mobility. Altering positions in research is more difficult, so universities showing low research performance and quality cannot easily move into the high-performance group. The higher the barriers to mobility built up by other universities by investing in research, the more difficult it is to change groups. So differences in research across universities can, or even will, remain unchanged, while universities change their strategies in teaching and move to the most favorable position. Heterogeneity in research is higher than in teaching as barriers to mobility are higher in research (Section 4.2). For example, all universities conduct teaching, but not all institutions focus on high research quality. The following hypothesis on the relation of teaching and research summarizes this reasoning for the characteristics of teaching and research.

H1: Heterogeneity across universities is greater in research than in teaching.

As it takes more time and is more costly to build up reputation with high research quality, not all institutions make these specific and long-term investments. Additionally, while the German university system rewards the number of students directly with financial incentives, it offers only a limited reward mechanism for research that results from the impact of resource allocation for universities. In the distributional process the weight attached to the number of students at an institution is higher than the weight attached to research grants for example.[2] Furthermore, teaching and research positions were based on number of students only.

For illustration assume two extreme situations: on the one hand there is a university with a high number of students enrolled but conducting no valuable research. This kind of institution will survive, at least for a certain period. On the other hand, however, consider a university with only very few or even no students but with excellent research record. It is hard to believe that this university might be able to get public financing for a longer time. Consequently, the incentive to invest in teaching is greater than in research. However universities having previously invested in research quality gain the advantage of an additional factor to attract students. Therefore, some universities decide to invest in research quality while all of them invest in teaching quality which leads to the hypothesis of higher heterogeneity in research than in teaching.

To test the relation of teaching and research across universities directly, Chapter 6 compares scores from Data Envelopment Analysis (DEA) in teaching and research. Given such indicators for both dimensions over four years, we expect a higher correlation across models within the same dimension, teaching or research, than across models. A high correlation across teaching models is expected as well as across research models. A low correlation across scores from the same model over time suggests that changing positions of universities is easier in the dimension with lower cost of moving or repositioning which goes along with lower barriers to mobility.

While hypothesis *H1* concentrates on the strategic dimensions teaching and research solely, the second hypothesis *H2*, originating from the concept of strategic groups, tackles heterogeneity in performance across groups. According to this theory, different performance levels characterize the groups in the university sector. Consequently, in the simplest case, two groups arise, one showing high-performance (called the high-ranked group) and the other low-performance (the low-ranked group). Generally, higher quality levels in teaching as well as in research have a positive impact on performance in all groups. However the impact of qualities is not a linear one over the low-ranked and the high-ranked universities. There is an increasing rate of return from teaching quality and research quality. Returns are higher in the high-ranked group than in the low-ranked group as small changes in quality do not affect the perception of the university's general quality among students or in the public. Students and the public know top-ranked universities by their names, while lower ranked institutions are treated similarly.

Stated differently, parameter heterogeneity across teaching quality and research quality across groups arises, which leads to hypothesis *H2*:

H2a: The effect of research quality on productivity is greater in the high-ranked group than in the low-ranked group.

The second part of the hypothesis claims the analogous relation for teaching quality:

H2b: The effect of teaching quality on productivity is greater in the high-ranked group than in the low-ranked group.

More specifically, as a consequence of higher barriers to mobility in research compared to teaching, the impact of research is expected to be greater in the high-ranked group than in the low-performance group. Universities in the high-ranked group built up barriers to mobility in research, while universities in the lower group have not. Furthermore, universities in the low-ranked group cannot enter the high-ranked group easily because overcoming the barriers to mobility would be costly and a long-term process. The opposite reasoning holds for teaching quality.

Basic microeconomic thinking suggests that hypotheses *H2a* and *H2b* together offer the potential for global gains by switching activity form the low-ranked to the high-ranked group. However there are important institutional barriers to switching resources between universities in the German higher education system. First, there is no legal possibility to shift resources between universities of different states. Second, even within a state university administrations and local and regional politicians fiercely resist any attempt to reallocate resources from one university to another.

In order to test this hypothesis, Section 7.3 clusters universities on the basis of their performance into low- and high-performance groups using cluster analysis and the Zivot-Andrews test. Interaction variables for teaching quality and research quality capture the impact on the high- and the low-performance groups. Generalized least squares (GLS) regressions then reveal the impact of the variables separated by groups. Testing for equality of the coefficients in the high-ranked group and the low-ranked group for research quality (respectively, teaching quality) can then indicate the different impacts of the strategic variables across groups.

To sum up, for analyzing the structure of the German university system in terms of strategy and performance, the concept of strategic groups turns out to be an appropriate framework. Thus, the well known elements of competitive analysis as performance, strategy, and structure apply not only to ordinary for-profit firms but also deliver a suitable framework for analyzing the structure of higher education, if universities are mainly publicly funded, as in Germany.

Although the concept of strategic groups offers an explanation on how strategic variables, i.e., teaching quality and research quality, affect performance of universities and vice versa, it does not argue on the final positions universities choose in teaching and research quality in equilibrium. Taking, however, results from the concept of strategic groups on the relation between teaching and research into account, a formal model could close this gap. Chapter 5 provides such a positioning model for universities centering on teaching quality and research quality.

NOTES

1 For an extensive discussion of barriers to mobility in social sciences and natural sciences in universities, see Warning (2004).
2 See Section 2.4 for some more details of financing of universities.

5 A Model of Competition: Positioning in the University Sector

Universities in German higher education are far from homogenous. No doubt, they are still much less heterogenous than US universities. However they differ considerably more than the politicians who designed the system wanted them to. Despite a relatively high level of regulation in the system they act strategically, mainly in competition for students, but also research has gained importance as a competitive parameter over the last few years. Thus, the main strategic variables – also currently discussed by politicians and in the media – are teaching and research, both in terms of quality and quantity.

In the continuing discussion about competition between universities, governments as well as universities themselves focus on the positioning of academic institutions with respect to teaching and research. While the preceding chapter on strategic groups was based more on intuition and verbal argumentation, this chapter provides a formal analysis of university positioning. A model of two-dimensional differentiation is presented, familiar from industrial economics, while paying attention to the specifics of the university sector. First, it takes into account that most universities in Germany are publicly financed and that students currently do not have to pay tuition and fees to attend. Second, in contrast to standard differentiation models (Hotelling 1929 and D'Aspremont et al. 1979 for horizontal differentiation; Shaked and Sutton 1982 for vertical differentiation), universities require two dimensions – teaching and research – to be considered.

It can be assumed that students prefer higher teaching quality over lower teaching quality to finish their studies quickly and successfully. As research is one component building up the reputation of a university, students favor quality research in order to take advantage of a degree from a high reputation university on the labor market. These considerations motivate universities to vertically differentiate in teaching and research quality.

To analyze positioning in the university sector, I use a three-stage game. Universities first choose teaching and research quality, in the second stage they decide on student support levels which are independent of teaching and research qualities but capture additional services a university provides for its students. In the third stage, students decide which university to attend.

This model is a variant of the general two-dimensional vertical differentiation model by Vandenbosch and Weinberg (1995). Apart from the fact that they analyze a general framework and not a university context, there are two main differences between their model and mine. First, while in Vandenbosch and Weinberg (1995) firms receive a specific price for their product paid by customers, in my model universities receive a constant payment from the state ministry for each student. Second, universities pay support to students to attract them, while Vandenbosch and Weinberg (1995) assume zero costs of production. Starting with this slightly different framework, the qualitative results remain similar.

Considering the number and importance of publicly financed university systems, theoretical analyses and results in this area are surprisingly rare. In particular, the positioning decision and the resulting structure within the higher education sector have not been widely evaluated. The three-stage model explicitly accounts for the characteristics of a publicly funded university system, like the German one, and shows that the well-known result of 'maximum differentiation' holds. Basically, universities differentiate maximally in one dimension while differentiation in the other dimension is minimal.

The structure of this chapter is as follows: Section 5.1 presents the framework and basic assumptions for the positioning model of publicly funded universities. Demand for education at the universities is introduced in Section 5.2 where I also discuss the student decision in stage three. In Sections 5.3 and 5.4 the equilibria in the second and the first stage are derived which leads to a positioning equilibrium for the universities. Discussing the results of the model in Section 5.5, particularly in the context of general differentiation models, leads to a testable hypothesis in the final Section 5.6. Briefly, the model explains how universities position themselves in teaching and research.

5.1   ASSUMPTIONS AND FRAMEWORK

A three-stage game between two universities each of which offers one 'product' facing direct demand is the theoretical framework developed here. Characterized by two attributes – teaching quality and research quality – the product is called 'higher education'. Consequently, a teaching-research combination represents each university. Recalling that university attendance has been free in Germany for a long time, we consider a publicly funded university system, where students do not have to pay tuition.

However universities not only provide teaching and research for free, but also invest in location-specific infrastructure, like dormitories, to attract students. This spending, which will also be called 'support', is not directly related to teaching and research quality. Instead, these investments can be interpreted as university-specific support for the students deliberately chosen by the university. Students are assumed to be heterogenous and choose the university they want to apply to based on teaching and research quality and on the support level, which are observable for them. There are no admission standards and universities accept all students who apply. For almost all fields of study this assumption fits the situation at German universities until the late 1990s perfectly well. When formal admission criteria are applied, student ability in most cases is only one element of a set of criteria, including proximity to parents' home and social indicators and is typically dominated by these other criteria.

This framework reflects the specific situation of a publicly funded university system: Students gain support from the university they attend and, in addition, receive the product of higher education with the attributes teaching and research. Universities receive a fixed amount per student from the government and do not get tuition or fees from the students.

Two representative universities are indexed with $j = 1, 2$. Both offer one product called higher education which is characterized by two dimensions, teaching quality t_j and research quality r_j. A pair (r_j, t_j) represents the product of each university j, where these characteristics take positive values from the intervals $r_j \in [\underline{r}, \overline{r}]$ and $t_j \in [\underline{t}, \overline{t}]$, with $\underline{r}$ and $\underline{t}$ denoting minimum qualities, $\overline{r} \geq 0$ and $\overline{t} \geq 0$ denoting maximum research and teaching qualities.

Teaching quality t_j and research quality r_j are funded by fixed, publicly provided basic financing (principally spending on personnel and on buildings). Both teaching quality and research quality can be measured in resources spent on quality to make those two dimensions comparable. Universities receive a fixed budget and, in addition, government pays a fixed amount per student to adjust for differing enrollment, i.e. government transfers a lump sum p per student to each university. Furthermore, university j decides about the indirect financial support level s_j it wants to provide to every student attending. This subsidy is independent of teaching and research quality but depends on other university characteristics, including spending on dormitories, for example .

Assume university j faces demand $D_j (s_1, s_2)$ which is the mass of students who prefer higher education from university j over higher education from university i. Then it maximizes its performance function:

$$P_j (s_1, s_2) = (p - s_j) D_j (s_1, s_2), \text{ for } j = 1, 2. \tag{5.1}$$

If the support expenditure is higher than the transfer from government, which is usually the case for public universities, the difference $(p - s_j)$ representing the surplus per student of university j is negative.

The specification captures via the demand function two aspects of prime importance for a German public university: the quality of teaching and research which – as we will see later – influences the number of students. For a nonprofit institution like a public university we can imagine a number of different objective functions, ranging from social welfare to individual objectives of a university administration, such as size or number of fields offered. The objective function used here includes the size of a university as an important factor, but acknowledges that this size is influenced directly or indirectly by the choice of a support level and of teaching and research quality. It is, therefore, neither a mere bureaucratic objective function, nor is it a single profit function.

Before applying students observe the teaching and research quality of a university. They prefer higher teaching quality over low teaching quality, and they prefer higher research quality over lower research quality. With regard to their evaluation of teaching and research quality students are heterogenous, where two parameters θ_t and θ_r capture this heterogeneity: θ_t denotes the valuation of teaching quality, θ_r the valuation of research quality. A pair (θ_r, θ_t) characterizes each student in (θ_r, θ_t)-space. These two research and teaching valuation parameters can be interpreted as representing the students' opportunity costs and are a signal for their ability. Both parameters of valuation are assumed to be uniformly and independently distributed over the students and without loss of generality restricted to $[0, 1]$. As the intervals for the characteristics t_j and r_j can be scaled arbitrarily, this normalization does not limit the analysis or influence the results. While alternative, more complicated distributional assumptions can be imagined, there is no compelling reason or convincing story to apply one of them. Therefore, I stick to the simplest distribution possible which is common in the literature on differentiation and leads to an analytically tractable version of the model.

Students receive a basic utility b that is high enough to induce them to attend university. Although there is no tuition in Germany, studying has costs for students which are to an extent university-specific and can be influenced by the institution through investment in infrastructure. Consequently, students prefer universities that provide a high level of support to compensate for university-specific costs. Therefore, the support level s_j of university j enters positively into a student's objective function. Students can only attend one single university and apply to the institution, which maximizes their indirect utility function. So when attending university j, a student receives utility $u(r_j, t_j; \theta_r, \theta_t)$:

$$u(r_j, t_j; \theta_r, \theta_t) = b + \theta_r r_j + \theta_t t_j + s_j, \text{ for } j = 1, 2. \qquad (5.2)$$

As the model focuses on the question which university students choose to attend and not whether they attend, every student receives the same basic utility which is normalized to zero in the following analysis. This utility function, in a wider context, can be seen as utility function of government in terms of a paternalistic utility function.

The timing of the three-stage game is as follows: In the first stage, universities choose teaching and research qualities, mostly via hiring. These are long-term decisions which cannot be easily changed, as shifts from a teaching-oriented university to a research-oriented one are costly and can only be realized over time by changing hiring policies. In the second stage, universities choose their support level in order to reduce university-specific costs for students. As this support contains the provision of cheap public transportation or subsidized housing, universities can revise this decision within a relatively short time period. Prices for public transportation of students can be negotiated almost every year and additional apartments can be rented or housing subsidies changed. Based on these actions of the university, in stage three under complete information students choose which university to attend. Backward induction solves the game applying the concept of a non-cooperative Nash equilibrium. After determining the indifferent student, the equilibrium support levels are derived and finally, the positioning equilibrium in terms of r_j and t_j is analyzed.

5.2   THE DEMAND FUNCTIONS OF THE UNIVERSITIES

In this section the demand functions for the two representative universities are derived and the third stage of the game is solved. To begin with the location in (θ_t, θ_r)- space where students are indifferent between university 1 or university 2 is determined. The characteristics of this geographic location are discussed to prepare for calculating the demand both universities face. From characterizing the indifferent students four cases arise that will be analyzed separately throughout the entire model. After some general explanations for the computation of the demand functions, the explicit forms of the different sections are derived. Some remarks on concavity and convexity conclude the section.

5.2.1   Computation Procedure of the Demand Functions

Within the aforementioned framework, the (θ_t, θ_r)-space is a unit square presenting the position of students in terms of valuations of teaching and research quality. It is defined by the corners (0,0), (0,1), (1,0) and (1,1). While Vandenbosch and Weinberg (1995) use trigonometry to determine the demand functions for the institutions, I determine demand in a straightforward and more general way by integrating. Students who are indifferent between applying at university 1 and 2 are located on the indifference line defined by

$$\theta_r r_1 + \theta_t t_1 + s_1 = \theta_r r_2 + \theta_t t_2 + s_2.$$

Given (r_j, t_j, s_j) for both universities from stage one and stage two, this indifference condition results in a line called the indifference line. In (θ_t, θ_r)-space it is given by

$$\theta_r (\theta_t) = \frac{s_1 - s_2}{r_2 - r_1} + \frac{t_1 - t_2}{r_2 - r_1} \theta_t. \tag{5.3}$$

The position of the indifference line within the (θ_t, θ_r)-space depends on the slope $(t_1 - t_2) / (r_2 - r_1)$ and the intercept $(s_1 - s_2) / (r_2 - r_1)$. Then, the indifference line divides the mass of students, given by the square with an area of one, into two groups. Students below the line choose to attend university 1, while students above the line decide to attend university 2. Consequently, university 1's demand is the area under the given indifference line which is characterized by its slope and its intercept. Given the slope of the indifference line, the demand function for university 1 (and university 2) depends on the axis intercept $(s_1 - s_2)/(r_2 - r_1)$.

To illustrate the basic idea of determining the demand functions, demand is calculated for a positive slope and a negative θ_r intercept as in Figure 5.1, by integrating along the indifference line. In general, the minimum value for the lower limit of the integral is 0, the maximum value for the upper limit is 1 as both θ_t and θ_r are defined over the interval $[0; 1]$. Computing the area under the indifference line $\theta_r (\theta_t)$ and considering the parameter restrictions of the (θ_t, θ_r)-space leads to a sum of two areas, one is a triangle, the other is a rectangle.

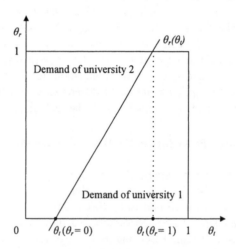

Figure 5.1   Demand with a Sample Indifference Line

Computing the integral along the indifference line within the valid limits, leads to the first part, the triangle. The lower limit of the integral is the point where the indifference line intersects the θ_t-axis, $\theta_t (\theta_r = 0)$; this lower limit is $\theta_t (\theta_r = 0) = - (s_1 - s_2) / (t_1 - t_2)$. The upper limit of the integral is the point where the indifference line intersects the upper bound of the (θ_t, θ_r)-space; that is $\theta_t (\theta_r = 1) = [(r_2 - r_1) - (s_1 - s_2)] / (t_1 - t_2)$. Integrating from $\theta_t (\theta_r = 1)$ to 1 over the constant 1 – as the maximum value of θ_r is 1 by assumption – produces the second part of the area, the remaining rectangle. Adding both areas, given the indifference line $\theta_r (\theta_t)$, leads to the demand of university 1:

$$D_1 = \int_{\theta_t(\theta_r=0)}^{\theta_t(\theta_r=1)} \theta_r\left(\theta_t\right) d\theta_t + \int_{\theta_t(\theta_r=1)}^{1} 1 d\theta_t.$$

Given the slope in Figure 5.1, the lower integration limit of the first area, the triangle, will be 0, when the intercept is equal to zero or larger. The upper integration bound of the first area will be 1, if the intercept becomes small enough for the indifference line to intersect at the corner $(1,1)$ or even at a lower level of θ_r. Then the second area, the rectangle, becomes zero and demand for university 1 is computed as one area, the triangle. Given the assumption that the two universities cover the complete market of mass 1 of students, the demand for university 2 will be $D_2 = 1 - D_1$.

As illustrated in the example, the demand functions for university 1 and university 2 depend on the characteristics of the indifference line: its slope $(t_1 - t_2)/(r_2 - r_1)$ and intercept $(s_1 - s_2)/(r_2 - r_1)$. Before determining the demand functions explicitly by integrating, the effect of these two characteristics on the demand function is examined in more detail.

The slope of the indifference line varies with the differences in teaching and in research between the two universities, specifically, the relation between $(t_1 - t_2)$ and $(r_2 - r_1)$. Based on the values of the slope, there exist four possible cases, which capture the different positions of the universities. First, the slope can either be positive or negative which leads to two basic types of university positioning: comparative dominance and absolute dominance. In the comparative dominance case each university has an advantage in one dimension. If university 1 has an advantage in teaching over university 2, i.e., $(t_1 - t_2) > 0$ and university 2 has an advantage in research over university 1, i.e., $(r_2 - r_1) > 0$, this results in a positively sloped indifference line. Likewise the opposite distribution of advantages is given by $(t_1 - t_2) < 0$ and $(r_2 - r_1) < 0$ and leads to a positive slope, too. In the absolute dominance case, one university has an advantage in both dimensions, research and teaching, over the other university. This corresponds to a negative slope of the indifference line: $((t_1 - t_2) > 0$ and $(r_2 - r_1) < 0)$ or $((t_1 - t_2) < 0$ and $(r_2 - r_1) > 0)$.

Second, the absolute value of the slope of the indifference line can be greater or smaller than one. If absolute differentiation is greater in research than in teaching, then the situation is called 'research dominance'. Consequently, the absolute difference $|r_2 - r_1|$ in this case is larger than $|t_1 - t_2|$ and the slope of the indifference line is smaller than 1 as equation (5.3) shows. If there is research dominance, depending on the sign of the slope 'comparative research dominance' (crd) and 'absolute research dominance' (ard) can be distinguished. In the case of 'comparative research dominance' each university has an advantage in one dimension, whereas in the 'absolute research dominance' case one university has an advantage in both dimensions. The opposite of research dominance is teaching dominance. Under teaching dominance, the absolute difference of teaching qualities $|t_1 - t_2|$ between the universities is greater than the absolute difference in research qualities $|r_2 - r_1|$, which results in a slope of the indifference line greater than one. Under teaching dominance, comparative teaching dominance and absolute teaching dominance can occur. In 'comparative teaching dominance' (ctd) each university has an advantage in one dimension, while 'absolute teaching dominance' (atd) implies an advantage of one university in both teaching and research. In summary, there are four possible cases: research dominance and teaching dominance with comparative dominance and absolute dominance.

Without loss of generality, in the absolute dominance case, assume the advantage in both dimensions to be at university 2, so that $(r_2 - r_1) > 0$ and $(t_1 - t_2) < 0$. Also, without loss of generality, in the comparative dominance case university 1 is assumed to have an advantage in teaching, whereas university 2 has an advantage in research, which is denoted by $(r_2 - r_1) > 0$ and $(t_1 - t_2) > 0$. That is, $(r_2 - r_1) > 0$ is used throughout the analysis. Combining the assumptions about the parameters leads to four cases summarized in Table 5.1.

Table 5.1   The Four Cases of the Analysis

	Comparative Dominance *slope > 0*	Absolute Dominance *slope < 0*
Research Dominance $|slope| < 1$	$|t_1 - t_2| \le |r_2 - r_1|$ and $(t_1 - t_2) > 0$ and $(r_2 - r_1) > 0$	$|t_1 - t_2| \le |r_2 - r_1|$ and $(t_1 - t_2) < 0$ and $(r_2 - r_1) > 0$
Teaching Dominance $|slope| > 1$	$|t_1 - t_2| \ge |r_2 - r_1|$ and $(t_1 - t_2) > 0$ and $(r_2 - r_1) > 0$	$|t_1 - t_2| \ge |r_2 - r_1|$ and $(t_1 - t_2) < 0$ and $(r_2 - r_1) > 0$

The intercept of the indifference line, $(s_1 - s_2) / (r_2 - r_1)$, influences the position of the line separating university 1's demand from university 2's demand. For given choices of the universities with regard to teaching and research, the support level difference of university 1 and university 2 $(s_1 - s_2)$ are crucial for the intercept. Changes in $(s_1 - s_2)$ shift the indifference line up or down and in this way influence the demand for the universities. In stage two the universities set the support to levels they want to provide their students, given their teaching and research quality. To analyze in more detail the characteristics of the intercept, assume that the research quality difference $(r_2 - r_1)$ and the teaching quality difference $(t_1 - t_2)$ are given. Depending on the difference in support levels $(s_1 - s_2)$, those indifference lines are described that intersect the corners of the (θ_t, θ_r)-square because demand functions of the universities change, whenever the indifference line intersects such a corner. Therefore, different demand areas within the four cases of Table 5.1 have to be distinguished.

Figure 5.1 already suggests that the indifference line can be shifted up and down by varying the support level difference. For a smaller intercept, for example, the indifference line is shifted down and passes the corner $(\theta_t = 1, \theta_r = 1)$ which changes the computation of the demand. The way in which the computation of the demand changes depends on the intervals of the indifference line. As these intervals result form the support levels of the two universities, boundary support levels for the demand regions can be determined. Assuming the support level of university 2 is given, then from (5.2) the support level of university 1 is

$$s_1^{(\theta_t, \theta_r)}(s_2) = s_2 - \theta_t(t_1 - t_2) + \theta_r(r_2 - r_1). \tag{5.4}$$

The superscript (θ_t, θ_r) indicates which corner in the (θ_t, θ_r)-space is met by the indifference line. For example, $s_1^{(1,0)}(s_2) = s_2 - (t_1 - t_2)$ represents the limit of the support level interval for university 1, given the support level of university 2, where the corner is described by $\theta_t = 1$ and $\theta_r = 0$. Geometrically, this is the lower right-hand corner. By substituting the corner coordinates for θ_r and θ_t the three demand regions are described, assuming the support level of university 2 is given.

The area below an indifference line describes the demand for university 1's education. The support level for university 2 can be expressed as function of the support level of university 1, leading to

$$s_2^{(\theta_t, \theta_r)}(s_1) = s_1 + \theta_t(t_1 - t_2) - \theta_r(r_2 - r_1). \tag{5.5}$$

Again, the boundary levels for the demand functions arising from the support level corner solutions are derived. These four boundary support levels differ in their ordering depending on the slope of the indifference line and the cases introduced earlier: absolute research dominance (ard), absolute teaching dominance (atd), comparative research dominance (crd) and comparative teaching dominance (ctd). Based on these cases the demand functions for research and teaching dominance can be derived. Each university's demand function consists of three sections in which the computation procedure differs. Depending on where the indifference line intersects the unit square, the demand function is: convex (region B), linear (region A) and concave (region C). To identify the different demand regions in the proceeding analysis the labels A, B and C will be used.

As total demand is represented by the area of the unit square in (θ_t, θ_r)-space, the demand of university 2 follows from the demand function of university 1 immediately as

$$D_1\left(s_1, s_2\right) + D_2\left(s_1, s_2\right) = 1. \tag{5.6}$$

If university 1 captures all demand, then $D_1\left(s_1, s_2\right) = 1$ and all students attend university 1 independent of its positioning with respect to r_1 and t_1. In the other extreme $D_1\left(s_1, s_2\right) = 0$ and consequently university 1 faces no demand. Between these two extreme situations, the demand function is continuous and consists of three sections.

Based on the four cases of Table 5.1 the demand functions can be developed. The demand of university 1 is the area between the indifference line and the line defined by $\theta_r\left(\theta_t\right) = 1$ for all θ_t within the square. $_iD_j^d\left(s_1, s_2\right)$ denotes the demand function for university $j = 1, 2$ in region $i = A, B, C$ for case $d = crd, ard, ctd, atd$. For example, $_AD_1^{ard}\left(s_1, s_2\right)$ represents the demand university 1 faces under absolute research dominance in region A. For given teaching qualities and research qualities and given support levels for both universities, the demand function is derived.

The following paragraphs illustrate the computation of demand functions for university 1 under comparative research dominance implying that the indifference line has a positive slope smaller than 1. From Figure 5.2 we observe the ordering of the intercepts of the boundary support levels as follows: $s_1^{(1,0)}\left(s_2\right) < s_1^{(0,0)}\left(s_2\right) < s_1^{(1,1)}\left(s_2\right) < s_1^{(0,1)}\left(s_2\right)$.

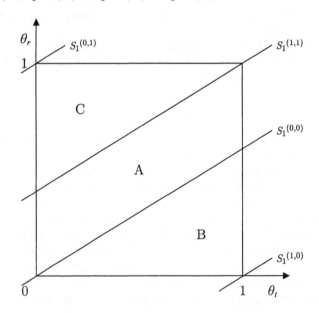

Figure 5.2   Indifference Line under Comparative Research Dominance

The demand function for university 1 is linear, if the indifference line intersects the square in region A, which is defined by the interval of boundary support levels $[s_1^{(0,0)}(s_2), s_1^{(1,1)}(s_2)]$:

$$AD_1^{crd}(s_1, s_2) = \int_0^1 \theta_r(\theta_t)\, d\theta_t$$

$$= \frac{2(s_1 - s_2) + (t_1 - t_2)}{2(r_2 - r_1)}. \tag{5.7}$$

If the indifference line intersects the square in region B, defined by the interval of boundary support levels $[s_1^{(1,0)}(s_2), s_1^{(0,0)}(s_2)]$, the demand function for university 1 is convex in s_1 and has the following form

$$BD_1^{crd}(s_1, s_2) = \int_{\theta_t(\theta_r)=0}^1 \theta_r(\theta_t)\, d\theta_t$$

$$= \frac{[(t_1 - t_2) + (s_1 - s_2)]^2}{2(r_2 - r_1)(t_1 - t_2)}. \tag{5.8}$$

For the indifference line intersecting the square in area C, the demand function for university 1 is defined by the interval $[s_1^{(1,1)}(s_2), s_1^{(0,1)}(s_2)]$ and has a concave form:

$$CD_1^{crd}(s_1, s_2) = \int_0^{\theta_t(\theta_r=1)} \theta_r(\theta_t)\, d\theta_t + \int_{\theta_t(\theta_r=1)}^1 1\, d\theta_t$$

$$= 1 - \frac{[(r_2 - r_1) - (s_1 - s_2)]^2}{2(r_2 - r_1)(t_1 - t_2)}. \tag{5.9}$$

Combining functions for regions A, B and C configures the demand function under comparative research dominance. Demand functions for the three remaining cases, absolute research dominance, comparative teaching dominance and absolute research dominance, are derived applying a similar procedure.[1] Recall that the slope of the indifference line is negative under absolute dominance which, however, does not change the computation procedure in general. Section 5.3 presents demand functions for all cases to build the performance functions of the universities.

5.2.2 Concluding Remarks on the Demand Functions

To sum up, the demand functions for the universities consist of three parts which are located in different regions defined by boundary support levels. In region B and region C demand functions are identical under absolute and comparative teaching dominance and under absolute and comparative research dominance. But the intervals on which these demand functions are defined vary. For region A, the linear section of the demand functions differ in functional form for all four cases.

As all students are assumed to start studying at a university, demand for university 2 is always the complement of demand of university 1. Consequently, the regions defined by the support levels are just the opposite from university 1. Figure 5.3 shows (similar to Vandenbosch and Weinberg (1995), p. 234) the shape of the demand function for university 1, D_1, and university 2, D_2, for a specific set of parameters and decisions on stage one of the game.

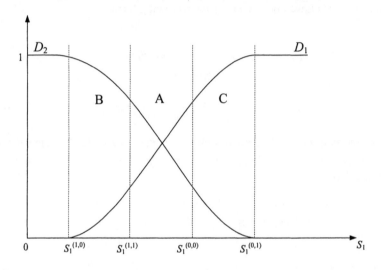

Figure 5.3   Demand Functions for a Given Support Level s_2 of University 2

In the case presented in Figure 5.3 the indifference line is positively sloped and the intercept leads to the following ordering of the boundary support levels of university 1: $s_1^{(1,0)}(s_2) < s_1^{(1,1)}(s_2) < s_1^{(0,0)}(s_2) < s_1^{(0,1)}(s_2)$. This ordering corresponds to comparative teaching dominance. However for all other cases the characteristics of the shape of the demand functions are the same while the shape always changes at the boundary support levels. Recall that the boundary support levels reflect the corners of the (θ_t, θ_r)-space of student preferences for teaching quality and research quality. For support levels smaller than the smallest boundary, here $s_1^{(1,0)}(s_2)$, the demand for university 1 is zero and all students study at university 2. In region B – defined by $[s_1^{(1,0)}(s_2), s_1^{(1,1)}(s_2)]$ – the demand of university 1 is convex. The shape of the demand function changes at the boundary level $s_1^{(1,1)}(s_2)$ and becomes linear over the interval $[s_1^{(1,1)}(s_2), s_1^{(0,0)}(s_2)]$ called region A. Demand of university 1 in region C, defined by the interval $[s_1^{(0,0)}(s_2), s_1^{(0,1)}(s_2)]$, is concave. Support levels larger than the maximum support level, here $s_1^{(0,1)}(s_2)$, lead to a demand of 1 for university 1, so that it covers the entire market.

5.3 THE SUPPORT LEVEL UNIVERSITIES PROVIDE TO STUDENTS

This section solves the second stage of the model by deriving the optimal support levels of university 1 and 2. The cases of comparative research dominance, absolute research dominance, comparative teaching dominance and absolute teaching dominance are examined separately. I determine a non-cooperative support level equilibrium $(s_1^\star, s_2^\star)$ that can be characterized by performances $P_i(s_i^\star, s_j^\star) \geq P_i(s_i, s_j^\star)$ for all support levels $s_i \geq 0$ with $i, j = 1, 2$ and $i \neq j$. Equilibria under research dominance are denoted with superscript $\star$, while equilibria in teaching dominance are denoted with $\dagger$.

The analysis always starts in region A where the demand function is linear. Taking the boundary support levels into account, it turns out that not all regions of the demand functions have to be considered to find the positioning equilibria of the universities. Under comparative dominance the support level equilibrium always lies in the linear part of the demand function so that in the cases of crd and ctd only the A regions have to be analyzed. Under absolute dominance the equilibria can be found in regions A or B so that region C needs not to be analyzed. These statements will be verified by varying the values of teaching and research quality of both universities after analyzing the support levels in the single regions and before determining the exact positioning equilibria.

5.3.1 Research Dominance

Under research dominance the difference of teaching qualities is smaller than the difference between research qualities of the universities, i.e., $|t_1 - t_2| \leq |r_2 - r_1|$. Thus, the absolute value of the slope of the indifference line is always smaller than 1 which occurs in two situations. Under comparative research dominance university 1 has an advantage in teaching while university 2 has an advantage in research. Therefore, under comparative research dominance the slope is positive. This will be discussed in the next paragraph in detail. Then the case of absolute research dominance will be examined where the advantage of university 2 in both teaching and research leads to a negative slope of the indifference line.

5.3.1.1 Comparative Research Dominance
If university 2 has an advantage in research and university 1 in teaching, i.e., $(r_2 - r_1) > 0$ and $(t_1 - t_2) > 0$, there is comparative research dominance.

In combination with the condition for research dominance, the ordering of the support levels of university 1 is

$$s_1^{(1,0)}(s_2) < s_1^{(0,0)}(s_2) < s_1^{(1,1)}(s_2) < s_1^{(0,1)}(s_2).$$

We start with region A, defined by the interval $[s_1^{(0,0)}(s_2), s_1^{(1,1)}(s_2)]$. The performance function of university 1 in region A is

$$_A P_1^{crd}(s_1, s_2) = (p - s_1)_A D_1^{crd}(s_1, s_2)$$

$$= (p - s_1) \frac{1}{2(r_2 - r_1)} [2(s_1 - s_2) + (t_1 - t_2)]. \qquad (5.10)$$

The first-order condition of university 1 leads to its reaction function

$$s_1 = \frac{1}{2}p + \frac{1}{2}s_2 - \frac{1}{4}(t_1 - t_2). \qquad (5.11)$$

Observe from (5.11) that the support levels are strategic complements. For university 2 the performance function in region A is given by

$$_A P_2^{crd}(s_1, s_2) = (p - s_2)_A D_2^{crd}(s_1, s_2)$$

$$= \frac{(p - s_2)}{(r_2 - r_1)} \left(s_2 - s_1 + r_2 - r_1 - \frac{1}{2}(t_1 - t_2) \right). \qquad (5.12)$$

Solving the first-order condition for s_2 leads to the reaction function for university 2:

$$s_2 = \frac{1}{2}p + \frac{1}{2}s_1 + \frac{1}{4}(t_1 - t_2) - \frac{1}{2}(r_2 - r_1). \qquad (5.13)$$

Solving the system (5.11) and (5.13) for s_1 and s_2, the optimal support levels for university 1 and university 2 are[2]

$$s_1^* = p - \frac{1}{6}(t_1 - t_2) - \frac{1}{3}(r_2 - r_1) \qquad (5.14)$$

$$s_2^* = p + \frac{1}{6}(t_1 - t_2) - \frac{2}{3}(r_2 - r_1). \qquad (5.15)$$

Since the demand region is defined by the support level interval $[s_1^{(0,0)}(s_2), s_1^{(1,1)}(s_2)]$, these optimal values must belong to this interval, though, the conditions $s_1^* \in [s_1^{(0,0)}(s_2^*), s_1^{(1,1)}(s_2^*)]$ and $s_2^* \in [s_2^{(1,1)}(s_1^*), s_2^{(0,0)}(s_1^*)]$ must hold. For the support level of university 1 we get

$$s_1^{(0,0)}(s_2^*) \leq s_1^* \Leftrightarrow s_2^* \leq s_1^* \Leftrightarrow (t_1 - t_2) \leq (r_2 - r_1)$$

and

$$s_1^* \leq s_1^{(1,1)}(s_2^*) \Leftrightarrow s_1^* \leq s_2^* - (t_1 - t_2) + (r_2 - r_1) \Leftrightarrow (t_1 - t_2) \leq (r_2 - r_1),$$

which is true for the case of comparative research dominance examined here. Analogously, for the support level of university 2:

$$s_2^{(1,1)}(s_1^*) \leq s_2^* \Leftrightarrow s_1^* + (t_1 - t_2) - (r_2 - r_1) \leq s_2^* \Leftrightarrow (t_1 - t_2) \leq (r_2 - r_1)$$

and

$$s_2^* \leq s_2^{(0,0)}(s_1^*) \Leftrightarrow s_2^* \leq s_1^* \Leftrightarrow (t_1 - t_2) \leq (r_2 - r_1). \tag{5.16}$$

Given the optimal support levels demand for university 1 is

$$_AD_1^{crd}(s_1^*, s_2^*) = \frac{1}{(r_2 - r_1)} \left(\frac{1}{6}(t_1 - t_2) + \frac{1}{3}(r_2 - r_1) \right). \tag{5.17}$$

As the demand of university 2 results as complement of the demand function of university 1, it is given by

$$_AD_2^{crd}(s_1^*, s_2^*) = \frac{1}{(r_2 - r_1)} \left(-\frac{1}{6}(t_1 - t_2) + \frac{2}{3}(r_2 - r_1) \right). \tag{5.18}$$

Under comparative research dominance, the dominance condition equals exactly the region condition of the boundary support level. There will not occur any equilibrium in region B or C that leads to a potential positioning equilibrium as will be discussed later.

5.3.1.2 Absolute Research Dominance
Under absolute research dominance university 2 has an advantage both in teaching and in research, i.e. $(t_1 - t_2) \leq 0$ and $(r_2 - r_1) > 0$. Combining these constraints with the research dominance inequality leads to $-(t_1 - t_2) \leq (r_2 - r_1)$ which implies for the ordering of the boundary support levels

$$s_1^{(0,0)}(s_2) < s_1^{(1,0)}(s_2) < s_1^{(0,1)}(s_2) < s_1^{(1,1)}(s_2).$$

Again, the analysis for university 1 starts in region A, defined by the interval $[s_1^{(1,0)}(s_2), s_1^{(0,1)}(s_2)]$. Under absolute research dominance with region A, the demand functions equal the ones of the comparative research dominance case. Consequently, the performance function and also the resulting optimal support levels are the same as before.

But the ordering of the boundary support levels differs between comparative and absolute research dominance. Under absolute research dominance the following conditions must hold for (s_1^{**}, s_2^{**}) to be an equilibrium: $s_1^{**} \in$

$[s_1^{(1,0)}(s_2^{**}), s_1^{(0,1)}(s_2^{**})]$ and $s_2^{**} \in [s_2^{(0,1)}(s_1^{**}), s_2^{(1,0)}(s_1^{**})]$.

(s_1^{**}, s_2^{**}) only define a support level equilibrium, if $-(t_1 - t_2) \leq 2(r_2 - r_1)$ and $-(t_1 - t_2) \leq 1/2(r_2 - r_1)$ are valid. These two inequalities reduce to one restriction because $-(t_1 - t_2) \leq 1/2(r_2 - r_1)$ is always stronger and can be interpreted as 'very strong' research dominance. The restriction is even stronger than $-(t_1 - t_2) \leq (r_2 - r_1)$ from absolute research dominance.

Further support level equilibria might exist in regions B and C. The analysis continues with region B, where demand of university 1 is convex and demand of university 2 is concave. Region B is defined by boundary support levels in the interval $[s_1^{(0,0)}(s_2), s_1^{(1,0)}(s_2)]$. The performance function of university 1 in region B is

$$_B P_1^{ard}(s_1, s_2) = (p - s_1)_B D_1^{ard}(s_1, s_2)$$

$$= (p - s_1) \frac{-(s_1 - s_2)^2}{2(t_1 - t_2)(r_2 - r_1)}. \tag{5.19}$$

This leads to a first-order condition of the performance function which is quadratic in the support levels and has two solutions for s_1

$$s_1 = s_2 \text{ or } s_1 = \frac{2}{3}p + \frac{1}{3}s_2. \tag{5.20}$$

Since for $s_1 = s_2$ the demand for university 1 is zero, $_A D_1^{ard}(s_1, s_2) = 0$, the second solution is used. Solving the first-order condition for university 2's performance function for s_2 delivers the corresponding results for university 2, and using restrictions from absolute dominance finally leads to the optimal support levels for university 1 and university 2:

$$s_{11}^{***} = p + \frac{1}{4}\sqrt{-2(t_1 - t_2)(r_2 - r_1)} \tag{5.21}$$

$$s_{21}^{***} = p + \frac{3}{4}\sqrt{-2(t_1 - t_2)(r_2 - r_1)} \tag{5.22}$$

or

$$s_{12}^{***} = p - \frac{1}{4}\sqrt{-2(t_1 - t_2)(r_2 - r_1)} \tag{5.23}$$

$$s_{22}^{***} = p - \frac{3}{4}\sqrt{-2(t_1 - t_2)(r_2 - r_1)}. \tag{5.24}$$

The second order condition does only hold for $(s_{12}^{***}, s_{22}^{***})$, so that we continue with these equilibrium support levels. Due to the boundary support levels s_{12}^{***} and s_{22}^{***}, the following conditions must hold:

$$s_{12}^{***} \in [s_1^{(0,0)}(s_{22}^{***}), s_1^{(1,0)}(s_{22}^{***})] \text{ and } s_{22}^{***} \in [s_2^{(1,0)}(s_{12}^{***}), s_2^{(0,0)}(s_{12}^{***})].$$

In combination with the absolute research dominance inequality we get the inequality $-(t_1 - t_2) \leq (r_2 - r_1) \leq -2(t_1 - t_2)$. In region C the positioning equilibrium cannot occur, as will be shown later. Therefore, no support level equilibrium will be calculated here.

5.3.2 Teaching Dominance

Under teaching dominance the difference between teaching qualities is greater than the difference between research qualities of the universities, i.e. $|r_2 - r_1| \leq |t_1 - t_2|$. Therefore, under teaching dominance the slope of the indifference line is always greater than 1. We can distinguish two cases: in comparative teaching dominance university 1 has an advantage in teaching while university 2 has an advantage in research implying a positive slope of the indifference line. I will discuss this case in the next paragraph, and the absolute teaching dominance case will be analyzed after that where the advantage of university 2 in both teaching and research leads to a downward sloping indifference line.

5.3.2.1 Comparative Teaching Dominance

University 2 has an advantage in research and university 1 has an advantage in teaching. The ordering of the boundary support levels in comparative teaching dominance is

$$s_1^{(1,0)}(s_2) < s_1^{(1,1)}(s_2) < s_1^{(0,0)}(s_2) < s_1^{(0,1)}(s_2).$$

Starting with region A defined by the interval $[s_1^{(1,1)}(s_2), s_1^{(0,0)}(s_2)]$, the performance function of university 1 is linear

$$_A P_1^{ctd}(s_1, s_2) = (p - s_1)_A D_1^{ctd}(s_1, s_2)$$
$$= (p - s_1) \frac{(s_1 - s_2) + (t_1 - t_2) - \frac{1}{2}(r_2 - r_1)}{(t_1 - t_2)}. \quad (5.25)$$

Writing an analogous performance function for university 2 and solving the system of first-order conditions for s_1 and s_2, the optimal support levels of university 1 and university 2 are

$$s_1^\dagger = p - \frac{2}{3}(t_1 - t_2) + \frac{1}{6}(r_2 - r_1) \quad (5.26)$$

$$s_2^\dagger = p - \frac{1}{3}(t_1 - t_2) - \frac{1}{6}(r_2 - r_1). \quad (5.27)$$

Since the support level interval $[s_1^{(1,1)}(s_2), s_1^{(0,0)}(s_2)]$ defines the demand region, $s_1^\dagger$ and $s_2^\dagger$ can only be equilibrium values, if $s_1^\dagger \in [s_1^{(1,1)}(s_2^\dagger), s_1^{(0,0)}(s_2^\dagger)]$ and $s_2^\dagger \in [s_2^{(0,0)}(s_1^\dagger), s_2^{(1,1)}(s_1^\dagger)]$.

All constraints reflect the inequalities defining the comparative teaching dominance case. The support equilibrium is $(s_1^\dagger, s_2^\dagger)$ in region A while there are no support equilibria in the areas B and C as will be discussed later.

5.3.2.2 Absolute Teaching Dominance

Under absolute teaching dominance university 2 has an advantage in both teaching and research, i.e. $(t_1 - t_2) \leq 0$ and $(r_2 - r_1) > 0$. Teaching dominance then implies $-(t_1 - t_2) \geq (r_2 - r_1)$, and the ordering of the boundary support levels is

$$s_1^{(0,0)}(s_2) < s_1^{(0,1)}(s_2) < s_1^{(1,0)}(s_2) < s_1^{(1,1)}(s_2).$$

Starting the analysis with region A, the linear performance function of university 1 is

$$\begin{aligned}
{}_A P_1^{atd}(s_1, s_2) &= (p - s_1)_A D_1^{atd}(s_1, s_2) \\
&= (p - s_1) \frac{1}{(t_1 - t_2)} \left(-(s_1 - s_2) + \frac{1}{2}(r_2 - r_1) \right). \quad (5.28)
\end{aligned}$$

Using (5.27) and the analogous function for university 2, we derive first-order conditions which lead to the optimal support levels for university 1 and university 2:

$$s_1^{\dagger\dagger} = p + \frac{1}{3}(t_1 - t_2) + \frac{1}{6}(r_2 - r_1) \qquad (5.29)$$

$$s_2^{\dagger\dagger} = p + \frac{2}{3}(t_1 - t_2) - \frac{1}{6}(r_2 - r_1). \qquad (5.30)$$

These optimal values must belong to the support interval $[s_1^{(0,1)}(s_2), s_1^{(1,0)}(s_2)]$. Therefore, conditions have to be identified which ensure that $s_1^{\dagger\dagger} \in [s_1^{(0,1)}(s_2^{\dagger\dagger}), s_1^{(1,0)}(s_2^{\dagger\dagger})]$ and $s_2^{\dagger\dagger} \in [s_2^{(1,0)}(s_1^{\dagger\dagger}), s_2^{(0,1)}(s_1^{\dagger\dagger})]$. In essence, for an equilibrium in region A to exist, we need strong absolute teaching dominance, $(t_1 - t_2) \leq -2(r_2 - r_1)$.

Demand functions under absolute teaching dominance and absolute research dominance are equal in region B. Consequently, the performance functions are identical and the resulting support level equilibria under absolute teaching dominance are the same as under absolute research dominance. Also, as in absolute research dominance, only the second pair of support levels fulfills the second-order condition and is an equilibrium. However the support level intervals differ between absolute research dominance and absolute teaching dominance. The second solution of region B must belong to the boundary intervals: $s_{12}^{\dagger\dagger\dagger} \in [s_1^{(0,0)}(s_{22}^{\dagger\dagger\dagger}), s_1^{(0,1)}(s_{22}^{\dagger\dagger\dagger})]$ and $s_{22}^{\dagger\dagger\dagger} \in [s_2^{(0,1)}(s_{12}^{\dagger\dagger\dagger}), s_2^{(0,0)}(s_{12}^{\dagger\dagger\dagger})]$ The only condition which imposes a binding constraint is $(t_1 - t_2) \geq -2(r_2 - r_1)$. Combining this inequality with the constraint from absolute teaching dominance it turns out that $(r_2 - r_1) \leq -(t_1 - t_2) \leq 2(r_2 - r_1)$ must hold. In region C the positioning equilibrium cannot occur as will be explained later.

5.4 UNIVERSITY POSITIONING IN TEACHING AND RESEARCH

Now we analyze the first stage of the game. Based on the optimal support levels from stage two, the positioning equilibria of the two universities are determined. Identifying the regions of possible positioning equilibria is the first step. Then, in the second step I determine the performance functions of the universities based on the support level equilibria from the preceding section. After that, the first-order conditions of each university's research and teaching quality are examined, given the position of the other university.

Interpreting these first derivatives as unilateral incentives, they thus describe the directions of performance improving behavioral changes. The third step identifies the best responses for each case and each university. From these best responses, the one that yield the highest performance are selected. Based on these best responses with maximum performance, Nash equilibria of the positioning game are derived. But before beginning our analysis of the performance of the universities, we need to follow the lead of Vandenbosch and Weinberg (1995) and clarify in which regions equilibria may occur.

5.4.1 Regions for Product Equilibria

This subsection explains why under comparative dominance there is an equilibrium neither in region B nor in region C. Furthermore, it states why under absolute dominance no equilibrium exists in region C. Both facts were mentioned before while solving the second stage of the game. The basic idea is to use the fact that the demand functions are continuous and that regions move continuously.

Under comparative research dominance, all constraints from the boundary support levels reflect the relations of teaching and research differences exactly. They are always satisfied in region A which implies that the only support equilibrium in the comparative research dominance case is in region A. From Figure 5.3 it becomes apparent that there cannot be any support equilibria in the other regions, B or C. Consequently, (s_1^*, s_2^*) is a unique equilibrium under comparative research dominance. Assume t_1 and t_2 are given with $(t_1 - t_2) > 0$ and the corresponding research qualities are changed. For identical research qualities with $(r_2 - r_1) = 0$ the conditions of teaching dominance hold and the optimal support levels fall into the interval defined by teaching dominance. For that reason the support level equilibrium under comparative teaching dominance is in region A. If $(r_2 - r_1)$ increases, the difference could be greater than $(t_1 - t_2)$ so that research dominance holds. The intervals defined by the boundary support levels of teaching dominance will not hold anymore, but the boundary support levels of research dominance will become valid so that the support level equilibrium will be under comparative research dominance in area A.

Similar arguments hold, assuming that when r_1 and r_2 are given $(r_2 - r_1) > 0$, the teaching qualities of the two universities are changed. For $(t_1 - t_2) = 0$ research dominance conditions are binding. As the difference in research qualities is greater than in teaching qualities, the optimal support levels fall into the interval defining research dominance so that the support level equilibrium under comparative research dominance is in region A. If $(t_1 - t_2)$ increases, the difference can become larger than $(r_2 - r_1)$ so that teaching dominance maintains. Then, the intervals defined by the boundary support levels under teaching dominance will hold, so that the support equilibrium will be in area A under comparative teaching dominance. As the conditions resulting from the boundary support levels are identical for the lower and upper boundaries, the support level equilibria move directly from comparative research dominance to comparative teaching dominance. Therefore, the positioning equilibrium will not occur in either regions B or C.

Assume t_1 and t_2 are given with $(t_1 - t_2) < 0$ and the corresponding research qualities are changed. For identical research qualities with $(r_2 - r_1) = 0$ the conditions of teaching dominance hold and the optimal support levels fall into the interval defined by teaching dominance. Consequently, the support level equilibrium under comparative teaching dominance is in region A. If $(r_2 - r_1)$ increases, the difference might become larger than $(t_1 - t_2)$ so that research dominance holds. The intervals defined by the boundary support levels of teaching dominance will not hold anymore, but the boundary support levels of research dominance will become valid so that the support equilibrium will be under comparative research dominance in area A.

When r_1 and r_2 are given with $(r_2 - r_1) > 0$ and the teaching qualities of the two universities are varied, the opposite reasoning holds. For $(t_1 - t_2) = 0$ the conditions for research dominance hold and the optimal support levels fall into the interval defining research dominance. As a result, the support level equilibrium under comparative research dominance is in region A. If $(t_1 - t_2)$ increases the difference might become larger than $(r_2 - r_1)$ so that teaching dominance holds. The intervals defined by the boundary support levels of research dominance will no longer hold, but the boundary support levels of teaching dominance will become valid so that the support equilibrium will be under comparative teaching dominance in area A. As the conditions resulting from the boundary support level are equal for the lower bound and the upper bound, the support level equilibria move directly from comparative research dominance to comparative teaching dominance and the positioning equilibrium will not occur in regions B or C of the demand function.

As a consequence of these considerations, no positioning equilibrium will exist in regions B and C under comparative dominance. Furthermore, there is no equilibrium in region C under absolute dominance. Therefore, these regions need not to be taken into account for the positioning equilibrium analysis.

5.4.2 Performance of the Universities

Prior to the analysis of positioning equilibria, the performance functions under the cases identified before have to be derived. Recall that the performance function of university i is given by

$$P_i\left(s_1^*, s_2^*\right) = \left(p - s_i^*\right) D_i\left(s_1^*, s_2^*\right). \tag{5.31}$$

Under comparative research dominance, performance of university 1 in area A equals performance under absolute research dominance in area A

$$
\begin{aligned}
_A P_1^{crd}\left(s_1^*, s_2^*\right) &=_A P_1^{ard}\left(s_1^{**}, s_2^{**}\right) \\
&= \frac{1}{(r_2 - r_1)}\left(\frac{1}{3}\left(r_2 - r_1\right) + \frac{1}{6}\left(t_1 - t_2\right)\right)^2 \\
&=: P_1^*\left(r_1, t_1; r_2, t_2\right) = P_1^{**}\left(r_1, t_1; r_2, t_2\right).
\end{aligned}
\tag{5.32}
$$

The corresponding performance for university 2 is

$$
\begin{aligned}
_A P_2^{crd}\left(s_1^*, s_2^*\right) &=_A P_2^{ard}\left(s_1^{**}, s_2^{**}\right) \\
&= \frac{1}{(r_2 - r_1)}\left(\frac{2}{3}\left(r_2 - r_1\right) - \frac{1}{6}\left(t_1 - t_2\right)\right)^2 \\
&=: P_2^*\left(r_1, t_1; r_2, t_2\right) = P_2^{**}\left(r_1, t_1; r_2, t_2\right).
\end{aligned}
\tag{5.33}
$$

Performance of university 1 under absolute research dominance turns out to be equal to performance under absolute teaching dominance in area B. However conditions for existence differ.

$$
\begin{aligned}
_B P_1^{ard}\left(s_1^{***}, s_2^{***}\right) &=_B P_2^{atd}\left(s_1^{\dagger\dagger\dagger}, s_2^{\dagger\dagger\dagger}\right) \\
&= \frac{1}{16}\sqrt{-2\left(r_2 - r_1\right)\left(t_1 - t_2\right)} \\
&=: P_1^{***}\left(r_1, t_1; r_2, t_2\right) = P_1^{\dagger\dagger\dagger}\left(r_1, t_1; r_2, t_2\right).
\end{aligned}
\tag{5.34}
$$

University 2's performance for this case is

$$
\begin{aligned}
_B P_2^{ard}\left(s_1^{***}, s_2^{***}\right) &=_B P_1^{atd}\left(s_1^{\dagger\dagger\dagger}, s_2^{\dagger\dagger\dagger}\right) \\
&= \frac{9}{16}\sqrt{-2\left(r_2 - r_1\right)\left(t_1 - t_2\right)} \\
&=: P_2^{***}\left(r_1, t_1; r_2, t_2\right) = P_2^{\dagger\dagger\dagger}\left(r_1, t_1; r_2, t_2\right).
\end{aligned}
\tag{5.35}
$$

Under comparative teaching dominance, performance of university 1 equals minus the performance under absolute teaching dominance of university 2 in region A.

$$
\begin{aligned}
{}_A P_1^{ctd}\left(s_1^\dagger, s_2^\dagger\right) &= -{}_A P_2^{atd}\left(s_1^{\dagger\dagger}, s_2^{\dagger\dagger}\right) \\
&= \frac{1}{(t_1 - t_2)}\left(-\frac{1}{6}(r_2 - r_1) + \frac{2}{3}(t_1 - t_2)\right)^2 \qquad (5.36) \\
&=: P_1^\dagger\left(r_1, t_1; r_2, t_2\right) = -P_2^{\dagger\dagger}\left(r_1, t_1; r_2, t_2\right).
\end{aligned}
$$

For university 2 we find

$$
\begin{aligned}
{}_A P_2^{ctd}\left(s_1^\dagger, s_2^\dagger\right) &= -{}_A P_1^{atd}\left(s_1^{\dagger\dagger}, s_2^{\dagger\dagger}\right) \\
&= \frac{1}{(t_1 - t_2)}\left(\frac{1}{6}(r_2 - r_1) + \frac{1}{3}(t_1 - t_2)\right)^2 \qquad (5.37) \\
&=: P_2^\dagger\left(r_1, t_1; r_2, t_2\right) = -P_1^{\dagger\dagger}\left(r_1, t_1; r_2, t_2\right).
\end{aligned}
$$

While the results in the different cases are very similar, recall that conditions for existence differ.

To determine the positioning equilibria of each university i, the performance functions of the universities are evaluated. Universities are in a Nash equilibrium position, if both universities cannot improve their performance by repositioning. For the analysis, the four cases of comparative research dominance, absolute research dominance, comparative teaching dominance, and absolute teaching dominance have to be considered as well as the validity intervals defined by the boundary support levels.

Calculating the derivatives of the performance function of university i with respect to its own research and teaching quality, r_i and t_i, reveals the directions of performance improving behavioral changes. The sign of the first-order condition indicates if a university improves its performance by increasing or decreasing teaching and research quality. Assuming university 2's qualities are given, the derivatives of the performance function of university 1 with respect to teaching quality or research quality are always strictly positive or strictly negative within a certain case. Table 5.2 provides a summary of the signs of the first derivatives and adds the conditions for these performance functions to be relevant.[3]

Columns 1 and 2 present the unilateral incentives for the universities to increase performance by choosing teaching and research quality. The first column gives the signs of the first derivatives of the performance function for university 1. Column 2 reports the corresponding results for university 2, again for research quality and teaching quality. The third column presents the conditions

Table 5.2 *Unilateral Incentives of Universities (Corresponding Conditions)*

University 1	University 2	Dominance	Region
$\dfrac{\partial_A P_1^{crd}}{\partial r_1} < 0$	$\dfrac{\partial_A P_2^{crd}}{\partial r_2} > 0$		
$\dfrac{\partial_A P_1^{crd}}{\partial t_1} > 0$	$\dfrac{\partial_A P_2^{crd}}{\partial t_2} > 0$	$(t_1 - t_2) \le (r_2 - r_1)$	$(t_1 - t_2) \le (r_2 - r_1)$
$\dfrac{\partial_A P_1^{ard}}{\partial r_1} < 0$	$\dfrac{\partial_A P_2^{ard}}{\partial r_2} > 0$		
$\dfrac{\partial_A P_1^{ard}}{\partial t_1} > 0$	$\dfrac{\partial_A P_2^{ard}}{\partial t_2} > 0$	$-(t_1 - t_2) \le (r_2 - r_1)$	$-(t_1 - t_2) \le \dfrac{1}{2}(r_2 - r_1)$
$\dfrac{\partial_B P_1^{ard}}{\partial r_1} < 0$	$\dfrac{\partial_B P_2^{ard}}{\partial r_2} > 0$		
$\dfrac{\partial_B P_1^{ard}}{\partial t_1} < 0$	$\dfrac{\partial_B P_2^{ard}}{\partial t_2} > 0$	$-(t_1 - t_2) \le (r_2 - r_1)$	$(t_1 - t_2) \le -\dfrac{1}{2}(r_2 - r_1)$
$\dfrac{\partial_A P_1^{ctd}}{\partial r_1} > 0$	$\dfrac{\partial_A P_2^{ctd}}{\partial r_2} > 0$		
$\dfrac{\partial_A P_1^{ctd}}{\partial t_1} > 0$	$\dfrac{\partial_A P_2^{ctd}}{\partial t_2} < 0$	$(t_1 - t_2) \ge (r_2 - r_1)$	$(t_1 - t_2) \ge (r_2 - r_1)$
$\dfrac{\partial_A P_1^{atd}}{\partial r_1} > 0$	$\dfrac{\partial_A P_2^{atd}}{\partial r_2} > 0$		
$\dfrac{\partial_A P_1^{atd}}{\partial t_1} < 0$	$\dfrac{\partial_A P_2^{atd}}{\partial t_2} > 0$	$-(t_1 - t_2) \ge (r_2 - r_1)$	$-(t_1 - t_2) \ge 2(r_2 - r_1)$
$\dfrac{\partial_B P_1^{atd}}{\partial r_1} < 0$	$\dfrac{\partial_B P_2^{atd}}{\partial r_2} > 0$		
$\dfrac{\partial_B P_1^{atd}}{\partial t_1} < 0$	$\dfrac{\partial_B P_2^{atd}}{\partial t_2} > 0$	$-(t_1 - t_2) \ge (r_2 - r_1)$	$(t_1 - t_2) \ge -2(r_2 - r_1)$

for the dominance region, absolute or comparative dominance, and teaching or research dominance. Column 4 shows the conditions that define the regions in which the support level equilibria are valid. Row 1 of Table 5.2, for example, indicates in the first column that under comparative research dominance university 1 has an incentive to decrease its research quality, given any teaching and research combination of university 2. Furthermore, row 2 (in the first cell) states a positive first derivative of the performance function with respect to teaching so that university 1 under comparative research dominance has an incentive to increase teaching quality independent of the strategic choices of university 2. The dominance condition and the region condition must always hold simultaneously.

5.4.3 Equilibrium Analysis

Depending on the parameters of the indifference line, four cases were defined which are examined separately throughout the entire analysis. Although demand for each university consists of three different parts, each one valid in an interval defined by so-called boundary support levels, only six regions are relevant for the equilibrium analysis. As discussed in Subsection 5.4.1, positioning equilibria can only exist in region A under comparative dominance (crd and ctd) and in regions A and B under absolute dominance (ard and atd).

This section solves the first stage of the model, i.e. the positioning of universities. The derivation of the equilibrium position of the universities follows three steps. First, it is assumed that one university, e.g. university 2, chooses the maximum values for both research quality and teaching quality. Given this position of university 2, the best response of university 1 is determined for each case and region in which an equilibrium exists. The unilateral incentives in Table 5.2 indicate performance improving directions for the universities. Additionally, dominance as well as regional conditions for each case must hold simultaneously. Based on the best response in each region, the corresponding performance levels are computed. Given the position of university 2, the best response research-teaching quality pair that exhibits the maximum performance level will also be called the 'best best response' of university 1.

Second, the best best response of university 1 serves as starting point for identifying the best reply of university 2. Again, for all relevant cases and regions the best response of university 2 is identified, and the performance levels in each case are determined. As before, I select the best response of university 2 revealing the highest performance level of all best responses and called it the 'best best response' of university 2, given university 1's position. Finally, in a third step, these best best responses are combined to yield a subgame perfect Nash equilibrium.

Although the underlying model differs in the third and the second stage from the game in Vandenbosch and Weinberg (1995), my analysis of the positioning equilibria is similar to theirs.[4] The analysis starts by assuming university 2 chooses maximum quality in both attributes teaching and research. An intuitive explanation is that students prefer higher quality over lower quality. Consequently, a university providing maximum quality in both dimensions will attract most students. Therefore, one university always chooses maximum research quality and maximum teaching quality which yields highest performance.

Proposition 1 *Assume* $(\bar{t} - \underline{t}) \leq (\bar{r} - \underline{r})$.

(1.1) Assume university 2 chooses maximum research quality and maximum teaching quality $(r_2 = \bar{r}, t_2 = \bar{t})$. *Then the best best response for university 1 is* $(r_1 = \underline{r}, t_1 = \bar{t})$.

(1.2) Assume university 1 chooses minimum research quality and maximum teaching quality $(r_1 = \underline{r}, t_1 = \bar{t})$. *Then the best best response for university 2 is* $(r_2 = \bar{r}, t_2 = \bar{t})$.

(1.3) Combining (1.1) and (1.2) leads to a Nash equilibrium $(r_1, t_1; r_2, t_2) = (\underline{r}, \bar{t}; \bar{r}, \bar{t})$.

Proof. The proof of Proposition 1 proceeds in three steps. After proving (1.1) and (1.2) the third part (1.3) follows immediately. For the proof see Appendix E. ■

If the range of possible teaching qualities is smaller than the range of the possible research qualities, differentiation in research is maximal in equilibrium and minimal in teaching. Universities choose to increase the distance in the dimension in which they can go farthest away from the other university.

Proposition 2 *Assume* $(\bar{t} - \underline{t}) > (\bar{r} - \underline{r})$.

(2.1) Assume university 2 chooses maximum research quality and maximum teaching quality $(r_2 = \bar{r}, t_2 = \bar{t})$. *Then the best best response for university 1 is* $(r_1 = \bar{r}, t_1 = \underline{t})$.

(2.2) Assume university 1 chooses minimum research quality and maximum teaching quality $(r_1 = \bar{r}, t_1 = \underline{t})$. *Then the best best response for university 2 is* $(r_2 = \bar{r}, t_2 = \bar{t})$.

(2.3) From (2.1) and (2.2) follows that $(r_1, t_1; r_2, t_2) = (\bar{r}, \underline{t}; \bar{r}, \bar{t})$ *is a Nash equilibrium.*

Proof. The proof is very similar to the one of Proposition 1 and therefore it is not presented here. See Appendix E for the proof of Proposition 1. ■

Universities maximize their distance in teaching and minimize distance in research, if the interval of teaching qualities is larger than the interval of research qualities. There are two further propositions by symmetry which are not presented here for two reasons: First, they follow immediately from the analysis above, and second, they do not provide further insights for the positioning of universities.[5]

5.5   GENERAL DISCUSSION

Within the framework of a publicly financed higher education system, the model presented exhibits maximum differentiation in research quality (respectively, teaching quality) and minimum differentiation in teaching quality (respectively, research quality). This section discusses the results of the positioning model for publicly funded universities and relates them to the conventional wisdom of product differentiation in for-profit firms. The finding of minimum differentiation in one dimension and maximum differentiation in the other at universities is consistent with the literature on product differentiation among profit maximizing firms.

Universities offer higher education characterized by two attributes: teaching quality and research quality. Students prefer higher quality over lower quality in both research and in teaching. Students demand both high quality teaching and high quality research. Their demand for teaching is direct, while demand for research is indirect and is reflected in students' choices of universities based upon a university's reputation. Evidence suggests that students indeed demand high quality teaching. At the same time, research improves a university's reputation which personnel managers can observe. Therefore students are also interested in high research quality.

In a framework of strategic interaction, universities in equilibrium choose to differentiate minimally in one attribute and maximally in the other, depending on the range of possible qualities. If the interval for measuring research (respectively, teaching) quality is greater than the interval measuring teaching (respectively, research) quality, then universities differentiate maximally in research (respectively, teaching) and minimally in teaching (respectively, research) quality. Strategies lead to equilibria which differ across the intervals, but exhibit maximum differentiation in one attribute with minimum differentiation in the other. Different strategic choices then determine the positions of universities within the higher education sector.

Similar to Vandenbosch and Weinberg (1995), universities in the positioning model differentiate vertically in both dimensions. Students always prefer better teaching and research quality over lower quality levels, but instead of the classical case of for-profit firms, where consumers have to pay a price to buy the product, here universities attract students by supporting them. Relaxation of the intensity of price competition in one dimension and using the advantages of a position 'in the middle' of all other dimensions drives the results of multi-dimensional models. Consequently, universities cluster in one attribute while differentiating maximally in the other. It depends on the teaching and research quality intervals to help determine in which dimensions minimal and maximal differentiation occurs.

A demand force and a strategic force, both familiar from one-dimensional differentiation, drive the result of maximum differentiation (Tirole 1988, pp. 296–298). The demand force implies that universities want to have as many students apply as possible in order to increase performance. Consequently, with one-dimensional differentiation, universities would share the market for students equally by having the same teaching-research combinations. However there is an additional strategic force that leads to an effect in the opposite direction. Given maximum quality in both attributes at university 2, university 1 differentiates in one dimension to reduce the influence of competition in support levels. At the same time quality in the other attribute remains at the maximum. This maximum quality ensures that some students still want to study at university 1, although quality in one dimension has not achieved the maximum value. Heterogeneity of students implies a trade-off between support and quality. Students get compensated with higher support levels in response to lower teaching or research quality.

Equilibrium results depend on the size of the research and the teaching quality intervals. Both universities aim for maximum quality in both dimensions, but the strategic forces only allow only one of them to locate there. The university that cannot pursue the high quality strategy for both dimensions chooses to offer minimum quality in the second dimension. In this way, support level competition is reduced and students are willing to apply at the university with low quality in one attribute because it still offers high quality in the other dimension.

In the literature on multi-dimensional product differentiation for for-profit firms we find similar results. Profit-maximizing firms tend to differentiate maximally in one dimension, while differentiation in the other dimension is minimal. This is true for two-dimensional vertical differentiation, for two-dimensional horizontal differentiation and for mixed differentiation. In particular, the result is in line with Economides (1989) for multiple horizontal differentiation and with Neven and Thisse (1990) for the combination of horizontal and vertical differentiation (see Section 3.3).

Consequently, there are indications that the results of the university positioning model presented here are not confined to the assumed vertical preference functions but are also robust for horizontal or combinations of horizontal and vertical differentiation (see Section 3.3). Briefly, there are clear signs that the results of university positioning are robust against variations in the utility function of the students.

Furthermore, the model can easily be extended to situations in which (public) universities charge tuition and fees. Since (a unique amount of) tuition could be in principle regarded as a negative component of the support level s_i, the positioning model from above is also capable to capture a much more general situation of public higher educations systems.

5.6 DERIVATION OF THE HYPOTHESES

One interpretation of the positioning model from the previous sections suggests that universities choose to differentiate minimally in the teaching quality dimension, while they differentiate maximally in research quality. In this way the positioning model can be interpreted as an additional foundation of the strategic groups concept. Both theoretical explanations for the heterogeneity of German universities focus on the principal variables of higher education, the strategic variables of teaching and research. While the model of strategic groups emphasizes the importance of common strategic variables for group formation based on similar performance, the positioning model explicitly reveals which positions universities choose. Postulating that in a state of equilibrium not all universities will choose identical levels of quality, one university will choose to maximize both teaching and research quality while the other university chooses also maximum teaching quality but minimal research quality. Furthermore, the symmetric solution is also an equilibrium, where both universities choose maximum research quality, but one goes for maximum teaching quality while the other chooses minimum teaching quality. They either differentiate maximally in teaching or in research quality while minimally differentiating in the other attribute.

The strategic choice of the quality levels is interesting as it determines the positioning of universities directly. Large quality intervals suggest a stronger strategic force and thus a lower demand effect. Therefore, universities differentiate maximally in the dimension exhibiting greater strategic force, i.e. the dimension with the larger dispersion over the interval of qualities. For given parameters measuring the interval of research qualities and measuring teaching qualities, there is always a Nash equilibrium. When the relations of the quality intervals for teaching and research change, the equilibrium positions of the universities move. When differentiation in research is at its maximum and the differentiation in teaching is minimal in the positioning model, the finding corresponds to the theoretical result of maximum differentiation in one dimension and minimum differentiation in the other. Due to higher mobility barriers in research than in teaching, the model of strategic groups suggests for the empirical investigation that universities differentiate maximally in research and minimally in teaching.

In the selected equilibrium stage both universities choose maximum teaching quality, while in research quality one chooses the minimum level and the other the maximum level, leading to the hypothesis that weights attached to teaching are greater than those attached to research.

H3: Universities attach greater weights to teaching than to research.

Subsection 6.4.2 will test this hypothesis by analyzing the weights of the DEA model for teaching and research. Larger average weights for teaching are consistent with the hypothesis above and therefore to confirm the results of the positioning model.

A hypothesis on group influence, even stronger than the implication from the concept of strategic groups discussed earlier would not only propose a different influence on being in the high- or in the low-ranked group, but also that the impact of teaching quality and research quality differs. The positioning model yields this result when the research interval is larger than the teaching interval. The implication from the positioning model suggests that since there is a high variance in research (as indicator of maximal differentiation) and a low variance in teaching (as indicator of minimal differentiation), research quality determines the group membership of universities.

H4: The probability that a university will be in the high-ranked group is mainly influenced by research quality, while teaching quality asserts only a minor influence.

Section 7.3 will test this hypothesis by running probit regressions and then evaluating the influence of research quality (respectively, teaching quality) – while all other variables are set to their means – on the predicted probability of being in the high-performance or low-performance group. Larger differences in predicted probabilities suggest a more heterogeneous impact of the variables. Thus, a low variation in conditional predicted probabilities for varying teaching quality and given other variables indicates a higher degree of homogeneity in teaching quality across German universities.

NOTES

1 Warning (2006) discusses all cases in detail.
2 The second-order conditions were calculated and proven to hold. This result holds also for the following maximization problems and will not be mentioned in the other cases.
3 Vandenbosch and Weinberg (1995) present similar results in a general context, i.e., not for universities.
4 Recall that the first-stage results will deviate from Vandenbosch and Weinberg (1995) as a consequence of the different sign of a first derivative discussed earlier.
5 Warning (2006) provides the full proofs of Proposition 2 as well as the two remaining propositions.

6 Performance of German Universities: A DEA Approach

This chapter applies a production-theoretic framework to test for differences in teaching, research and overall performance across universities in Germany. The concept of strategic groups (Chapter 4) focuses on performance differences between groups of universities and suggests higher barriers to mobility in research than in teaching, which makes changing positions in research more difficult than in teaching.

To measure performance in the presence of multiple inputs and multiple outputs in a framework where no output prices are available, Data Envelopment Analysis (henceforth DEA) is the most appropriate method. It not only reveals if a university is efficient or not, but also provides a score indicating the degree of efficiency for each university. To illustrate the main advantages of DEA, Section 6.1 briefly introduces the method. Section 6.2 specifies the DEA models for teaching, research and both. Section 6.3 presents the data sources and descriptive statistics of the input and output factors. DEA results in Section 6.4 reveal the relation and degree of heterogeneity of teaching and research across universities in Germany. Section 6.5 presents results on overall performance, taking teaching and research into account simultaneously. Finally, Section 6.6 interprets the empirical findings in the light of the concept of strategic groups.

6.1 DATA ENVELOPMENT ANALYSIS: BASIC IDEAS

Performance measurement using DEA is based on the idea that an output-to-input ratio is an indicator of the degree of efficiency. DEA extends the one-input–one-output case to multiple dimensions both in inputs and outputs and enables us to identify a best-practice production function without specifying the functional form of the production function or assuming information about the efficiency term. In this way DEA easily incorporates multiple outputs and multiple inputs. Constructing a virtual input and a virtual output integrates multiple dimensions, and the ratio of virtual output to virtual input leads to the DEA efficiency score that indicates the level of efficiency for each university. Maximizing the ratio of virtual output to virtual input, subject to constraints capturing theoretical properties of the technology, determines aggregation multipliers to construct the virtual values endogenously.

Basically, DEA calculate the efficiency scores for universities in two steps. First, shaping the empirical production frontier in terms of best-practice identifies fully efficient universities. All universities on the efficiency frontier are declared technically efficient and have a DEA-efficiency score of 1. The frontier describes the best input-output combinations in the sample and envelops the remaining universities that are relatively inefficient. Consequently, DEA compares only universities within the sample. The position of a university in the input-output space, and by implication the efficiency score, depends upon the observed units in the sample. In this way the evaluation procedure follows a concept of relative efficiency.

Second, projecting the inefficient universities onto the frontier generates hypothetical units on the frontier. Linear combinations of efficient universities on the frontier construct these hypothetical units. The distance of the inefficient university to its corresponding hypothetical unit on the efficiency frontier represents the level of efficiency of each institution. Thus, determining distances to the frontier yields a DEA efficiency score for each university.

Typically, DEA has been utilized in non-profit sectors where market prices for inputs and, in particular, outputs are not available. Furthermore, researchers applied the method to various sectors and organizations for which it is difficult to aggregate performance indicators to one single performance measure, such as return on assets or return on investment. DEA also allows for the analysis of multi-objective situations. Public sector evaluations using DEA have dealt with, for example, police service (Diez-Ticio and Mancebon 2002), schools (Chakraborty et al. 2001) and hospitals (Oleson and Peterson 2002). The method has also been used to evaluate the banking industry (Berger and Humphrey 1997; Ali and Gstach 2000) and the efficiency of mergers (Ralston et al. 2001).

DEA is a non-parametric method to determine an empirical production function using linear programming. Considering the multiple input and multiple output character of a university, the basic idea is to generalize the single input and single output case. A ratio of a weighted sum of outputs to a weighted sum of inputs captures the multiple dimensions. Attaching an individual multiplier to every input (output) and summing these over products yields the weighted sum of inputs (outputs). In line with the single-input–single-output case the ratio of the virtual output to the virtual input is a measure of efficiency. The DEA model treats the observed inputs and outputs as given constants, while the attached multipliers are the variables which have to be determined by solving the model.

To present DEA in more formal terms, assume there are n universities that are denoted by the index j. Each institution uses m inputs to produce s outputs. University j consumes the quantity x_{ij} of input i to produce the quantity y_{rj} of output r. At least one input or output value must be positive. The assigned multiplier to output r is u_r and the multiplier assigned to input i is v_i. In the basic model for each university k of the n institutions a program must be solved, maximizing the ratio of weighted outputs to weighted inputs. This leads to a multi-dimensional framework efficiency score for university k, indicated by e_k. Adding several constraints to ensure a solid production-theoretic basis of the maximal efficiency score e_k of university k, a fractional program:

$$\max e_k = \max_{u_r, v_i} \frac{\sum_{r=1}^{s} y_{rk} u_r}{\sum_{i=1}^{m} x_{ik} v_i} \qquad (k = 1, \ldots, n) \qquad (6.1)$$

$$\text{subject to} \frac{\sum_{r=1}^{s} y_{rj} u_r}{\sum_{i=1}^{m} x_{ij} v_i} \leq 1 \qquad (j = 1, \ldots, n)$$

$$u_r \geq 0 \qquad (r = 1, \ldots, s)$$

$$v_i \geq 0 \qquad (i = 1, \ldots, m).$$

The first constraint ensures that the maximum efficiency score does not exceed 1 for any university. In addition, the second and the third constraint limit the multipliers attached to the inputs and outputs to non-negative values. In this way neither virtual inputs nor virtual outputs can be negative. Furthermore, the lower boundary of the efficiency score will always be zero. Assuming that university k is evaluated, the objective is to obtain multipliers u_r and v_i maximizing the ratio of virtual output to virtual input for university k. By definition, all computed efficiency scores always vary between 0 and 1, with 1 indicating a university that is fully efficient in the sample.

This specification is the starting point for efficiency measurement with DEA, developed by Charnes et al. (1978). The objective is is to maximize the ratio of outputs to inputs, interpreted as efficiency score. A value of $e_k = 1$ implies that university k transforms inputs into outputs at maximum efficiency compared to the other units in the sample, while a value of $e_k < 1$ implies some degree of inefficiency. In graphical terms all efficient units lie on the piece-wise linear (production) frontier, which envelops the inefficient units and results from linear programming. The relations of the solutions for the multipliers u_r and v_i indicate the rate of substitution between inputs or outputs.

The following paragraphs present the main elements of DEA models briefly (for a detailed description of various models see for example Cooper et al. 2000 or Thanassoulis 2001). Apart from the input-output specification, there are two further principal elements in DEA to formulate the program: assumptions about technology and about orientation. An important assumption concerning returns to scale establishes characteristics of the technology, distinguishing between constant and variable returns to scale.

In addition to using different technological constraints, DEA models distinguish between being oriented or additive. This distinction is based on the way of determining the distance to the efficiency frontier. Oriented models assume proportional reduction of inputs or augmentation of outputs – keeping the other dimension constant – to determine the efficiency level for a university. Inefficiency arises as a consequence of 'too much input consumed' or as a consequence of 'too little output created'. Efficiency analysis using DEA then means that the projection of unit k follows a line from the origin through the production frontier. This is called radial projection.

We classify DEA models as input-oriented and as output-oriented models. Those models that reveal a potential to reduce input quantities at given output levels are called input-oriented, assuming that decision-makers can control the inputs but not the outputs. Contrary to that, output-oriented DEA models assume fixed inputs. Increasing output levels while inputs remain at a constant level achieves efficiency.

Independent of the technology and orientation assumptions made, there are two main modes of presentation for all DEA models: the multiplier form and the envelopment form. The latter refers to the name of the method where a frontier envelopes inefficient units. Duality theory shows that both formulations lead to the same solution of the objective value e_k, the efficiency level of university k.

The seminal paper introducing DEA by Charnes, Cooper and Rhodes (Charnes et al. 1978) assumes constant returns to scale. Starting with the idea of the fractional program (6.1), they add an additional constraint to ensure a unique solution of the program. Several model extensions followed, such as the one by Banker-Charnes-Cooper (Banker et al. 1984) (BCC) which incorporated variable returns to scale and thus generalized the assumption of constant returns to a more flexible technology. Given that the technology in the BCC-model is more flexible, efficiency scores that are based on this specification will turn out to be higher than those assuming constant returns to scale.

The output-oriented DEA model with variable returns to scale (VRS) in multiplier form differs from the constant returns to scale output-oriented DEA model in that the absolute value ω is added to the virtual input:

$$\min_{\mu_r, \nu_i} \sum_{i=1}^{m} x_{ik} \nu_i + \omega \tag{6.2}$$

$$\text{subject to} \quad -\sum_{r=1}^{s} y_{rj} \mu_r + \sum_{i=1}^{m} x_{ik} \nu_i + \omega \geq 0 \qquad (j = 1, \dots, n)$$

$$\sum_{r=1}^{s} y_{rk} \mu_r = 1$$

$$\mu_r \geq 0 \qquad (r = 1, \dots, s)$$

$$\nu_i \geq 0 \qquad (i = 1, \dots, m).$$

Instead of maximizing $1/\left(\sum_{i=1}^{m} x_{ik} \nu_i + \omega\right)$, the objective function turns to minimizing $\sum_{i=1}^{m} x_{ik} \nu_i + \omega$ with the same constraints. The value of the objective function consequently will be the reciprocal value. Economically, this program minimizes the objective function – which is the virtual input – subject to a unit virtual output. But even if a weighted sum of inputs is minimized, in a geometric way this reflects searching for maximal proportional augmentation of the outputs at given the inputs levels. This becomes more clearly, when looking at the dual program, the envelopment form:

$$\max_{\eta_k^{VRS}, \lambda_j} \eta_k^{VRS} \tag{6.3}$$

$$\text{subject to} \sum_{j=1}^{m} \lambda_j x_{ij} \leq x_{ik} \qquad (i = 1, \ldots, m)$$

$$\eta_k^{VRS} y_{rk} - \sum_{j=1}^{n} \lambda_j y_{rj} \leq 0 \qquad (r = 1, \ldots, s)$$

$$\sum_{j=1}^{n} \lambda_j = 1 \qquad (j = 1, \ldots, n)$$

$$\lambda_j \geq 0 \qquad (j = 1, \ldots, n).$$

The efficiency score in the output-oriented DEA model with variable returns to scale is $e_k = 1/\eta_k^{VRS}$. η_k^{VRS} indicates the proportion by which all inputs of unit k can be reduced without violating the constraints and without reducing output levels by radially projecting the university onto the efficient frontier. The envelopment form of the output-oriented DEA model with variable returns to scale differs from the constant returns to scale model only by adding the convexity constraint, $\sum_{j=1}^{n} \lambda_j = 1$.

In terms of efficiency analysis the CRS assumption delivers more differentiated results than the VRS assumption. The efficiency score for each university in a VRS model will always be at least as high as in the CRS model. Efficiency measures for input and output orientation are the same when we assume constant returns to scale. The weights λ_j in the envelopment model indicate the importance of the fully efficient universities j in building the hypothetical unit for an inefficient university. These universities on the efficient frontier are called reference universities. For an inefficient university k, the set of efficient universities with $\lambda_j > 0$ for all $j = 1, \ldots, n$ defines the reference set for that university.

6.2   SPECIFICATION OF THE DEA MODELS

To explore the hypothesis of higher barriers of mobility in research than in teaching, separate DEA models will be used to provide scores for these two dimensions. Subsection 6.2.1 briefly presents DEA models – examining teaching and research separately using the method to aggregate various output dimensions. Subsection 6.2.2 introduces DEA models to create an overall performance measure for universities considering teaching and research simultaneously. The following paragraphs outline the three crucial elements of the models: the input-output specification, its orientation and finally the assumption about returns to scale of the production process of the university.

6.2.1 Separate DEA Models for Teaching and Research

Introducing separate DEA models for teaching and research in German universities suggests a measure to reveal different positions of institutions in these areas. Traditional production theory and the DEA literature use labor and capital as inputs. Typical inputs of universities are the number of teachers and researchers, library spending and expenditures on computers (see Subsection 3.2.2). Consuming these inputs, universities produce two outputs: teaching and research. However there is no generally accepted indicator for measuring these outputs, so the models will cover different aspects of both output factors applying various input-output specifications, providing important information on the robustness of the results.

The research models concentrate on publications in different fields, on research grants and on the number of habilitations, the formal qualification to get a professorship in Germany. To measure teaching, the models focus on the type of degree conferred. We start by specifying the research models and continue with a description of the teaching model specifications. Labels for teaching and research models indicate the main characterizing input or output factors. All specifications include identical numbers of input and output factors. Therefore different numbers of inputs and outputs do not bias DEA scores but ensure comparability across the different specifications.

The number of scientific personnel in the social sciences (according to the Social Science Citation Index, henceforth SSCI) and in the natural sciences (according to the Science Citation Index, henceforth SCI) captures the labor input and allows us to consider the different foci of universities on social sciences and natural sciences. Due to the lag in observing research outputs in terms of publications as well as in other dimensions, these output variables are taken as four year averages in the DEA models. Consequently, *SSCI staff av4* denotes scientific staff in the social sciences and *SCI staff av4* the scientific staff in the natural sciences as a four-year average. The *library expenditure* in t captures the capital input including the availability of literature, books as well as journals, and serves as proxy for general research conditions.

First, the outputs of the Grants Model (*R1*) consist of the number of refereed publications. Articles written and published serve as one principal measure of research. Differentiating between the different publications strategies across fields, the output factors measure publications in the natural sciences (*Publications SCI*) and in the social sciences (*Publications SSCI*) separately. Additionally, selecting publications from the widely accepted Citation Indices by the

Institute of Scientific Information (ISI) ensures both a quantity and quality dimension. To be listed in the index, special requirements of journal quality have to be fulfilled. Additionally, the model includes the total value of research *grants* as one more measure of research. A university's reputation and past research facilitate receiving research grants. Note that the inclusion of research grants as an output also carries the benefit of capturing applied research.

Second, in contrast to the Grants Model the Habilitation Model (*R2*) focuses on human capital as the research output. It differs in only one output factor from the Grants Model: the number of *habilitations* replaces the total value of research grants. Post-docs, who are looking to complete their habilitation and then become professors, conduct large portions of the research at German universities. There is only limited incentive for universities to provide persons with the habilitation, if they do not stand a fair chance on the job market which is in large parts based on research performance of the candidates. Furthermore, incentives for habilitation candidates to go to those universities that do not offer a competitive research environment may be small. Briefly, the Habilitation Model apart from publications covers the human-capital component of research by accounting for the number of habilitations.

Third, the Total Research Model (*R3*) combines the Grants Model and the Habilitation Model in taking the number of habilitations and the total value of research grants simultaneously into consideration. Total publications from social sciences and natural sciences covers the theoretical research part and is the third output factor of model (*R3*). Table 6.1 summarizes the input-output specifications of the different research models.

Table 6.1   Specification of the Research Models

Model	Inputs	Outputs
Grants Model (*R1*)	*SCI staff av4* *SSCI staff av4* *Library expenditure*	*Publications SCI* *Publications SSCI* *Grants*
Habilitation Model (*R2*)	*SCI staff av4* *SSCI staff av4* *Library expenditure*	*Publications SCI* *Publications SSCI* *Habilitations*
Total R Model (*R3*)	*SCI staff av4* *SSCI staff av4* *Library expenditure*	*Total publications* *Grants* *Habilitations*

While all research models apply the same set of inputs, the three teaching models differ not only on the output, but also on the input side. The number of staff in the social sciences and in the natural sciences separately measure labor input in all three models. Although it takes about six years to finish studying at German public universities, the years just before graduating seem to have a significant influence on a student's success. For that reason, the average number of staff over the last five years before student graduation is employed as a measure of the labor input in all teaching specifications (*SCI staff av5*, *SSCI staff av5*). Furthermore, two models, the Qualification Model and the Field Model, apply *library expenditure* as a common capital input. This is meant to capture university infrastructure, such as availability of textbooks and access to computing. To cover the success of a university in teaching, these models include the number of incoming students, lagged by the regular study time of four years. Models *T1* and *T2* use the total number of beginners, whereas model *T3* distinguishes between new entrants in social sciences and in natural sciences, and treats these beginners as inputs to the production process.

Given these common input factors, the teaching outputs are twofold. The Qualification Model (*T1*) discriminates between the two main kinds of qualifications German universities award: teaching qualification and diploma. Students pursuing a teaching qualification study two or more subjects simultaneously, students aiming for a diploma usually specialize in one subject. While universities focused on conferring diploma degrees specialize, universities providing teaching qualifications often structure their studies in a more interdisciplinary fashion. Briefly, it maps the contrast between providing more general knowledge (teaching qualifications) and specialized knowledge (diploma) in a field. To denote these two dimensions of teaching output, the qualification model includes the number of *teaching qualifications* and the number of *diplomas* awarded.

In contrast to the Qualification Model, the Field Model (*T2*) emphasizes the different fields students graduate in, instead of the different kinds of qualification. In line with the inputs of staff from social sciences and natural sciences model, *T2* considers graduates from these areas as a teaching output. While studying social sciences takes place in relatively large classes, studying natural sciences contains practical components conducted in smaller student groups. This is especially true in physics, chemistry, biology and medicine. The Field Model includes the numbers of graduates in the social sciences (*SSCI graduates*) and in the natural sciences (*SCI graduates*) as teaching outputs.

Finally, the Beginner Model (*T3*) makes an explicit distinction between new entrants in social sciences (*SSCI beginner in t−4*) and in natural sciences (*SCI beginner in t−4*) as inputs and graduates in these fields as outputs. Therefore, the Beginner Model captures importance differences between these two fields. Table 6.2 shows the input-output specifications of the three teaching models proposed.

Based on these input-output specifications the DEA model generates individual scores for all universities in each year of the observation period 1997–2000. Consequently, DEA solves 24 (6 models, each solved for 4 years) programs for each university, assuming constant returns to scale to ensure a high discriminating power. Note, that these DEA models do not measure performance in a traditional production-theoretic way. They should rather be interpreted as aggre-

Table 6.2   Specification of the Teaching Models

Model	Inputs	Outputs
Qualification Model (*T1*)	*SCI staff av5* *SSCI staff av5* *Library expenditure*	*Diplomas* *Teaching qualifications*
Field Model (*T2*)	*Beginner in t − 4* *SCI staff av5* *SSCI staff av5* *Library expenditure* *Beginner in t − 4*	*SCI graduates* *SSCI graduates*
Beginner Model (*T3*)	*SCI staff av5* *SSCI staff av5* *SCI beginner in t − 4* *SSCI beginner in t − 4*	*SCI graduates* *SSCI graduates*

gating outputs in one specific area of interest. This is consistent with numerous studies in the area of higher education (see Subsection 3.2.2.2). Overall performance will be addressed in the next section.

6.2.2   Modeling Overall Performance

DEA models for universities must take both teaching and research outputs into account. To determine the robustness of the results, four different input-output specifications are used, leading to four DEA models. All of them include the same set of input factors, capturing the impact of labor and capital. The number of staff in the social sciences and the number of staff in the natural sciences represent labor input. In this way the input variables control for the relative weight of different fields at each university, as some concentrate either on social sciences or on natural sciences while others do both. As previously explained, library spending is a proxy for the capital input of universities. High expenditure on libraries suggests a good infrastructure for students and professors by assuring availability of textbooks and journals.

Universities use their inputs to produce teaching and research, which is modeled in four different ways, labeled *TR1* through *TR4*. Four different sets of outputs capture various foci of the university and gain insights into the stability of the DEA results. The first model, *TR1*, applies the total number of graduates as teaching outputs and the number of publications and the total value of research grants as research output. In the second specification, *TR2*, the number of habilitations replaces the value of grants. While the value of grants in the first model focuses on reputation and research output, the number of habilitations in the second model emphasizes the human capital production of research. Models *TR3* and *TR4* utilize four outputs, two for teaching and two for research.

These DEA models explicitly consider differences of the fields in the output dimensions. Both treat publications in the natural sciences and the social sciences as separate outputs. Additionally, *TR3* includes the number of graduates separated in the social sciences and natural sciences, while *TR4* distinguishes graduates by type: teaching qualification or diploma. Table 6.3 summarizes the four DEA models for overall performance considering teaching and research outputs simultaneously.

Table 6.3   Specification of the Overall DEA Models

Model	Inputs	Outputs
TR1	*SCI staff av4* *SSCI staff av4* *Library*	*Total graduates* *Total publications* *Grants*
TR2	*SCI staff av4* *SSCI staff av4* *Library*	*Total graduates* *Total publications* *Habilitations*
TR3	*SCI staff av4* *SSCI staff av4* *Library*	*Graduates SCI* *Graduates SSCI* *Publications SCI* *Publications SSCI*
TR4	*SCI staff av4* *SSCI staff av4* *Library*	*Teaching qualifications* *Diplomas* *Publications SCI* *Publications SSCI*

As for the orientation of the DEA models, the production process of universities suggests the use of output-orientation as the second crucial element (the first was the assumption about returns to scale), assuming maximization of outputs for given inputs. This is because German universities are publicly funded by the state ministry with a budget that can be considered fixed. Universities differ in size, and therefore the DEA models are specified under variable returns. The four DEA models *TR1–TR4* are run for all universities and all years which leads to 272 observations (4 years and 68 universities).

6.3   DATA AND DESCRIPTIVE STATISTICS

The underlying dataset for the DEA models described above consists of 68 state-funded universities in Germany for the years from 1997 to 2000, excluding specialized universities in medicine (e.g., the medical universities at Lübeck and Hannover), in sports ('Deutsche Sporthochschule Köln'), in politics (e.g., 'Hochschule für Politik in München') and several other specialized universities. The sample excludes private universities as well because they either focus on business or on business and medicine. I also exclude the two Universities of the

Armed Forces at Hamburg and Munich because their orientation and structure means that comparisons with other German universities would be misleading. For example, they have an atypical recruitment process for their students (young officers), atypical financing (by the Federal Government) and a completely different organization of study (trimester instead of semester). Furthermore, the dataset does not contain newly founded universities that started just before the observation period. In this way this sample is a subgroup of the group of all scientific universities described in Chapter 2.

As there is no standardized database for German universities, the data originate from different sources. The following paragraphs introduce the descriptive statistics of input and output measures used in the various models. This subsection also provides an overview of the data sources and a discussion of data quality.

Various publications by the German Science Council ('Wissenschaftsrat') contain information on the size of scientific staff. Categorized by states, the Council publishes recommendations on investments of the universities. In this context several university-related measures turn out to be available. Aggregating different fields leads to data that fit into the categories of social sciences and natural sciences. The group of natural sciences consists of mathematics, natural sciences, medicine, agricultural, forestry, dietetics and engineering. Social sciences include arts, law, economics, as well as languages and cultural studies.

Table 6.4 summarizes descriptive statistics of the input factors for the single years as well as the four-year average. Starting with the scientific staff in the research models all variables were lagged by two years. For all four years, the average staff in natural sciences (*SCI staff av4*) is 895 with a minimum of zero for universities without natural sciences and a maximum of 2,517. The four-year average of scientific staff in the social sciences at 360 is much smaller across the 272 observations for the four year period from 1997 to 2000. Values for the five-year average of scientific staff (*SCI staff av5*, *SSCI staff av5*) are almost identical for the four-year averages, indicating almost fixed input variables for German universities over time. A large dispersion in the number of scientific staff within a field reflects the different size and focus of universities. Scientific staff in the natural sciences is much greater than in the social sciences. The average number of new students in natural sciences (*SCI beginner t−4*) was only 933, while the number of beginners in social sciences (*SSCI beginner t−4*) was 1,450 students on average. The maximum number of new entrants in social sciences is twice the maximum numbers of new entrants in the natural sciences.

Finally, the German Library Statistics provides data on library expenditure which covers information on all libraries in Germany, and the university libraries in particular. Average library expenditure on new material over the time period 1997 to 2000 was 2.3 million Euros in our sample. Clearly, there is variation across universities which, to a large extent, is due to size of the institutions. Total expenditure has decreased from 1997 to 2000.

Table 6.4 Descriptive Statistics of the Input Factors

		1997	1998	1999	2000	All years
SCI staff av4	Mean	897.91	895.12	894.03	895.17	895.56
	Std. Dev.	642.95	641.72	640.00	643.38	638.45
	Min	0.00	0.00	0.00	0.00	0.00
	Max	2,446.75	2,469.50	2,477.75	2,477.50	2,477.75
SSCI staff av4	Mean	363.60	360.97	358.94	354.98	359.62
	Std. Dev.	259.16	253.06	248.96	244.62	250.13
	Min	0.00	0.00	0.00	0.00	0.00
	Max	1,201.75	1,141.25	1,116.50	1,092.75	1,201.75
SCI staff av5	Mean	897.96	897.10	895.82	894.32	896.30
	Std. Dev.	645.06	642.29	643.05	641.36	639.38
	Min	0.00	0.00	0.00	0.00	0.00
	Max	2,442.40	2,455.60	2,462.00	2,480.80	2,480.80
SSCI staff av5	Mean	365.14	362.15	359.72	356.31	360.83
	Std. Dev.	261.61	255.77	251.36	246.49	252.48
	Min	0.00	0.00	0.00	0.00	0.00
	Max	1,229.40	1,170.00	1,132.00	1,107.00	1,229.40
SCI be- *ginner in* $t-4$	Mean	994.51	921.65	899.99	916.56	933.18
	Std. Dev.	693.49	627.80	610.51	619.23	636.09
	Min	0.00	0.00	0.00	0.00	0.00
	Max	2,776.00	2,434.00	2,692.00	2,548.00	2,776.00
SSCI be- *ginner in* $t-4$	Mean	1,420.15	1,415.41	1,463.66	1,501.02	1,450.06
	Std. Dev.	1,055.01	1,055.37	1,072.35	1,101.34	1,065.81
	Min	0.00	0.00	0.00	0.00	0.00
	Max	4,722.00	5,444.00	5,061.00	5,514.00	5,514.00
Total be- *ginner in* $t-4$	Mean	2,414.66	2,337.06	2,363.65	2,417.57	2,383.24
	Std. Dev.	1,430.98	1,366.31	1,399.31	1,444.11	1,403.09
	Min	204.00	287.00	211.00	244.00	204.00
	Max	6,280.00	6,425.00	6,295.00	6,848.00	6,848.00
Library *(in mill.)* €	Mean	2.31	2.32	2.24	2.26	2.28
	Std. Dev.	1.22	1.19	1.13	1.18	1.17
	Min	0.69	0.56	0.41	0.21	0.21
	Max	6.35	6.24	6.59	6.23	6.59

Notes: av4: average number over the current and the last three years (four-year average); *av5:* average number over the current and the last four years (five-year average); SSCI number refers to the social sciences in general; SCI number refer to natural sciences in general

All DEA models for the research specifications use the number of publications in the Citation Indices provided by the Institute of Scientific Information. For the social sciences I searched the SSCI (Social Science Citation Index) and the AHI (Arts and Humanities Index) for each university for the years 1997 to 2000, for the natural sciences I did the same in the SCI (Science Citation Index). Not only does the average number of publications in the two categories differ considerably, a four-year average of 810 publications in the natural sciences versus 68 in the social sciences during the same time period, but there are also great differences in the maximum numbers of publications. Averaged over four years, they are 5,032 in the natural sciences and 360 in the social sciences, indicating a high variance within the fields and also heterogeneity across universities.

The number of habilitations captures another research output of universities. With up to 112 habilitations and an average of 23 there are large differences across universities. As our third output variable in research, the total value of research grants amounts on average over the four-year period considered to 26.2 million Euros, with a maximum of 121 million Euros in 2000. Table 6.5 presents the descriptive statistics for the research output factors for the individual years and on average for the years 1997 to 2000.

Table 6.5   Descriptive Statistics of the Research Outputs

		1997	1998	1999	2000	All years
	Mean	801.76	815.28	815.00	811.15	810.80
SCI	Std. Dev.	833.94	819.49	847.43	829.51	828.05
Publications	Min	1.00	0.00	0.00	1.00	0.00
	Max	4,748.00	4,396.00	5,032.00	4,850.00	5,032.00
	Mean	64.34	60.24	69.06	77.90	67.88
SSCI	Std. Dev.	65.24	57.01	67.54	70.65	65.28
Publications	Min	0.00	0.00	0.00	0.00	0.00
	Max	321.00	236.00	336.00	360.00	360.00
	Mean	866.10	875.51	884.06	889.04	878.68
Total	Std. Dev.	890.12	866.53	903.95	891.01	883.12
Publications	Min	2.00	9.00	8.00	5.00	2.00
	Max	5,069.00	4,632.00	5,368.00	5,210.00	5,368.00
	Mean	24.26	26.88	26.68	29.72	26.89
Habilitations	Std. Dev.	22.33	24.41	22.94	25.37	23.74
	Min	0.00	0.00	1.00	1.00	0.00
	Max	95.00	112.00	88.00	103.00	112.00
	Mean	31.80	33.60	35.60	37.80	34.70
Grants	Std. Dev.	26.30	27.20	27.60	30.10	27.80
(in mill.) €	Min	0.95	0.80	0.73	0.98	0.73
	Max	117.00	121.00	128.00	141.00	141.00

There are two basic sets of outputs to measure teaching outputs. First, the average number of diplomas was 1,352 with a minimum of 78 and a maximum of 3,820. In contrast, the number of teaching qualifications was much smaller, with an average of 344. Some universities do not provide any teaching qualifications at all.

Second, information on graduates from different fields is the basis for the second set of teaching outputs. The average number of graduates in the social sciences was 1,033, whereas the average number of graduates in the natural sciences was 1,022 in the four-year average from 1997 to 2000. Showing nearly identical average values, the maximum number of graduates across fields varies substantially. For the social sciences the maximum was 4,150 graduates in 2000, while the maximum number of graduates in the natural sciences was 3,461 in 1997. Whereas the number of graduates in the natural sciences has decreased over the four years in the data, the number of social sciences graduates increased. Table 6.6 presents descriptive statistics for the singles years separately as well as the average values over the four-year period.

Table 6.6   Descriptive Statistics of the Teaching Outputs

		1997	1998	1999	2000	All years
	Mean	1,468.06	1,374.87	1,310.72	1,254.15	1,351.95
Diploma	Std. Dev.	946.04	882.64	847.13	802.86	870.06
	Min	78.00	164.00	179.00	183.00	78.00
	Max	3,795.00	3,820.00	3,784.00	3,573.00	3,820.00
	Mean	347.22	349.91	345.69	336.75	344.89
Teaching	Std. Dev.	301.38	312.06	318.31	325.09	312.63
qualifications	Min	0.00	0.00	0.00	0.00	0.00
	Max	1,462.00	1,372.00	1,464.00	1,615.00	1,615.00
	Mean	1,100.49	1,043.88	989.54	955.28	1,022.30
SCI	Std. Dev.	795.96	744.60	694.32	677.48	727.61
graduates	Min	0.00	1.00	0.00	0.00	0.00
	Max	3,461.00	3,115.00	2,719.00	2,674.00	3,461.00
	Mean	1,065.19	1,039.34	1,022.21	1,006.06	1,033.20
SSCI	Std. Dev.	799.30	795.89	786.93	786.42	788.07
graduates	Min	0.00	0.00	0.00	0.00	0.00
	Max	3,693.00	3,973.00	3,991.00	4,150.00	4,150.00

Comparing output factors in teaching and research, it turns out that heterogeneity across German universities tends to be greater in research than in teaching. Finally Table 6.7 summarizes details on the sources of the data used. Some remarks on data availability and data sources may be valuable to conclude this section. Inputs and outputs of universities consist of multiple dimensions that our variables cannot cover completely. For this reason, four different output combinations are used to capture different dimensions. To comment on validity of the data and problems with data sources, let me first review the input factors. Staff is an appropriate input variable in a model of the production process of universities. Even if averaging over four year seems somehow arbitrary at first glance, it turns out that another or even no averaging procedure leads to highly correlated outcomes and does not change our results at all.

Sources for data on labor inputs are the official ones and, therefore, ought to be reliable sources. A more preferable labor input might be the qualification of staff. However there would be other drawbacks: First, splitting the staff variable

Table 6.7 *Sources of Data Input and Output Factors*

Variable	Source
SCI Staff SSCI Staff	Wissenschaftsrat (1993, 1994, 1995, 1996, 1997, 1998, 1999, 2000b, 2001, 2002b); 4 different issues
SCI beginner SSCI beginner	Wissenschaftsrat (1993, 1994, 1995, 1996); 4 different issues
Library	Deutsche Bibliotheksstatistik (2003)
SCI publications SSCI publications	Science Citation Index (2003) Social Science Citation Index (2003) Arts and Humanities Index (2003)
Grants	Statistisches Bundesamt (2001b, 2002, 2003b)
Habilitations	Statistisches Bundesamt (2001c)
Diplomas Teaching Qualifications	Statistisches Bundesamt (1998, 1999, 2000, 2001a)
SCI graduates SSCI graduates	Statistisches Bundesamt (1998, 1999, 2000, 2001a); Abt.VII

into multiple factors increases the number of inputs which in turn leads to DEA results with less discriminating power. Second, staff data on qualification is only rarely and not systematically available. Data on library expenditure, of course, does not capture the entire capital dimension of inputs, but it covers a significant aspect. To the best of my knowledge there is no other variable available that would cover capital inputs better. Extracting data from a semi-official database and recalculating of increases from the preceding year was necessary to generate observations for some institutions in some years.

In a context where universities select students based on their abilities, the quality of students should have been considered as an input factor. However this kind of selection process was not used in Germany in the considered time period of this analysis. For that reason also the customer-input-technology approach is not appropriate here. To comment on the choice of outputs, I start with those for teaching that are exclusively from official sources. These sources ought to be the most reliable available in Germany. Note, however, that quality does depend on reporting by the universities. Undoubtedly, information on starting salaries or employment rates 6 months after graduation would have been desirable, but these data are not available for German universities.

Focusing on publications as one important research output is accepted in the literature – and also the general public. The decision about the database for searching publications, of course, is more controversial. I favor the ISI citation database as it is the only one covering all fields applying a similar standard on taking up journals or not. However there are some drawbacks. Checking the German as well as the English names of the universities ruled out the problem of misspelling of institutions and their addresses (a problem that occurs also in other databases). The citation indexes list for most years only the first author when searching for an institution. We can imagine at least two cases: First, alphabetical order of all authors. Then there is no reason why names of researchers are not uniformly distributed across universities. Second, the order of name is not alphabetical. Then publications count for the first mentioned author, and it is plausible to assume that it is the first mentioned author who led the team or who carried out the most important research of the joint project.

All in all, there exists no university-specific database which made it necessary to construct a dataset from different sources. More data and also more detailed data in the future may lead to more specific insights. The main direction of the results, however, can be expected to be fairly robust.

6.4   DEA RESULTS FOR TEACHING AND RESEARCH

This section reports the DEA results to test validity of hypothesis *H1* that there is greater heterogeneity in research than in teaching at universities. Subsection 6.4.1 reports the results of the separate DEA models. Analyzing the multipliers of teaching and research of the overall models, Subsection 6.4.2, investigates the positioning of universities in these dimensions.

6.4.1   Results of the Separate Models

Stating higher heterogeneity in research than in teaching, this subsection reports the descriptive and correlation results of the scores for research and then for teaching. Testing heterogeneity measures in research models against those in the teaching models to support hypothesis *H1* concludes the subsection. Before interpreting the results of the teaching and the research models, some preparatory remarks may be helpful, as the measures used are not traditional performance measures, even if the literature in the field of higher education treats them in this way. DEA is a method to evaluate efficiency in a multiple-input–multiple-output setting and requires the inclusion of all outputs for given inputs. Therefore, the scores presented in this subsection cannot be interpreted as efficiency scores directly, as either only teaching or research outputs are taken into account.

Interpreting the score of a research or a teaching model as an indicator of research efficiency, teaching efficiency or even overall efficiency can be misleading. Imagine a university allocating only a small amount of its inputs to research and most of it to teaching. Suppose, furthermore, that the researchers at this university produce a relatively high research output, whereas output in the teaching dimension is low relative to input. Given the way inputs are measured for both the research and teaching models, this university will receive a low efficiency score from a DEA model focused on research and normal or average score from DEA based on teaching.

As a result of the unity of teaching and research, as described in Chapter 2, we cannot observe the allocation of resources to teaching or research separately in the German university system. However this initial drawback becomes an advantage in the analysis of the relation between teaching and research. The results of these scores indicate the degree of heterogeneity across models. To test the heterogeneity hypothesis, we are interested in the differences over time and across DEA models.

Interpreting the DEA scores in this subsection, two assumptions are very plausible: First, the technology does not change over the four-year period examined. Consequently, changes across years are conscious position changes of the university from one year to the other. Second, also the degree of inefficiency does not change over time. Then, teaching and research DEA scores can be interpreted as distributions of resources on the different tasks, teaching and research. Both assumptions can be safely made because in the time period observed German universities were not prone to rapidly change their production processes.

The mean of the DEA scores measures average relative efficiency. Comparisons across models indicates the degree of homogeneity. The standard deviation serves as direct measure for dispersion within and across models. With respect to their development over time DEA scores indicate relative efficiency. Table 6.8 displays the results of the DEA models in research under the assumption of constant returns to scale.

Table 6.8   Results of the DEA Research Models (68 observations each year)

		1997	1998	1999	2000
	Mean	0.659	0.673	0.716	0.706
	Std. Dev.	0.255	0.262	0.234	0.231
Grants Model (*R1*)	Min	0.216	0.215	0.225	0.275
	Max	1.000	1.000	1.000	1.000
	Eff. Univ.	13	15	13	16
	Mean	0.634	0.632	0.713	0.704
	Std. Dev.	0.281	0.277	0.261	0.237
Habilitation Model (*R2*)	Min	0.035	0.069	0.255	0.231
	Max	1.000	1.000	1.000	1.000
	Eff. Univ.	10	13	17	18
	Mean	0.681	0.685	0.766	0.746
	Std. Dev.	0.255	0.245	0.224	0.208
Total R Model (*R3*)	Min	0.208	0.195	0.272	0.302
	Max	1.000	1.000	1.000	1.000
	Eff. Univ.	10	11	18	16

There seems to be a trend towards higher research scores over time. Increasing minimum scores and a decrease in the standard deviation point to a decrease of heterogeneity (recall that the maximum DEA score is always one). These results are robust against a change to variable returns to scale technology. Also, the findings are robust across different model specifications, i.e., they do not depend on the selection of the input and output factors.

To point out this fact more clearly, Table 6.9 displays the correlations across the research models. Over time the correlation within the same model research is high for all specifications, even if correlations seem to decrease marginally. Correlation seems to be greatest within the Grants Model *R1* which can be explained by the fact that grants are usually provided over multiple years. They make universities appear stable over time in this category. Furthermore, this reflects the fact that universities attracting grants successfully will continue doing so in the future. Also, bold figures in Table 6.9 indicate that the results display a high correlation within the same year and across models. Finally, correlations are high across all specifications across all years, as only two values are less than 0.7 but still greater than 0.65. These observations suggest that universities did not change positions dramatically over the time period observed.

Table 6.9   Correlation of the Research Scores

		R1				R2				R3			
		1997	1998	1999	2000	1997	1998	1999	2000	1997	1998	1999	2000
R1	1997	1.00											
	1998	0.92	1.00										
	1999	0.80	0.84	1.00									
	2000	0.90	0.86	0.85	1.00								
R2	1997	**0.82**	0.78	0.57	0.69	1.00							
	1998	0.83	**0.88**	0.64	0.73	0.91	1.00						
	1999	0.79	0.78	**0.71**	0.73	0.67	0.75	1.00					
	2000	0.84	0.82	0.72	**0.83**	0.75	0.81	0.84	1.00				
R3	1997	**0.88**	0.83	0.73	0.80	**0.84**	0.81	0.72	0.74	1.00			
	1998	0.89	**0.93**	0.79	0.80	0.81	**0.89**	0.76	0.78	0.90	1.00		
	1999	0.79	0.81	**0.77**	0.74	0.69	0.73	**0.77**	0.68	0.77	0.83	1.00	
	2000	0.91	0.86	0.83	**0.90**	0.74	0.75	0.74	**0.87**	0.87	0.84	0.81	1.00

This paragraph presents the results from the teaching models. Compared to research, the scores vary more across the various specifications, and there is a decrease of the scores over time. Table 6.10 summarizes the results of the DEA teaching models.

Altogether, there is a significant decrease of the scores from 1997 to 2000 while the values do not differ substantially across specifications. As in the case of research, correlations indicate the relation of the teaching scores across various specifications and over time. Table 6.11 offers the correlation coefficients of the teaching models for all three specifications for 1997 to 2000.

Within models the teaching correlation coefficients are not very stable. Each

Table 6.10   Results of the DEA Teaching Models (68 observations each year)

		1997	1998	1999	2000
	Mean	0.828	0.779	0.807	0.790
	Std. Dev.	0.190	0.204	0.206	0.187
Qualification Model (*T1*)	Min	0.249	0.399	0.335	0.341
	Max	1.000	1.000	1.000	1.000
	Eff. Univ.	22	16	16	13
	Mean	0.849	0.808	0.823	0.819
	Std. Dev.	0.169	0.191	0.180	0.175
Field Model (*T2*)	Min	0.291	0.400	0.381	0.352
	Max	1.000	1.000	1.000	1.000
	Eff. Univ.	21	18	18	20
	Mean	0.851	0.844	0.826	0.815
	Std. Dev.	0.145	0.152	0.162	0.161
Beginner Model (*T3*)	Min	0.326	0.403	0.385	0.352
	Max	1.000	1.000	1.000	1.000
	Eff. Univ.	16	17	13	15

box in the table again gives the correlations within a model and over time. There appears to be no trend. However it is conspicuous that the correlations within the models over time are relatively low which suggests that changing positions in teaching is not too difficult. Across models the correlation within the same year is always greater than 0.68. Finally, correlation coefficients across years and across teaching models vary a lot with a number of coefficients being rather low.

The results from the correlation analysis, within a given model over time, can be interpreted as evidence that moving and repositioning in the teaching

Table 6.11   Correlation of the Teaching Scores

		T1				*T2*				*T3*			
		1997	1998	1999	2000	1997	1998	1999	2000	1997	1998	1999	2000
	1997	1.00											
T1	1998	0.78	1.00										
	1999	0.68	0.86	1.00									
	2000	0.61	0.79	0.90	1.00								
	1997	**0.95**	0.79	0.72	0.64	1.00							
T2	1998	0.63	**0.87**	0.85	0.80	0.74	1.00						
	1999	0.60	0.81	**0.94**	0.86	0.70	0.91	1.00					
	2000	0.51	0.76	0.81	**0.90**	0.61	0.86	0.88	1.00				
	1997	**0.82**	0.61	0.53	0.49	**0.86**	0.59	0.53	0.49	1.00			
T3	1998	0.44	**0.68**	0.66	0.61	0.53	**0.82**	0.73	0.70	0.58	1.00		
	1999	0.43	0.62	**0.79**	0.71	0.54	0.76	**0.85**	0.73	0.54	0.82	1.00	
	2000	0.40	0.67	0.74	**0.78**	0.53	0.78	0.79	**0.87**	0.54	0.75	0.80	1.00

dimension is rather easy and not very costly. Or, to put it another way, barriers to mobility are low for teaching compared to research.

Means as well as standard deviations differ significantly between teaching and research models. A low standard deviation within teaching hints at low differentiation and a high degree of homogeneity in teaching, while a high standard deviation in research signals a high degree of heterogeneity and high differentiation in research. These results remain stable across different specifications thus are consistent with hypothesis *H2*.

To detect the direct relation between teaching and research, Table 6.12 presents the correlations between all scores from teaching models and all scores from research models. In addition, a test on equality of the means of all teaching models and the means of all research models was run. Furthermore, an F-test examines the empirical variance of the scores from the teaching and research models. Asterisks in the brackets indicate the level of significance where the first position relates to the test for equality of means and the second to the test for equality of variances. As usual, ***, **, * represent the 1 percent, 5 percent and 10 percent level, respectively.

Table 6.12   The Relationship between the Teaching and Research Scores

Corr	1997	1998	1999	2000
(R1,T1)	0.3628	0.3944	0.4269	0.5163
	(***, ***)	(***, **)	(***, no)	(***, **)
(R1,T2)	0.3867	0.3636	0.4618	0.4410
	(***, ***)	(***, ***)	(***, **)	(***, **)
(R1,T3)	0.3623	0.2095	0.4090	0.3400
	(***, ***)	(***, ***)	(***, ***)	(***, ***)
(R2,T1)	0.3076	0.3501	0.3283	0.4338
	(***, ***)	(***, ***)	(***, **)	(***, **)
(R2,T2)	0.3388	0.2546	0.3548	0.3574
	(***, ***)	(***, ***)	(***, ***)	(***, ***)
(R2,T3)	0.2405	0.1408	0.3600	0.3258
	(***, ***)	(***, ***)	(***, ***)	(***, ***)
(R3,T1)	0.3953	0.3812	0.5039	0.5791
	(***, ***)	(***, *)	(*, no)	(**, no)
(R3,T2)	0.4305	0.3652	0.5054	0.5093
	(***, ***)	(***, **)	(**, **)	(***, *)
(R3,T3)	0.3707	0.2711	0.4771	0.4532
	(***, ***)	(***, ***)	(***, ***)	(***, **)

Table 6.12 shows a positive, but relatively low correlation between teaching and research models, ranging from 0.2095 to 0.5791 implying that universities with high teaching scores tend to have high research scores. The mean and the variance between teaching and research scores differ significantly in 33 out of 36 cases. For example, in 1997 the correlation between the DEA scores of research

model *R1* and teaching model *T1* is 0.3628. The means of the two models differ significantly at the 1 percent level, while the variances differ only at the 5 percent level. This finding supports the hypothesis of heterogeneity across teaching and research, and in this way suggests different barriers to mobility between teaching and research.

Examining the relation between teaching and research on the basis of descriptive statistics, results hint to a group structure within the German university system with respect to teaching and research. The correlation between teaching and research is positive for all specifications and all years. Assuming there is no technology change over the four-year period, DEA scores map the distribution of resources to teaching and research and thus indicate the degree of heterogeneity between the teaching and research models.

Summarizing the results of the teaching and the research models, there are two main insights that confirm hypothesis *H1*, stating that heterogeneity across universities in research is greater than in teaching because barriers to mobility are higher in research compared to teaching. First, the correlation analysis indicates almost stable positions over time in research, but at the same time universities tend to change positions in teaching. Second, the correlation between teaching and research is always positive. However average scores and standard deviations across models differ significantly, which implies that universities choose different positions in teaching and research.

6.4.2   Analysis of the Multipliers from the Overall Models

The positioning model from Chapter 5 predicts that greater weights are attached to teaching than to research. Furthermore, variation is expected to be smaller in teaching than in research. Examining the multipliers attached to teaching and research in the DEA overall model, especially of those multipliers related to the output factors, tests hypothesis *H3* from the positioning model. DEA determines these multipliers for both dimensions as the solution of an optimization program so that a university cannot find any better multipliers that would increase its overall efficiency value.

To test the relative importance of teaching and research for the universities, I analyze the output multipliers. As DEA incorporates multiple outputs, combining all teaching multipliers constructs a teaching index for each of the four models. Analogously, all research multipliers of a model are used to compose a research index for each university and each model. These indexes capture the importance each university attaches to these two dimensions, teaching and research.

Constructing the index proceeds as follows: First, the weights μ_r from equation (6.2) for teaching and research are added separately. Second, normalizing these indexes are normalized to the interval [0,1]:

$$\frac{index - \min(index)}{\max(index) - \min(index)}$$

Following this procedure for all four overall models of Subsection (6.2.2) leads to an index Ti in teaching and in research Ri for each model $i = 1, ..., 4$. To observe and control for developments in different years, normalization is done separately for the years. Due to the normalization procedure, minimum values are always zero and maximum values are always equal to one.

I first present the teaching indexes for each year separately. Table 6.13 shows the descriptive statistics for all four models. On average the teaching indexes are different from zero and that they do not follow a time trend. The same observation is true for the standard deviation and for the coefficient of variation which defines the ratio between the standard deviation and the mean.

Table 6.13   Teaching Multipliers of the Overall DEA Models

		1997	1998	1999	2000
	Mean	0.185	0.088	0.138	0.090
T1	Std. Dev.	0.189	0.139	0.175	0.187
	Coeff. Var.	1.023	1.586	1.267	1.567
	Mean	0.155	0.117	0.103	0.114
T2	Std. Dev.	0.185	0.172	0.155	0.172
	Coeff. Var.	1.193	1.471	1.513	1.510
	Mean	0.096	0.016	0.119	0.107
T3	Std. Dev.	0.157	0.121	0.203	0.181
	Coeff. Var.	1.631	7.594	1.708	1.692
	Mean	0.265	0.177	0.201	0.218
T4	Std. Dev.	0.213	0.202	0.232	0.237
	Coeff. Var.	0.806	1.144	1.153	1.088

Second, the analysis of the research indices shows a different picture. Table 6.14 presents the descriptive statistics on research for all models. Contrary to the teaching indexes the research indexes show very small average values which are close to zero in several cases. However there seems to be an increasing trend in the mean. While the standard deviation remains almost constant over time, relative dispersion appears to decrease slightly, as the coefficient of variation indicates.

The preceding two tables give a first hint on the link between teaching and research. For a more thorough investigation, three analytical steps examine the relation between the teaching index Ti and the research index Ri of each model TRi for $i = 1, ..., 4$. A t-test tests for the equality of the means of Ti and Ri for each year; a Chi-square test tests for equality of the coefficients of variation measuring relative dispersion; bivariate correlation coefficients identify the direct relation.

Table 6.14   Research Multipliers of the Overall DEA Models

		1997	1998	1999	2000
	Mean	0.040	0.030	0.045	0.052
R1	Std. Dev.	0.158	0.121	0.128	0.126
	Coeff. Var.	3.990	2.998	2.858	2.427
	Mean	0.065	0.053	0.093	0.082
R2	Std. Dev.	0.170	0.144	0.233	0.164
	Coeff. Var.	2.595	2.717	2.498	1.992
	Mean	0.094	0.074	0.067	0.133
R3	Std. Dev.	0.188	0.164	0.141	0.177
	Coeff. Var.	1.989	2.204	2.086	1.327
	Mean	0.071	0.032	0.100	0.185
R4	Std. Dev.	0.159	0.124	0.164	0.198
	Coeff. Var.	2.246	3.938	1.641	1.072

Table 6.15 provides three pieces of information in each cell: First, the correlation coefficient between the teaching and the research index for each model; second, the t-value for the test on equality of the means; and third the Chi-value of the test on equality of the coefficient of variation.

Correlation coefficients between the teaching and the research indexes show a very low positive relation that seems to be more or less constant over time within models. The absolute t-value ($t(67; 0.05)$) of the test on equality of means of the teaching index Ti and the research index Ri reveals in 11 out of 16 cases a significant difference at the 5 percent level which points to different strategies of universities in teaching and research. Relative dispersion also seems to differ between the two dimensions, as the Chi-value($X = 2.706$) demonstrates, even if these results are less striking than those of the test on equality.

All in all, this analysis of the multipliers for teaching and research supports the theoretical findings of the positioning model: All universities put a high weight on teaching while only some do on research.

Table 6.15   Relationship between the Teaching and Research Multipliers

Corr	1997	1998	1999	2000
(R1,T1)	0.019	0.139	0.277	0.116
	(4.911, 4.309)	(2.758, 2.695)	(4.129, 4.076)	(1.758, 1.723)
(R2,T2)	0.077	0.058	−0.136	0.163
	(1.205, 4.466)	(0.262, 2.753)	(2.406, 2.610)	(3.067, 0.899)
(R3,T3)	0.168	−0.056	0.593	0.185
	(0.061, 0.439)	(2.299, 0.573)	(2.580, 0.415)	(0.947, 0.662)
(R4,T4)	0.314	0.222	0.351	0.314
	(0.811, 8.521)	(3.609, 3.105)	(5.633, 1.976)	(7.202, 0.005)

6.5   RESULTS FOR OVERALL PERFORMANCE

This section provides descriptive statistics for the DEA efficiency scores, which serve as endogenous variable in subsequent chapters. As an efficiency measure for each university the score reveals not only whether a university is efficient or not, but also the degree of (in-)efficiency for each institution. With a score of 1 a university is efficient compared to all other universities. For scores below 1, the difference, 1-score, indicates the level of inefficiency. Table 6.16 displays the descriptive statistics for the four output-oriented DEA models under variable returns to scale.

Table 6.16   Overall Efficiency for German Universities

		1997	1998	1999	2000	All years
	Mean	0.793	0.787	0.781	0.772	0.783
	Std. Dev.	0.211	0.201	0.182	0.191	0.196
TR1	Min	0.239	0.240	0.262	0.274	0.239
	Max	1.000	1.000	1.000	1.000	1.000
	Eff. Univ.	17	14	9	9	53
	Mean	0.793	0.786	0.783	0.782	0.786
	Std. Dev.	0.215	0.214	0.195	0.182	0.201
TR2	Min	0.229	0.219	0.247	0.307	0.219
	Max	1.000	1.000	1.000	1.000	1.000
	Eff. Univ.	15	14	10	10	49
	Mean	0.818	0.806	0.805	0.802	0.808
	Std. Dev.	0.212	0.217	0.205	0.192	0.206
TR3	Min	0.243	0.233	0.227	0.278	0.227
	Max	1.000	1.000	1.000	1.000	1.000
	Eff. Univ.	21	18	14	14	69
	Mean	0.814	0.793	0.792	0.787	0.796
	Std. Dev.	0.211	0.220	0.206	0.198	0.208
TR4	Min	0.224	0.218	0.223	0.271	0.218
	Max	1.000	1.000	1.000	1.000	1.000
	Eff. Univ.	20	16	12	12	66

The average efficiency of all four models varies between 0.772 (*TR2* in 2000) and 0.814 (*TR4* in 1997), and standard deviations range from 0.182 (*TR1* in 1999) to 0.220 (*TR4* in 1998). Both series suggest a considerable degree of similarity for the results of the different models.

Correlations of the efficiency scores from the four models support the idea of relatively homogenous results across specifications and indicate robustness of the performance measure. Table 6.17 presents the correlation coefficients for the four models.

A minimum correlation of 0.8813 highlights the high degree of homogeneity across the different DEA specifications which supports the view that the results do not depend upon the outputs chosen. However within DEA models the scores exhibit considerable heterogeneity in performance, as can be seen in Table 6.16. The minimum for the four total models varies between 0.218 and 0.278. By design, the maximum efficiency score is 1. Consequently, there are differences in performance among universities, independent of the specifics of the production process modeling. Focusing on the level of inefficiency, defined as 1−*efficiency score*, kernel density estimates confirm this view. Figure 6.1 displays the Epanechnikov kernel density for the four DEA models.

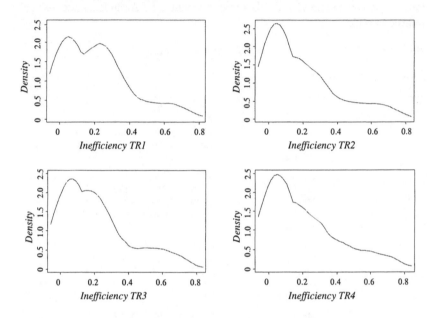

Figure 6.1   Kernel Density Estimate for the Overall DEA Scores

For all four DEA models, the shape of the kernel densities is similar which again supports the robustness of the performance measurement results. Densities are skewed to the left, which goes along with the median being greater than the mean. Evidently, low inefficiency scores are more frequent than high inefficiency scores. As the distribution of the scores is far from being normal, the

Table 6.17   Correlation of the Overall Efficiency Scores

	TR1	TR2	TR3	TR4
TR1	1.0000			
TR2	0.8969	1.0000		
TR3	0.9352	0.9222	1.0000	
TR4	0.8813	0.9662	0.9157	1.0000

flexible gamma distribution seems to capture the distribution of the scores fairly well.

To provide more information on the scores for the individual universities, Table B.1 in the Appendix displays the DEA scores in detail. They are averaged over the four years 1997 to 2000 for each model, and averaged over time and models in the last column. Results of the ranking position show a very high correlation, which again confirms the robustness of the results for the underlying models. Table 6.18 reports the correlation results of the ranking.

Table 6.18   Correlation of the Rankings

	TR1	TR2	TR3	TR4
TR1	1.0000			
TR2	0.9181	1.0000		
TR3	0.9592	0.9510	1.0000	
TR4	0.9031	0.9723	0.9428	1.0000

In summary, the results for overall efficiency of German universities do not depend upon the DEA model used. There is considerably high heterogeneity in the performance of the different institutions within one model. Examining whether this heterogeneity is based on strategic choice of university administrators or other factors will be the focus of the next chapter.

6.6   DEA RESULTS AND THE EXISTENCE OF STRATEGIC GROUPS

To determine the levels of heterogeneity in teaching, research and overall performance of German universities, DEA models were run for all three dimensions. Analyzing the scores from various models helps to identify the focus of each university. First, descriptive statistics of the teaching and the research models suggest the existence of higher barriers to mobility in research than in teaching. Second, direct comparisons across teaching and research models provide further evidence of heterogeneity across universities. Third, the analysis of the multipliers of the overall DEA performance model reveals substantial differences between teaching and research positions of universities. And fourth, universities show heterogeneity in overall performance.

Examining the descriptive statistics of the teaching models, it appears that there are more changes over time in teaching than in research scores which suggests that it is more difficult to change positions in research than in teaching. Furthermore, correlations across research models are higher than across teaching models. This remains true over different input-output specifications as well as over time which indicates there are fewer impediments to change positions with respect to teaching. In this way, the analysis provides evidence for higher barriers to mobility in research than in teaching, thus lending support to hypothesis *H1* from Chapter 4.

There is evidence that it is easier to change positions in teaching than in research, and that heterogeneity is greater in research than in teaching. Both results are consistent with the existence of strategic groups in German higher education. First, significantly higher means and lower variances of DEA scores in teaching compared to research point to homogeneity in teaching and heterogeneity in research. Second, a low correlation over time and across teaching models on the one hand, and a relatively high correlation across research models on the other hand, suggest low impediments to mobility for changing positions in teaching as opposed to research. Therefore, a group structure emerges.

These results find support in the analysis of the multipliers of the overall DEA model which measures multi-dimensional performance of universities. Reflecting the weight and importance universities attach to the two dimensions, teaching and research, multipliers for teaching turn out to be smaller than those for research. In connection with the higher degree of dispersion in research multipliers, the results are consistent with hypothesis *H3* from the positioning model of Chapter 5.

Finally, a positive correlation between the teaching and research results implies that both dimensions should be considered simultaneously. It is important to examine the influence that teaching and research related variables have on total performance. In the next chapter an econometric analysis focuses on this topic, taking into account strategic variables and several control variables.

7 Teaching and Research as Strategic Variables of German Universities

The theoretical chapters predict a connection between university administrator's use of teaching and research for positioning and the structure of higher education. While the concept of strategic groups focuses on performance differences between groups, the positioning model concentrates on the different influences of strategic variables belonging to different groups. Both approaches imply heterogeneity of universities resulting in a group structure in the higher education sector. This chapter applies econometric methods to test these implications.

To explain productivity heterogeneity for German universities as overall performance from Section 6.5, will serve as endogenous variable in the regressions. The first section of this chapter, Section 7.1, divides the exogenous variables into four categories, strategic variables, university characteristics, environmental and competitive variables, which Chapter 4 already suggested, and introduces the data and descriptive statistics. Section 7.2 examines the influence of teaching and research on performance, while Section 7.3 studies the heterogeneous effect of teaching quality and research quality on productivity. Finally, Section 7.4 summarizes the empirical results of performance differences in higher education.

7.1 STRATEGIC AND OTHER EXOGENOUS VARIABLES

The DEA efficiency scores, also interpreted as productivity, suggest heterogeneity across universities. Theory predicts that strategic variables – teaching quality and research quality – explain to some extent the performance differences. This section discusses variables influencing the performance of universities, i.e., productivity. I divide exogenous variables into four groups: strategic variables, university characteristics, environmental variables and variables mapping the degree of competition the university faces.

In a multiple stage analysis with DEA in stage one and econometrics in stage two, variables over which the institution has no control should be incorporated in the second stage of the analysis (Lovell 1993). University administration controls strategic variables, while state ministries determine most of the university characteristics and the degree of competition within a state (see Chapter 2).

Theoretical analysis, especially the concept of strategic groups, suggests including the two strategic variables, teaching quality and research quality in regression, as they are hypothesized to influence performance. Performance of the universities does not cover these two indicators explicitly, thus they are not part of the production process assumed by DEA. State governments determine the variables in the category 'university characteristics' (or determined them decades ago). Therefore, we consider them given for universities as well as environmental variables that are not directly connected to the university. Environmental variables reflect locational characteristics of the university which neither the university itself nor the state ministry can change.

These four categories of variables are discussed in the following. First the definition and construction of the variables are presented, followed by descriptive statistics. Table 7.2 summarizes the data sources for the exogenous variables.

Strategic variables form the principal category of variables of universities in this context because university administration can directly influence them. In this way these strategic variables serve as instruments for a university to position itself. Germany lacks standardized teaching or research evaluations, such as are used in the United Kingdom for example, thus the strategic variables are operationalized with the graduate-to-student ratio and the grants per professor ratio.

While performance measurement with DEA captures several output dimensions of universities in quantities, strategic variables reflect the quality dimension of teaching and research. The graduate-to-student ratio measures teaching quality (*Teaching Quality*), the fraction of graduates of total number of students at a university per year. This variable refers to the ability of universities to graduate students. The higher this ratio, the more students pass their exams successfully compared to the total number of students. This interpretation assumes higher teaching quality at those institutions with higher graduate-to-student ratio. *Teaching Quality* shows a minimum value of 0.028 and a maximum of 0.156. On average 9.2 percent of university students are graduated each year.

To measure research quality of the universities, the value of research grants per professor provided by the German Research Foundation (DFG) is used. As the German Research Foundation supports high quality research the variable *Research Quality* encompasses various research dimensions and fields. Data consider all universities with more than a half million Euros awarded over three years and with more than 10 professors in a field. On average the DFG awards 39,105 Euros per professor to universities included in this analysis.

Both variables *Teaching Quality* and *Research Quality* range across different intervals as minimum and maximum values in Table 7.1 show, the following formula normalizes both variables to the interval $[0, 1]$:

$$normalized\ variable = \frac{variable - min(variable)}{max(variable) - min(variable)}$$

Normalization facilitates easy interpretation of estimated coefficients. Table 7.1 displays the descriptive statistics for the raw strategic variables as well as for the normalized strategic variables.

The university characteristics category includes attributes on student subsidies, size, composition of subjects and age of each university. Universities subsidize apartments for students to attract them. A large number of rooms in dormitories make moving for students easier since they do not need to find an apartment on the private housing market. The variable *Support* describes the number of apartments per students at the university location. The support level universities provide students compensates for low teaching or research quality, and works a subsidy for its students. Support is the number of apartments per student and ranges between 0.019 and 1.092. Conversely, the number of students per apartment is between 53.65 and 0.915. In one city there are more apartments available than requested, which the minimum number of 0.915 students per apartment indicates.

University size may be an important variable to determine performance. The number of students measures *University Size* and captures economies of scale and scope. While the smallest university has 2,422 students the largest institution in the sample has 60,704 students enrolled, which also points to large differences in size of universities.

Of course, the relation of social sciences and natural sciences at a university influences the results in teaching as well as in research. Teaching methods and publication strategies differ substantially between these two areas. In the social sciences teaching usually takes place in large classrooms, mostly as lecture or tutorial, meaning that the number of students plays a minor rule. Education in the natural sciences consumes a large amount of resources compared to the social sciences. Students in the natural sciences conduct research in laboratories in small groups accompanied by scientific staff. Consequently, the natural sciences require more scientific staff per student and laboratories with special apparatus. The fraction of social science staff, *Social Sciences*, captures the resulting lower costs for social sciences dominated institutions. On average, natural sciences staff dominates with 67.3 percent of the staff at universities. As the analysis takes place on the university level, this variable captures differences due to various field philosophy. Clearly, distinguishing only between social sciences and natural sciences is rather rough, but it ensures that results in the quality dimensions are not due to field specifics.

In addition, apart from the composition of fields in universities, the existence of a medical school impacts performance. Most universities with a medical program/degree run a hospital that results in a different cost and staff structure. Thus, the dummy variable *Medicine* takes the value 1 if the university has a medical department. At about 48.5 percent of German universities a medical department is present, either human, veterinary or both.

Important university characteristics for attracting students are reputation and being well known. The age of a university, *University Age*, captures both dimensions. Perhaps tradition affects some strategic decisions and in this way influences performance. Additionally, a dummy variable (*After WWII*) captures whether a university was founded after World War II. The youngest university in this sample in 1997 was four years old while the oldest institution was 614. Table 7.1 shows the descriptive statistics for the exogenous variables.

Table 7.1   Descriptive Statistics of the Exogenous Variables

Variable	Obs.	Mean	Std. Dev.	Min	Max
Teaching Quality (real)	272	0.092	0.024	0.028	0.156
Teaching Quality (normalized)	272	0.497	0.187	0.000	1.000
Research Quality (real)	272	39.105	22.444	0.000	104.955
Research Quality (normalized)	272	0.373	0.214	0.000	1.000
Support	272	0.172	0.142	0.019	1.092
University Size (in 1,000)	272	17.922	12.075	2.422	60.704
Social Sciences	267	0.347	0.234	0.000	1.000
Medicine	272	0.485	0.501	0.000	1.000
University Age	272	180.838	194.089	4.000	614.000
After WWII	272	0.456	0.499	0.000	1.000
Universities within 100 km	272	9.632	5.403	0.000	21.000
Concentration	272	0.291	0.231	0.094	1.000
Student Fraction in the City	264	0.083	0.047	0.015	0.223
City Size (in 1,000)	264	491.855	718.035	50.270	3,425.759
Unemployment	264	12.469	3.848	5.300	21.400
Western Germany	272	0.794	0.405	0.000	1.000

Note: The table displays the descriptive statistics for the four groups of exogenous variables: strategic variables, university characteristics, competitive variables and environmental variables.

The third category of exogenous variables measure the aspect of the competition an institution of higher education faces. As direct competition measure the analysis includes the number of universities located within 100 kilometers (*Univ in 100km*). The more universities nearby, the larger is the variety of institutions students can choose from. If several universities are located nearby, student moving costs for all these universities are similar. Therefore, students do not choose the university connected with lowest mobility costs, but they choose the university offering the most appropriate studies. This may force universities either to compete with a number of other universities or to position strategically in niches to avoid a high degree of competition.

The second competition measure is the Herfindhal-index encapsulating student concentration in states (*Concentration*). Computed for the students of each state, it accounts for the competitive situation within each state, especially on the input side. It influences the competition for financial resources in the ministry for education (or the corresponding ministry on state level). A higher concentration of students, i.e., lower competition, makes it easier for a university to receive additional resources from the state ministry. The index is normalized to the interval from 0 to 1, and on average it is 0.29 in the sample, which indicates a rather low concentration of students.

Environmental variables form the last category of control variables. While the preceding groups of exogenous variables refer more or less directly to the university, the environmental variables capture the location of the institution. To depict the importance of students in the city, the variable *Students in City* captures the number of students at the university location in relation to the number of inhabitants of the city. This value varies significantly and is between 1.5 and 22.3 percent. As not only university characteristics attract students, the number of inhabitants of the city where the university is located, *City Size*, captures this effect. Larger cities offer different outside opportunities for students than smaller cities. In this way, city size may have an effect on performance of a university due to student selection effects. The average city size where universities are located is around half a million inhabitants.

The unemployment rate in the area indicates the economic activity and wealth of the area around the university, implying higher living standards and higher public resource availability when unemployment is low. However the variable *Unemployment* also includes an indirect effect. High unemployment rates in a region suggest young people start studying instead of being unemployed and in this way decreases university performance (Plümper and Schneider 2006). The unemployment rate ranges from 5.3 percent to 21.4 percent with a mean of 12.5 percent. Data for inhabitants and the unemployment rate are researched for each university location individually from the online database of the German Federal Statistical Office. Finally, inserting a dummy for universities located in the Western part of Germany takes structural, regional differences into account. Table 7.2 summarizes the source of the data for exogenous variables.

Section 4.1.1 has already discussed the validity and quality of the strategic variables. Indicators measuring teaching quality directly in terms of success on the labor market of graduates by employment rates or salary would have been preferred, but this kind of data is not available for Germany. However the graduate-to-student ratio serves as a good proxy. An even more discriminating variable than the total value of grants approximates research quality here, it is the value of grants provided by the German Research Foundation (DFG), which requires very high quality applications before granting money. Official statistics from the Federal Statistical Office and from the Science Council (Wissenschaftsrat) provide data on most university characteristics. The support level of univer-

Table 7.2　Sources of the Exogenous Variables

Data	Source
DFG Grants (*Research Quality*)	DFG (2003), pp. 166–167
	DFG (2000), pp. 73–75
Number of students	Statistisches Bundesamt (2000)
	Statistisches Bundesamt (2002)
Number of graduates	Statistisches Bundesamt (2000)
	Statistisches Bundesamt (2002)
Students at public institutions	Statistisches Bundesamt (2000b)
	Statistisches Bundesamt (2002)
Number of apartments (*Support*)	Stern Magazin (1999), pp. 205–247
	Stern Magazin (2000), pp. 138–182
	Stern Magazin (2001), pp. 148–193
Founding year of the university	Stern Magazin (2001)
Staff in Social Sciences and in Arts and Humanities, Natural Sciences	Wissenschaftsrat (2002b, 2001, 2000b, 1999)
Presence of medical department	Statistisches Bundesamt (2002)
	Statistisches Bundesamt (2000)
Number of universities within 100km	Own Research
Number of students in the city	Statistisches Bundesamt (2002)
	Statistisches Bundesamt (2000)
Number of inhabitants in the city Unemployment rate in the city	Statistisches Bundesamt (2004)

sities provided to students, of course, can neither be observed nor measured directly – the same problem as for the teaching and research quality dimension. Therefore, a well selected proxy variable is to capture this effect. Environmental factors stem from official data sources and have been chosen in a way that they cover most aspects characterizing a university's location.

7.2　THE IMPACT OF TEACHING AND RESEARCH ON PERFORMANCE

Before testing heterogeneity in German higher education, this section deals with the explanation of performance differences across universities. It tests whether research quality has a larger impact than teaching quality on productivity.[1] To explain performance, as measured by DEA efficiency, the analysis examines the four groups of exogenous variables: strategic variables, university characteristics, competitive variables and environmental variables.

All regressions are run on inefficiency as the endogenous variable. Subsection 6.5 describes the characteristics of the variable *Inefficiency* and delivers two arguments for this procedure. First, either a university is efficient or it is not. Different degrees of efficiency economically do not make any sense, but the degree of inefficiency mirrors the extent to which universities do not reach efficiency. Second, a gamma distribution describes the inefficiency score quite well, which strongly suggests regressing the exogenous variables on the inefficiency score. A negative sign for a coefficient implies that the corresponding variable decreases the extent of inefficiency. Put differently, a negative sign indicates an efficiency enhancing influence of the corresponding variable. To ensure robustness of the results against various performance measures, the model considers the performance results of all four overall DEA specifications.

Considering the distributional characteristics of the endogenous variables, the DEA inefficiency score, the appropriate method is GLS regression. For the four DEA models it detects the effect of teaching and research quality on inefficiency as a performance measure. Inefficiency scores are approximately gamma-distributed as the kernel density estimate suggests. A generalized least squares estimator incorporates distributions other than the normal distribution and corrects for violation of the Gauss-Markov conditions (for GLS see Greene 2003).[2]

Both quality variables, the DFG research grants per professor and the graduation rate, are expected to have a negative effect on inefficiency, i.e., a positive effect on performance, thus higher qualities increase the performance of universities. Table 7.3 summarizes the results for the GLS estimations for the four DEA models.

The coefficients for the teaching and research quality variables in all four specifications show the theoretically expected signs. Teaching and research quality have statistically significant impact on performance. For all four DEA specifications higher quality levels lead to lower inefficiency. While research quality is always significantly different from zero at the 1 percent level, teaching quality is only significant at the 10 percent level in two specifications and once at the 5 percent level.

From the university characteristics group, the fraction of social sciences at the university has a significant influence on performance. A higher fraction of social sciences at an institution corresponds to a lower inefficiency. One basic explanation may be that class size in the natural sciences is much smaller than in the social sciences as a result of using laboratories and experiments for teaching. Competition variables also have impact on the performance of universities. The concentration of students in a state, the Herfindhal Index, in three out of four specifications shows positive significance and thus indicates that higher concentration goes along with greater inefficiency. In states with few universities there is less competition for state funding and additionally, in small states universities provide prestige for the state and therefore institutions may receive additional resources to enhance reputation without having to improve the quality of teaching or research.

Table 7.3   Results from the GLS Estimation

	Ineff *TR1*	Ineff *TR2*	Ineff *TR3*	Ineff *TR4*
Strategic Variables				
Research Quality	−2.75(6.63)***	−1.82(4.06)***	−1.77(4.81)***	−1.87(4.56)***
Teaching Quality	−1.26(2.88)***	−0.95(1.89)*	−0.95(2.30)**	−0.90(1.83)*
University Characteristics				
Support	0.47(0.91)	0.14(0.24)	0.25(0.47)	0.08(0.14)
University Size	−0.07(0.50)	0.55(1.98)**	0.21(1.08)	0.26(1.29)
Social Sciences	−2.30(5.12)***	−2.38(3.61)***	−2.44(4.56)***	−2.89(5.48)***
Medicine	0.34(2.11)**	−0.13(0.67)	−0.11(0.61)	−0.10(0.59)
University Age	0.08(0.95)	−0.07(0.67)	−0.01(0.16)	−0.02(0.16)
After WWII	−0.16(0.69)	−0.38(1.22)	−0.17(0.64)	−0.29(0.98)
Competition Variables				
Univ in 100km	0.01(0.41)	−0.01 (0.60)	−0.01(0.74)	−0.01(0.67)
Concentration	0.33(1.51)	0.67(3.01)***	0.62(3.53)***	0.59(2.86)***
Environmental Variables				
Students in City	−4.10(2.49)**	−8.07(3.46)***	−4.67(2.63)***	−7.64(3.81)***
City Size	−0.13(1.71)*	−0.52(3.21)***	−0.22(2.33)**	−0.39(3.16)***
Unemployment	0.20(0.08)	1.54(0.48)	−0.36(0.15)	−0.21(0.07)
West Germany	−0.07(0.36)	−0.58(2.38)**	−0.42(2.15)**	−0.34(1.27)
Constant	2.76(1.79)*	2.69(1.46)	1.90(1.05)	3.75(1.90)*
Observations	259	259	259	259

Note: This table presents the results from GLS estimations with the inefficiency score of DEA as endogenous variable. The underlying distribution is gamma, the link function is a log-function. Absolute values of z statistics are shown in parentheses. Positive signs indicate an inefficiency increasing effect, i.e., a performance reducing effect. Coefficients for Unemployment are multiplied with 100. * significant at 10%; ** significant at 5%; *** significant at 1%.

In the fourth group, environmental variables, city size and the number of students in the city have a significantly negative effect on inefficiency. Universities in larger cities are less inefficient, which can be explained by network influences between industry, research institutes and university research. Lower inefficiency of universities in cities with a high fraction of students hints at competition between and for students. Briefly, results of the GLS regressions are in line with theory and robust across different specifications of the performance measure. Not only are signs robust across various models, coefficient magnitude is also very robust across models.

To test the hypothesis of different impacts from teaching quality and research quality we must calculate the normalized effects of the strategic variables on performance. Normalization of the coefficients allows for the comparison of the effects. However the GLS estimator is not linear thus relating the estimated coefficients to the standard deviation of the corresponding variable leads to a normalized effect of teaching quality on performance of $-1.265 * 0.187 = -0.237$, while the research quality effect is much higher ($-2.751 * 0.214 = -0.589$). The normalized effects thus show a much larger impact of research quality on performance than teaching quality. Table 7.4 displays the normalized coefficients by conditioning them on the standard deviation of the strategic variable.

Table 7.4   Normalized Effects of the GLS Model

	Research Quality	Teaching Quality
TR1	−0.589	−0.237
TR2	−0.391	−0.178
TR3	−0.380	−0.179
TR4	−0.400	−0.168

Note: This table shows the normalized effects of teaching quality and research quality on productivity. Normalization results from relating the coefficients of the four models, *TR1*, *TR2*, *TR3* and *TR4* to the standard deviations of the strategic variables, which is 0.187 for teaching quality and 0.214 for research quality.

The rows of Table 7.4 show the normalized effects of teaching and research quality for the four models. Obviously, the influence of research quality on inefficiency is always at least twice as large as the impact of teaching quality. Taking the significant results about the sign of the coefficients and the size of the coefficient together, the empirical results lend support to the hypothesis *H2* from the concept of strategic groups as well as for the hypothesis from the positioning model: teaching quality and research quality have different impact on performance. Higher values in both dimensions reduce inefficiency with a greater effect from research quality than from teaching quality.

To get further information about the different impact of teaching and research quality on inefficiency, quantile regression is used next on all inefficiency scores. This robust method does not depend on the distribution of the endogenous variable (Hallock and Koenker 2001) and therefore it is helpful for the gamma-distributed inefficiency score. Focusing on different quantiles, these regressions concentrate on low-performing universities by running regressions onto the 90 percent inefficiency quantile instead of the mean. The 90 percent quantile denotes the value at which 90 percent of the universities have a lower degree of inefficiency and only 10 percent show higher inefficiency scores. Table 7.5 represents the results for the quantile regression onto the 90 percent quantile with bootstrapping and 1,000 repetitions.

The results are consistent with the results of the GLS estimations for teaching quality and research quality. Research quality and teaching quality illustrate significantly negative coefficients and thus support the finding that higher qualities reduce inefficiency. Control variables exhibit the expected signs and statistical significance is similar to the results from the GLS regressions. To evaluate the effect of regressions on quantiles other than the 90 percent value, many regres-

Table 7.5   Results for Quantile Regression

	Ineff *TR1*	Ineff *TR2*	Ineff *TR3*	Ineff *TR4*
Strategic Variables				
Research Quality	−0.32(3.62)***	−0.06(0.81)	−0.16(2.36)**	−0.09(0.97)
Teaching Quality	−0.20(1.92)*	−0.08(0.88)	−0.18(2.23)**	−0.16(1.21)
University Characteristics				
Support	−7.81(0.39)	4.59(0.34)	−3.35(0.22)	−0.01(0.00)
University Size	−3.60(0.96)	0.40(0.13)	−5.90(1.50)	−1.00(0.23)
Social Sciences	−0.25(3.01)***	−0.19(1.98)**	−0.25(3.17)***	−0.24(2.00)**
Medicine	0.08(1.73)*	0.03(0.79)	0.04(1.06)	0.04(1.02)
University Age	0.05(1.70)*	0.01(0.35)	0.03(1.22)	0.02(0.78)
After WWII	0.04(0.61)	−0.07(1.47)	−0.02(0.41)	−0.04(0.63)
Competition Variables				
Univ in 100km	0.06(0.24)	−0.05(0.24)	0.07(0.29)	0.12(0.37)
Concentration	0.07(1.25)	0.15(3.31)***	0.09(2.42)**	0.13(2.53)**
Environmental Variables				
Students in City	−0.03(1.50)	−0.06(3.34)***	−0.02(1.04)	−0.07(2.50)**
City Size	−0.84(2.69)***	−1.18(3.30)***	−0.85(2.23)**	−1.39(2.93)***
Unemployment	0.28(0.60)	1.37(3.37)***	0.72(1.68)*	0.73(1.11)
West Germany	−0.13(2.68)***	−0.19(4.32)***	−0.16(3.92)***	−0.19(3.33)***
Constant	1.08(2.42)**	1.09(3.54)***	1.23(2.98)***	1.34(3.20)***
Pseudo R^2	0.44	0.44	0.46	0.40

Note: This table presents the results from quantile regressions with the inefficiency score of DEA as endogenous variable regressing at the 90 percent quantile using bootstrapping. Robust z statistics are given in parentheses. Positive signs indicate an inefficiency increasing effect, i.e., a performance reducing effect. Coefficients for Support, Universities in 100km and Unemployment are multiplied with 100. * Significant at 10%; ** significant at 5%; *** significant at 1%

sions on various quantiles are conducted. Focusing on the two strategic variables Figure 7.1 presents the coefficients of teaching quality and research quality for model *TR1* graphically.

For different quantiles on the horizontal axis, the graph demonstrates the resulting coefficients from quantile regression on the vertical axis. The left hand graph in Figure 7.1 shows that regression on the 90 percent quantile (indicated by 0.9 on the horizontal axis) leads to a coefficient of research quality of −0.410 which is consistent with the results in Table 7.5. Analogously, the coefficient for teaching quality, −0.262, in the right graph on the vertical axis results for a value of 0.9 on the horizontal axis. The vertical axis exhibits coefficients for different quantiles on the horizontal axis. Regressing on the median (0.5 on the horizontal line) for example, leads to a coefficient of −0.322 for research quality and −0.198 for teaching quality. Note, that for each point in the graph one quantile regression is run. All results hold for the remaining three models, *TR2*, *TR3* and *TR4*. The Appendix provides the corresponding figures.

The main insight from these figures is the fact that the coefficients for teach-

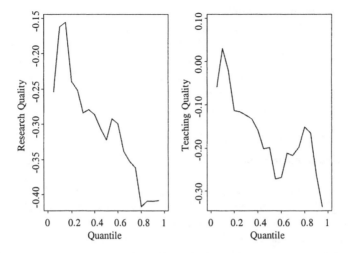

Note: This figure displays the coefficients of several quantile regressions for teaching quality and research quality with inefficiency from the *TR1* model being the endogenous variable. The left-hand side graph shows the coefficients for research quality while the right-hand side graphs the coefficients of the teaching quality.

Figure 7.1   Coefficients for Teaching and Research Quality in TR1 *Model*

ing quality and research quality are always negative, almost independent of the quantile. Consequently, higher quality levels lead to lower inefficiency. Furthermore there is a tendency for the coefficients to decrease with higher quantiles, implying a stronger impact with higher values of inefficiency. In this fashion the quantile regressions also suggests a heterogeneous impact of the strategic variables on performance, which the following section will examine.

7.3   HETEROGENEOUS IMPACT OF TEACHING AND RESEARCH

The concept of strategic groups and the positioning model hypothesize heterogeneity across universities, but concentrate on different aspects. While the hypothesis *H2* from the concept of strategic groups points to heterogeneous impact in low- and high-ranked groups, the positioning model centers on the different influence of the strategic variables, teaching and research quality on group membership (*H4*). This section examines both aspects of heterogeneity across universities, especially focusing on the impact of teaching quality and research quality on group structure which is a special form of heterogeneity.

Subsection 7.3.1 presents two methods for grouping universities based on performance, i.e., productivity, into heterogenous clusters. Traditional cluster analysis and the more sophisticated Zivot-Andrews test lead to groups that show a high degree of homogeneity within the group and a high degree of heterogeneity across groups. The second Subsection 7.3.2 tests the hypothesis from the concept of strategic groups by running GLS regressions with interaction terms across the strategic variables and testing for equality. Finally, Subsection 7.3.3 tests hypothesis *H4* from the positioning model focusing on differing impact of strategic variables for being in the high-ranked group or in the low-ranked group.

7.3.1   Group Formation

Mirroring the concept of strategic groups, this subsection divides universities into two groups based on performance. The efficiency score from DEA, a multi-dimensional productivity measure for universities, describes performance. Applying different grouping mechanisms two groups of universities arise: a lower ranked group consisting of low-ranked universities (i.e., the high-inefficiency universities) and a high-ranked group consisting of high-performance universities (i.e., the low-inefficiency universities). Cluster analysis, a prominent method for identifying group structure, determines groups endogenously. Additionally, a more sophisticated method, the Zivot-Andrews test, detects structure as well.

While literature commonly builds structure on almost arbitrary factors, this section groups universities on the economically based performance measure of inefficiency. Non-hierarchical clustering, *kmeans*, utilizes the Euclidean norm as a distance measure and minimizes variance within groups. The dummy variable $high_{CA,TRi}$ refers to performance and takes 1 for a university in the high-ranked group and 0 for a university in the low-ranked group.

$$high_{CA,TRi} = \left\{ \begin{array}{l} 1, \text{ if inefficiency is low} \\ 0, \text{ else} \end{array} \right\}$$

$$= \left\{ \begin{array}{l} 1, \text{ if performance is high} \\ 0, \text{ else} \end{array} \right\}$$

Consequently, the complement is $low_{CA,TRi} = 1 - high_{CA,TRi}$, and a '1' indicates universities showing low performance, i.e., a high inefficiency score. Table 7.6 displays the descriptive statistics of the groups derived by cluster analysis and shows values for the degree of inefficiency so that low numbers indicate high performance.

Using cluster analysis as a grouping method the mean in the high-ranked group (low inefficiency group) varies between 0.096 and 0.129 across the different DEA models. In contrast the average in the low-ranked group varies between 0.452 and 0.550. The high-performance group is always larger than the high-inefficiency group. Again, results are similar across different DEA specifications. While cluster analysis is a multivariate method not accounting for

Table 7.6 Group Formation Applying Cluster Analysis

		High-Ranked Universities	Low-Ranked Universities
	Mean	0.110	0.452
	Std. Dev.	0.098	0.146
TR1	Min	0.000	0.281
	Max	0.276	0.761
	Obs.	187	85
	Mean	0.101	0.523
	Std. Dev.	0.102	0.135
TR2	Min	0.000	0.315
	Max	0.305	0.773
	Obs.	213	59
	Mean	0.129	0.550
	Std. Dev.	0.106	0.116
TR3	Min	0.000	0.351
	Max	0.339	0.781
	Obs.	217	55
	Mean	0.096	0.493
	Std. Dev.	0.095	0.141
TR4	Min	0.000	0.299
	Max	0.291	0.782
	Obs.	198	74

stochastic influences, the Zivot-Andrews test is a unit root test, developed in the econometric context of time series data to detect breaks (Zivot and Andrews 1992).

A Zivot-Andrews test identifies a break point based on the intercept, the trend or both. Ordering the inefficiency scores by size, the test statistics based on trend identifies a break point. However the results are robust for the break point based on the intercept and on both trend and intercept. For an inefficiency score below or equal to the break point the dummy variable $high_{ZA,TRi}$ equals 1 and for an inefficiency score above the break point score, the dummy variable equals 0. Formally:

$$
high_{ZA,TRi} \;=\; \left\{ \begin{array}{l} 1, \text{ if inefficiency is low} \\ 0, \text{ else} \end{array} \right\}
$$
$$
\;=\; \left\{ \begin{array}{l} 1, \text{ if performance is high} \\ 0, \text{ else} \end{array} \right\}
$$

Again, the complementary variable, $low_{ZA,TRi} = 1 - high_{ZA,TRi}$, indicates the low-ranked group of universities. Table 7.7 shows the average inefficiency scores for the groups by the Zivot-Andrews test and all four DEA models.

Conducting a Zivot-Andrews test leads to high-ranked groups composed of between 203 and 217 universities, which show an average inefficiency level between 0.093 and 0.138. While the average inefficiency in the high-inefficiency

Table 7.7   Group Formation Applying the Zivot-Andrews Test

		High-Ranked Group	Low-Ranked Group
	Mean	0.138	0.529
	Std. Dev.	0.115	0.126
TR1	Min	0.000	0.351
	Max	0.335	0.761
	Obs.	217	55
	Mean	0.093	0.496
	Std. Dev.	0.096	0.146
TR2	Min	0.000	0.295
	Max	0.292	0.773
	Obs.	205	67
	Mean	0.116	0.504
	Std. Dev.	0.097	0.138
TR3	Min	0.000	0.296
	Max	0.295	0.781
	Obs.	203	69
	Mean	0.104	0.514
	Std. Dev.	0.102	0.134
TR4	Min	0.000	0.327
	Max	0.325	0.782
	Obs.	206	66

group is between 0.496 and 0.529, the standard deviation remains almost constant across both groups, indicating homogeneity within groups. Testing via Zivot-Andrews identifies a group structure with low standard deviations within groups.

Both theoretical approaches suggest heterogeneity across universities that results in a group structure for higher education. Briefly, the preceding subsection has revealed two groups of universities based on performance. These groups show a high degree of heterogeneity across the identified clusters. Cluster analysis and the Zivot-Andrews test reveal very similar average inefficiency within the lower and higher ranked group of universities. However group size differs between the two grouping mechanisms. Although the two grouping methods show robust results, the most discriminating results are expected for the regressions in which the Zivot-Andrews test determines the break point endogenously. These groupings serve as the starting point for the following subsection, which examines the impact of teaching quality and research quality according to heterogeneity.

7.3.2   Grouping on the Strategic Variables

Strategic group theory hypothesizes a larger effect from research quality in the high-performance group than in the low-performance group. Correspondingly, teaching quality is predicted to have a larger effect in the low-performance group than in the high-performance group.

Measuring parameter heterogeneity, interaction variables categorize teaching and research quality. Dummy variables from cluster analysis and the Zivot-Andrews test indicate groups of high-ranked and low-ranked universities. Using these dummy variables, four interaction variables are generated, two for teaching quality (*TQ*low*, *TQ*high*) and two for research quality (*RQ*low*, *RQ*high*). For distributional reasons the endogenous variable is the inefficiency level of a university; the high-performance group is equivalent to the low inefficiency group and the low-performance group is equivalent to the high inefficiency group. From now on the terms high and low refer to performance and instead of inefficiency. For both methods described above, GLS regressions identify the influence of various strategic variables on inefficiency. Finally, a test for equality of the coefficients of the interaction variables detects different impact on high- and low-performance universities. Table 7.8 displays the results of the GLS regression with a gamma distribution and a log function as link function. The Zivot-Andrews test constructs the interaction terms with teaching and research.

The analysis starts with the results for the strategic variables, teaching quality and research quality. For research quality the interaction term, $RQ * low_{ZA, TRi}$, has a statistically significant negative coefficient for all specifications, i.e., for all $i = 1, \ldots, 4$. Higher research quality decreases inefficiency significantly in the low-ranked group. However in the high-ranked group, the estimated coefficient of research quality is significantly negative only in one specification *TR1*. For the remaining three regressions, these coefficients are positive. Consequently, research quality does not identify a robust significant effect in the high-ranked group. Nevertheless, the comparison of research quality coefficients shows significant differences between the low and the high group in all specifications. The test for equality of the coefficients of the interaction terms rejects equality.

Across different groups the impact of research quality is similar to those of teaching quality. Three out of four specifications always demonstrate negatively significant impact of the interaction variable for $TQ * low_{ZA, TRi}$. While higher teaching quality decreases inefficiency in the high-ranked group significantly, in the low-ranked group (high inefficiency) the teaching variable twice has positively significant influence, though the regressions suggest that high teaching quality increases inefficiency in the low-ranked group. Comparing the coefficients of the interaction variables between high and low, it turns out that these coefficients differ significantly for all four specifications.

Teaching quality and research quality show different impact in the low- and the high-ranked group. This finding supports the hypothesis, *H2*, from the strategic group concept, stating a group structure within the industry sector of higher education where groups exhibit different performance levels which can be explained by strategic variables whose impact differs across groups. Teaching

Table 7.8   Results from the GLS Estimation (Zivot-Andrews Test)

	Ineff *TR1*	Ineff *TR2*	Ineff *TR3*	Ineff *TR4*
Strategic Variables				
RQ*high$_{ZA,TR1}$	−2.43(5.23)***			
RQ*low$_{ZA,TR1}$	−0.95(1.65)*			
TQ*high$_{ZA,TR1}$	−1.22(2.41)**			
TQ*low$_{ZA,TR1}$	−0.66(1.48)			
RQ*high$_{ZA,TR2}$		−1.27(2.58)***		
RQ*low$_{ZA,TR2}$		0.09(0.17)		
TQ*high$_{ZA,TR2}$		−1.04(2.49)**		
TQ*low$_{ZA,TR2}$		1.23(3.28)***		
RQ*high$_{ZA,TR3}$			−1.39(3.43)***	
RQ*low$_{ZA,TR3}$			0.53(0.93)	
TQ*high$_{ZA,TR3}$			−0.85(1.78)*	
TQ*low$_{ZA,TR3}$			0.38(1.00)	
RQ*high$_{ZA,TR4}$				−1.45(3.32)***
RQ*low$_{ZA,TR4}$				1.03(1.76)*
TQ*high$_{ZA,TR4}$				−0.86(1.60)
TQ*low$_{ZA,TR4}$				0.68(1.44)
University Characteristics				
Support	−0.07(0.15)	−0.27(0.58)	−0.16(0.37)	−0.40(0.90)
University Size	−0.02(0.12)	0.54(1.92)*	0.35(1.52)	0.37(1.88)*
Social Sciences	−1.94(4.40)***	−1.72(2.87)***	−1.95(3.71)***	−2.25(5.04)***
Medicine	0.36(2.23)**	−0.09(0.47)	−0.03(0.16)	0.06(0.34)
University Age	0.04(0.41)	−0.20(1.87)*	−0.09(1.00)	−0.13(1.20)
After WWII	−0.25(1.04)	−0.76(2.36)**	−0.35(1.30)	−0.59(1.91)*
Competition Variables				
Univ in 100km	−0.01(0.01)	−2.56(1.51)	−1.68(1.05)	−2.25(1.35)
Concentration	0.38(1.78)*	0.74(3.22)***	0.77(4.32)***	0.73(3.39)***
Environmental Variables				
Students in City	−3.47(2.04)**	−3.88(1.58)	−4.39(2.40)**	−5.84(2.87)***
City Size	−0.15(1.85)*	−0.46(2.95)***	−0.35(3.12)***	−0.47(4.29)***
Unemployment	−0.41(0.18)	2.73(0.89)	−5.85(0.25)	0.41(0.14)
West Germany	0.16(0.68)	0.19(0.82)	0.22(0.94)	0.60(1.93)*
Constant	2.22(1.48)	1.07(0.63)	1.48(0.92)	2.78(1.62)
Test for Equality of Interaction Terms				
RQ Chi2(1)	6.57**	4.41**	8.95***	14.78***
TQ Chi2(1)	5.94*	16.74***	8.97**	11.79***

Note: This table presents the GLS estimations results with the inefficiency score as the endogenous variable. The underlying distribution is gamma, the link function is a log function. * significant at 10%; ** significant at 5%; *** significant at 1%. Coefficients for Universities in 100km and Unemployment are multiplied with 100. Absolute values of z statistics are in parentheses. Dummy variables for the interaction terms stem from the Zivot-Andrews test. Then, $high_{ZA,TRi}$ reflects the high-ranked group from the DEA model *TRi*, $i = 1, \ldots, 4$. The corresponding dummy variable $low_{ZA,TRi}$ is the complement and indicates the low-performance group. As the endogenous variable is inefficiency, positive signs indicate an inefficiency increasing effect, i.e., a performance reducing effect. The test for equality of the interaction variables examines whether the coefficients for the low- and the high-ranked group are statistically different. It tests whether $RQ * low_{ZA,TRi} = RQ * high_{ZA,TRi}$ for $i = 1, \ldots, 4$ and whether $TQ * low_{ZA,TRi} = TQ * high_{ZA,TRi}$ for $i = 1, \ldots, 4$.

quality as well as research quality have robust inefficiency decreasing influence in the high-performance group only. The effects differ significantly from the low-performance group and thus indicate higher returns on quality in the high-ranked group of universities. Briefly, there is empirical evidence for different impact of strategic variables on different groups which in turn supports the existence of strategic groups in the German university sector.

The effects of the control variables do not differ systematically from those in the section before, which used the GLS model. University characteristics, especially the composition of the university by fields, has significant influence. For all specifications a higher fraction of social sciences decreases inefficiency. Also competition matters, as a higher concentration of students in the state increases the inefficiency. Finally, from the set of environmental variables, the city size has a significantly negative impact on inefficiency, so does the fraction of students in the city. To demonstrate robustness of the results the corresponding regression incorporates dummy variables generated by traditional cluster analysis. Table 7.9 represents the results of the GLS estimations with interaction variables resulting form cluster analysis.

Results of the regression utilizing interaction variables, interacting the strategic variables with dummies from cluster analysis, tend to be similar to those clustering with the Zivot-Andrews test. The influence of research quality, $RQ *$ $high_{CA,TRi}$ in the high-ranked group is always negatively significant while the effect of research quality on performance in the low-ranked group shows no robustly significant coefficient. Signs of the interaction variables vary. This observation is also true for teaching quality. All specifications show a significantly negative impact of $TQ * low_{CA,TRi}$ on inefficiency. Also, higher teaching quality decreases inefficiency in the high-performance group. However the influence of teaching quality in the low-ranked group is statistically significant and positive. The coefficients of the interaction variables in teaching quality and in research quality differ significantly. Composition of the university, concentration of students and the fraction of students in the city are again significant. These effects of the control variables are similar to those under the Zivot-Andrews test groupings and the GLS estimations without interaction terms.

In summary, the GLS estimations with interaction variables show that the influence of teaching quality and research quality differs across the low-performance and the high-performance groups, which is consistent with hypothesis *H2* from the concept of strategic groups. There is significant impact of both qualities in the high-ranked group but robust significant effects of the qualities in the low-ranked group are not found; the impact under cluster analysis in the high-ranked group is significantly positive. The test for equality of research quality (and, respectively, teaching quality) coefficients across groups reveals always statistically significant results and thus is compatible with hypothesis *H2* from the concept of strategic groups. These results are robust as they neither depend on the grouping mechanism nor on performance measurement. Traditional clus-

Table 7.9   Results from the GLS Estimation (Cluster Analysis)

	Ineff $TR1$	Ineff $TR2$	Ineff $TR3$	Ineff $TR4$
Strategic Variables				
RQ*high$_{CA,TR1}$	−2.05(3.87)***			
RQ*low$_{CA,TR1}$	−0.96(2.20)**			
TQ*high$_{CA,TR1}$	−1.26(2.21)**			
TQ*low$_{CA,TR1}$	−0.15(0.37)			
RQ*high$_{CA,TR2}$		−1.00(2.04)**		
RQ*low$_{CA,TR2}$		0.67(1.53)		
TQ*high$_{CA,TR2}$		−1.04(2.23)**		
TQ*low$_{CA,TR2}$		1.45(4.03)***		
RQ*high$_{CA,TR3}$			−1.12(2.67)***	
RQ*low$_{CA,TR3}$			0.39(0.96)	
TQ*high$_{CA,TR3}$			−1.00(2.41)**	
TQ*low$_{CA,TR3}$			1.23(3.88)***	
RQ*high$_{CA,TR4}$				−1.28(3.09)***
RQ*low$_{CA,TR4}$				0.32(0.84)
TQ*high$_{CA,TR4}$				−1.08(2.61)***
TQ*low$_{CA,TR4}$				0.94(3.20)***
University Characteristics				
Support	0.12(0.28)	−0.51(1.05)	−0.29(0.67)	−0.38(0.85)
University Age	0.05(0.51)	−0.19(1.75)*	−0.10(1.06)	−0.09(0.80)
After WWII	−0.20(0.79)	−0.68(2.10)**	−0.32(1.18)	−0.57(1.83)*
Social Sciences	−1.68(3.97)***	−1.51(2.63)***	−1.95(3.68)***	−2.26(4.89)***
Medicine	0.34(2.10)**	−0.11(0.54)	−0.12(0.67)	−0.13(0.72)
University Size	−0.07(0.43)	0.64(2.16)**	0.32(1.48)	0.28(1.42)
Competition Variables				
Univ in 100km	−0.09(0.07)	−0.03(1.65)*	−0.03(1.54)	−0.03(1.53)
Concentration	0.28(1.22)	0.82(3.24)***	0.72(3.74)***	0.62(2.83)***
Environmental Variables				
Students in City	−0.94(0.51)	−4.13(1.71)*	−2.24(1.22)	−3.61(1.72)*
City Size	−0.08(0.93)	−0.49(3.05)***	−0.23(2.31)**	−0.36(3.26)***
Unemployment	1.77(0.78)	2.69(0.87)	−3.95(0.16)	1.70(0.58)
West Germany	0.24(1.07)	0.19(0.77)	0.24(1.07)	0.47(1.61)
Constant	0.79(0.55)	0.19(0.11)	0.01(0.01)	1.89(1.09)
Test for Equality of Interaction Terms				
RQ Chi2(1)	3.79*	6.06**	4.61**	8.12***
TQ Chi2(1)	5.46**	15.59***	14.58***	20.37***

Note: This table presents the GLS estimations results with the inefficiency score as the endogenous variable. The underlying distribution is gamma, the link function is a log function. * significant at 10%; ** significant at 5%; *** significant at 1%. Coefficients for Unemployment are multiplied with 100. Absolute values of z statistics are in parentheses. Dummy variables for the interaction terms stem from Cluster Analysis. Then, $high_{CA,TRi}$ reflects the high-ranked group from the DEA model TRi, $i = 1, \ldots, 4$. The corresponding dummy variable $low_{CA,TRi}$ is the complement and indicates the low-ranked group. As the endogenous variable is inefficiency, positive signs indicate an inefficiency increasing effect, i.e., a performance reducing effect. The test for equality of the interaction variables examines whether the coefficients for the low- and the high-performance group are statistically different. It tests whether $RQ * low_{CA,TRi} = RQ * high_{CA,TRi}$ for $i = 1, \ldots, 4$ and whether $TQ * low_{CA,TRi} = TQ * high_{CA,TRi}$ for $i = 1, \ldots, 4$.

ter analysis, as well as the Zivot-Andrews test, reveal similar results. Finally, controlling for university characteristics, competition effects and environmental variables, the results are consistent with the existence of performance based groups. Across groups the influence of strategic variables, teaching quality and research quality differs. These results is consistent with the hypothesis *H2* that there are performance based strategic groups in German higher education.

7.3.3   Probit Analysis to Test Heterogeneity

The preceding sections have revealed the determinants of inefficiency and detected the different influence of teaching quality and research quality on high- and low-ranked groups of universities. The next subsection inspects the impact of strategic variables for being in the high- or low-ranked group. Probit estimations test this hypothesis originated from the positioning model, maintaining heterogenous impact over the intervals measuring teaching quality and research quality. Dummy variables constructed by the Zivot-Andrews test serve as endogenous variables in the first step and those constructed by cluster analysis serve in the second step. The first subsection 7.3.3.1 discusses the estimation results, while the second subsection 7.3.3.2 focuses on the size of the coefficients for the strategic variables teaching quality and research quality, first graphically and then analytically.

7.3.3.1   Estimation Results
This section reveals the impact of different intervals of the teaching and the research quality variables, suggested by the positioning model of universities. Probit estimations estimating the likelihood for being in the low-ranked group rather than the high-ranked group. The two main strategic variables, teaching quality and research quality are the variables of primary concern. Table 7.10 shows the results for probit estimations with the heteroscedasticity consistent Huber-White estimator.

All estimated coefficients of the strategic variables, teaching quality and research quality, illustrate the theoretically expected signs. The likelihood of being in the low-performance group decreases significantly with higher quality levels in both dimensions. While the fraction of social sciences at a university significantly decreases the probability of being in the low-performance group as in Tables 7.8 and 7.9, none of the competition variables consistently demonstrates a significant influence.

However environmental variables have become more important. City size, the fraction of students in the city and location in the western part of Germany reduce the likelihood for being in the low-performance group. Again, the results for grouping by cluster analysis support the robustness of the estimation results. Table 7.11 reveals the results of the probit estimations in which cluster analysis derives the endogenous variable indicating the high-inefficiency group.

Table 7.10   Results from the Probit Estimation (Zivot-Andrews Test)

	low$_{ZA,TR1}$	low$_{ZA,TR2}$	low$_{ZA,TR3}$	low$_{ZA,TR4}$
Strategic Variables				
Research Quality	−13.40(4.36)***	−7.54(5.37)***	−13.87(3.38)***	−7.07(3.91)***
Teaching Quality	−4.95(3.53)***	−3.55(3.41)***	−6.03(3.23)***	−3.10(2.47)**
University Characteristics				
Support	3.17(2.10)**	−0.82(0.52)	2.45(1.29)	−1.92(0.99)
University Size	−0.41(0.91)	0.79(1.98)**	1.08(1.63)	1.06(2.20)**
Social Sciences	−12.41(4.72)***	−6.98(5.06)***	−13.81(3.59)***	−9.04(4.27)***
Medicine	−1.24(2.29)**	−0.67(1.87)*	−1.62(2.28)**	−1.36(2.79)***
University Age	0.39(1.39)	0.35(1.31)	0.15(0.51)	0.75(1.35)
After WWII	−0.80(0.87)	−0.27(0.35)	−1.02(1.09)	0.31(0.21)
Competition Variables				
Univ in 100km	0.14(2.05)**	−0.02(0.34)	0.05(1.01)	0.02(0.39)
Concentration	−1.48(0.97)	0.78(1.12)	0.64(0.75)	1.36(2.23)**
Environmental Variables				
Students in City	−12.05(1.60)	−34.10(3.20)***	−33.25(2.14)**	−54.42(3.09)***
City Size	−0.14(0.42)	−1.06(3.16)***	−0.63(1.17)	−1.39(2.89)***
Unemployment	0.08(1.35)	−0.10(2.49)**	−0.05(1.02)	−0.05(1.14)
West Germany	−2.19(3.11)***	−1.79(2.86)***	−2.74(3.69)***	−3.19(2.90)***
Constant	14.00(2.39)**	16.12(3.44)***	13.22(1.86)*	17.09(2.57)**
Pseudo R^2	0.77	0.61	0.77	0.72

Note: This table displays the probit estimations results using the dummy variable for being in the low-ranked group as endogenous variable. * Significant at 10%; ** significant at 5%; *** significant at 1%. Zivot-Andrews test generates the dummy variable low$_{ZA,TRi}$ based on the DEA inefficiency score. Robust z statistics are in parentheses. The Huber-White estimator ensures heteroscedasticity consistency.

For all four model specifications, the strategic variables teaching quality and research quality are consistent with the hypothesis that higher quality in both dimensions reduces the probability for the low-ranked group membership. Again, university characteristics and environmental variables have a strong and significant effect among the control variables. Results of the probit estimations clearly reveal robust results for the effect of strategic variables. Neither the grouping mechanism nor the performance measure changes the results. There seems to be evidence of a greater influence of research quality on performance than of teaching quality on performance.

7.3.3.2 The Size of the Coefficients
To test hypothesis *H4* from the positioning model, this section examines the size of the effects of teaching quality and research quality on performance. Due to nonlinearity of the probit estimators, the coefficients cannot be easily interpreted. Accordingly, two methods for comparing them are evaluated. First, this subsection displays the predicted probabilities conditional to the mean graphically. Second, Monte Carlo simulations support the results of these figures and

Table 7.11   Results from the Probit Estimation (Cluster Analysis)

	low$_{CA, TR1}$	low$_{CA, TR2}$	low$_{CA, TR3}$	low$_{CA, TR4}$
Strategic Variables				
Research Quality	−6.40(5.82)***	−3.74(2.29)**	−9.78(4.70)***	−5.66(5.49)***
Teaching Quality	−2.69(2.66)***	−2.07(1.67)*	−2.90(2.29)**	−2.18(2.48)**
University Characteristics				
Support	−0.17(0.13)	−1.94(1.43)	0.78(0.55)	−1.03(0.85)
University Size	0.47(1.44)	0.23(0.65)	−0.49(1.40)	0.73(2.02)**
Social Sciences	−5.78(6.45)***	−4.89(2.28)**	−9.58(5.44)***	−5.73(5.08)***
Medicine	−0.25(0.68)	−0.54(1.14)	−0.99(2.33)**	−0.45(1.42)
University Age	0.06(0.28)	0.44(1.43)	0.35(1.43)	0.24(0.87)
After WWII	−0.61(0.91)	−0.62(0.66)	−0.99(1.46)	−0.09(0.12)
Competition Variables				
Univ in 100km	−0.02(0.52)	0.11(3.29)***	0.10(1.85)*	−0.03(0.76)
Concentration	0.47(0.82)	0.27(0.36)	−1.41(1.46)	0.35(0.52)
Environmental Variables				
Students in City	−22.96(3.06)***	−30.56(3.14)***	−13.40(1.59)	−34.31(3.36)***
City Size	−0.79(2.88)***	−0.76(1.96)*	−0.13(0.37)	−0.86(3.03)***
Unemployment	−0.08(1.91)*	0.03(0.82)	0.07(1.36)	−0.05(1.53)
West Germany	−1.53(2.84)***	−2.41(3.98)***	−2.52(3.57)***	−1.82(2.78)***
Constant	14.62(3.43)***	11.49(1.97)**	13.33(2.15)**	12.28(3.58)***
Pseudo R^2	0.56	0.66	0.76	0.59

Note: This table displays the probit estimations results using the dummy variable for being in the low-ranked group as endogenous variable.* significant at 10%; ** significant at 5%; *** significant at 1%. Cluster analysis generates the dummy variable low$_{CA, TRi}$ based on the DEA inefficiency score. Robust z statistics are in parentheses. The Huber-White estimator ensures heteroscedasticity consistency.

ensure the numerical robustness of the graphical results.

The analysis above presents the results of the probit estimations. The more the influence of quality on the predicted probabilities varies over the quality intervals, the more heterogeneous the impact. Figure 7.2 displays the predicted probabilities for the low-ranked universities of the *TR1* model, on the left by applying the Zivot-Andrews test, on the right by applying cluster analysis.

When research quality is free and teaching quality as well as all other variables are normalized to the mean, the straight graph gives an idea about the shape of the probability. Thus, conditional probabilities are calculated and figured. When teaching quality is free, the dotted line establishes the shape for the predicted probability. Figure 7.2 displays the different influence of the strategic variables.

Apparently, the bearing of research quality on the likelihood for the low-ranked group differs more over the intervals measuring research quality than teaching quality does. As the figures for model *TR1* illustrate, the overall impact is not only greater for research quality but also more heterogeneous than for teaching quality. This observation is compatible with the hypothesis that

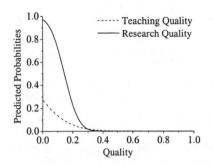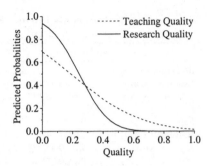

Note: This figure shows the conditional effects of teaching quality and research quality using different grouping mechanisms. The left-hand graph shows the conditional predicted probabilities for model *TR1* under the Zivot-Andrews test. The right-hand side graph shows the predicted probabilities when when all variables, except for teaching quality, are set to their mean. Bold lines show predicted probabilities when all variables except for research quality are set to their mean.

Figure 7.2   Graph of Predicted Probabilities for Model TR1

universities choose positions in which they differ more in research quality than in teaching quality. Appendix D displays the corresponding figures for the remaining models, *TR2*, *TR3* and *TR4* and supports the above results. Briefly, the graphical analysis of coefficients size confirms that the higher heterogeneity of universities positions in research than in teaching.

A procedure introduced by Tomz et al. (2003) proves the robustness of these results numerically; it not only shows a greater influence of research quality than of teaching quality but also shows greater heterogeneity in research quality than the impact of teaching quality is. The program by Tomz et al. (2003) computes the conditional effect of single variables. Applying Monte Carlo simulations the program reveals additional information about results, particularly about key variables. The procedure comprises three steps. First, it carries out 50,000 Monte Carlo simulations for each coefficient of the statistical model, here the probit regression. Second, it sets the values of the explanatory variables except for one equal to the mean of the corresponding variable. Third, given the assumption of fixed exogenous variables, the program simulates expected probabilities. Due to the high number of simulations, it detects the influence of single variables robustly. Tomz et al. (2003) and King et al. (2000) provide the formal algorithm and distributional assumptions.

For each of the strategic variables, teaching quality and research quality, the conditional impact on the expected probability being in the low-performance group is estimated. To determine the conditional effect of teaching quality, the strategic variable research quality is also set to the mean. Then, teaching quality takes various values over different quantiles: 10 percent, 25 percent, 50 percent.

In this way, the procedure isolates the impact of teaching quality on the probability for being in the low-ranked group. For each probit estimation model, I calculate five conditional influences (five quantiles) for each variable, teaching quality and research quality. In total, for the four different DEA models, this procedure leads 20 to conditional effects for teaching quality and to 20 conditional effects for research quality in the Zivot-Andrews case. Higher probabilities indicate a greater influence of the quantile of the strategic variable. A higher probability for the 10 percent quantile than for the 90 percent quantile means that lower values of the variable have higher impact than lower values.

Furthermore, computing probabilities across the same quantile of different variables contrasts the influence of teaching quality and research quality on the probability of being in the low-performance group. Table 7.12 displays the conditional effects after Monte Carlo simulation of teaching quality and research quality, when the Zivot-Andrews test determines the endogenous variable.

Table 7.12   Conditional Effects after MC Simulation (Zivot-Andrews Test)

	Teaching Quality				Research Quality			
	TR1	*TR2*	*TR3*	*TR4*	*TR1*	*TR2*	*TR3*	*TR4*
p10	0.0372	0.3347	0.1251	0.0934	0.6947	0.7763	0.8388	0.4375
	(0.0360)	(0.0926)	(0.0653)	(0.0482)	(0.1535)	(0.0860)	(0.1417)	(0.1139)
p25	0.0125	0.2147	0.0437	0.0515	0.1659	0.4642	0.3307	0.1661
	(0.0161)	(0.0667)	(0.0367)	(0.0306)	(0.0685)	(0.0822)	(0.0887)	(0.0527)
p50	0.0033	0.1128	0.0117	0.0246	0.0027	0.1034	0.0101	0.0225
	(0.0068)	(0.0499)	(0.0197)	(0.0212)	(0.0060)	(0.0481)	(0.0189)	(0.0206)
p75	0.0009	0.0532	0.0037	0.0122	0.0002	0.0239	0.0016	0.0053
	(0.0033)	(0.0380)	(0.0123)	(0.0166)	(0.0017)	(0.0228)	(0.0101)	(0.0100)
p90	0.0004	0.0268	0.0017	0.0073	0.0000	0.0019	0.0005	0.0008
	(0.0022)	(0.0286)	(0.0097)	(0.0148)	(0.0005)	(0.0057)	(0.0089)	(0.0046)

Note: This table displays the predicted probabilities for probit estimations using the dummy variable low-performance group membership as the endogenous variable. Standard deviations of the predicted probabilities are in parentheses. The Zivot-Andrews test generates the dummy variable, $high_{ZA, TRi}$, based on the DEA inefficiency score. The left side presents the conditional impact of teaching quality, the right side the conditional effects of research quality, while all other exogenous variables are fixed to their mean.

The impact on the likelihood of being in the low-ranked group decreases with higher quantiles of the strategic variable; at least for research quality which is consistent with theory. Higher quality levels decrease the probability of being in the low-ranked group. When teaching quality varies over the quantiles, the probability decreases at a lower rate than it did for variations in research quality. Interpreting this low probability, it seems that teaching quality has a relatively homogenous influence on being in different groups. Most frequently, the probability of being in the low-performance group is low at similar levels for the different quantiles given all other exogenous variables are fixed to the mean.

While the effect over the entire teaching interval is almost constant, research quality is not homogenous over the research quality interval. For small values of research quality (10 and 25 percent) the impact on the probability of being in the low-performance group is high. Low research quality values lead to a high probability of low-ranked group membership. Differently stated, high values of research quality make it more probable that a university is in the high-performance group. Differences in probabilities in research quality between quantiles tend to be maximal, while differences between quantiles in teaching quality tend to be minimal. Similar results for the conditional effects after Monte Carlo simulation are derived by requesting cluster analysis for generating the endogenous variable. Table 7.13 displays the corresponding results.

Table 7.13   Conditional Effects after MC Simulation (Cluster Analysis)

	Teaching Quality				Research Quality			
	TR1	*TR2*	*TR3*	*TR4*	*TR1*	*TR2*	*TR3*	*TR4*
p10	0.4134	0.0953	0.0433	0.2309	0.8068	0.2204	0.5681	0.6045
	(0.0869)	(0.0396)	(0.0298)	(0.0803)	(0.0722)	(0.0813)	(0.1488)	(0.1034)
p25	0.3095	0.0637	0.0216	0.1674	0.5571	0.1107	0.1759	0.3516
	(0.0577)	(0.0257)	(0.0152)	(0.0581)	(0.0680)	(0.0310)	(0.0628)	(0.0798)
p50	0.2034	0.0396	0.0096	0.1100	0.1909	0.0380	0.0080	0.1027
	(0.0463)	(0.0231)	(0.0089)	(0.0443)	(0.0453)	(0.0232)	(0.0079)	(0.0425)
p75	0.1247	0.0260	0.0044	0.0691	0.0626	0.0196	0.0007	0.0336
	(0.0499)	(0.0245)	(0.0065)	(0.0382)	(0.0306)	(0.0221)	(0.0019)	(0.0236)
p90	0.0798	0.0197	0.0027	0.0461	0.0075	0.0093	0.0000	0.0047
	(0.0505)	(0.0269)	(0.0061)	(0.0378)	(0.0096)	(0.0212)	(0.0004)	(0.0073)

Note: This table displays the predicted probabilities for probit estimations using the dummy variable for low-performance group membership as the endogenous variable. Standard deviations of the predicted probabilities are in parentheses. Cluster analysis generates the dummy variable, $high_{CA,TRi}$, based on the DEA inefficiency score. The left side presents the conditional impact of teaching quality, the right side the conditional effects of research quality, while all other exogenous variables are fixed to their mean.

Comparing across simulations, with one exception, the probability at corresponding quantiles for the same model is always higher fixing teaching quality to the mean than fixing research quality to the mean. Consequently, research quality has a higher impact on high-performance group membership. These findings are consistent with the results of the graphical presentation of the predicted probabilities in the preceding subsection. In all four model specifications the efficiency decreasing effect of research is higher than of teaching, which points to the higher impact of research on performance of universities. This result may be due to the characteristics of research that result in higher mobility barriers for research quality than for teaching quality.

In summary, the influence of teaching quality and research quality on the probability of being in the low-performance group is not homogenous. The impact of high research quality values is much greater than the impact of low research quality values. It is also higher than the effect of high teaching quality values. But most importantly, the different influence of high and low research quality levels is much greater than the difference in teaching quality. When minimum differentiation is in teaching quality and maximum differentiation is in research quality, this is analogous to the min-max differentiation result in the positioning model. Consequently, this is compatible with hypothesis *H4*. Research quality mainly determines the probability that a university is a member of the high-ranked group, while the impact of teaching quality is minor.

7.4   SUMMARY OF THE RESULTS ON STRATEGIC VARIABLES

Empirical investigation confirms the existence of heterogeneity across German universities, more specifically the existence of strategic groups, as suggested by the theory of strategic groups and the positioning model. Both theoretical approaches emphasize the major role of teaching quality and research quality as strategic variables for heterogeneity.

To identify the impact of the strategic variables, teaching quality and research quality the preceding sections examined their impact on performance. The inefficiency scores from Data Envelopment Analysis indicate the degree of inefficiency of each institution and serve as the endogenous variable. Apart from the strategic variables the empirical work incorporated university characteristics, competition variables and environmental variables as exogenous determinants of inefficiency. Within this framework, two hypotheses – derived from the model of strategic groups and from a positioning model – were tested.

Processing GLS regressions illustrates the negative impact of teaching quality as well as research quality on inefficiency, i.e., a positive influence on performance. However normalized coefficients reveal that the effects differ in size, in particular that in the effects of higher quality research are greater than the effects of higher quality teaching. Additionally, the results from quantile regression have suggested heterogeneity of the impact of these two variables. This heterogeneity was investigated in the light of the theoretically derived hypotheses.

Strategic group theory claims that there are groups in higher education – characterized by strategic variables – showing similar performance levels. Different methods have divided universities into two groups based on productivity so that a high-ranked group and a low-ranked group are identified. Results show that teaching quality and research quality have negatively impact on inefficiency within the high-ranked group. In contrast, neither teaching quality nor research quality has robust significant influence on inefficiency in the low-ranked group.

Likewise, the effect of research quality in the high- and the low-ranked groups differs significantly, which is also true for teaching quality. This finding of different impacts of research quality (and, respectively, teaching quality) in the high- and the low-performance group supports the hypothesis of the concept of strategic groups. German higher education exhibits a group structure because returns of quality vary across high-ranked and lower ranked universities.

While empirical investigations using the concept of strategic groups have mainly focused on performance differences, the positioning model focused on the differing impacts of teaching and research quality. Probit regressions confirm that both teaching and research quality have a significantly negative influence on inefficiency. Computing conditional predicted probabilities reveals a higher research quality effect not only compared to the impact of teaching quality but also higher heterogeneity of the variable over the interval of research quality. Graphical and numerical analyses strengthen this finding. These results provide strong support for the min-max results from the positioning model.

NOTES

1 The terms performance and productivity are used interchangeably, inefficiency from DEA is the complementary term.
2 A gamma distribution as family specification and a log function as link function are applied.

8 Concluding Remarks

To conclude the book, this final chapter summarizes in Section 8.1 the theoretical and empirical results on positioning and strategic groups in a university sector. Section 8.2 then describes recent developments in German higher education, which emphasize the increasing importance of strategic positioning and of the results presented in the previous chapters.

8.1 SUMMARY OF THE RESULTS

This study deals with positioning and performance of publicly funded universities where German universities serve as example throughout the entire analysis. It provides theoretical explanations for and empirical evidence of heterogeneity in a university system where government financing traditionally has been aimed at maintaining a high degree of homogeneity. Regardless of an education policy favoring equal conditions at German universities, the universities themselves feel motivated to compete in the dimensions of teaching and research. Theory suggests and empirical analysis confirms that it is rational for German universities to choose teaching quality and research quality such that these institutions of higher education differ from each other and form a group structure within the sector.

Two theoretical approaches – the model of strategic groups from management theory, and the differentiation model from industrial economics – were adapted to the (German) university sector. The concept of strategic groups focuses on performance differences between groups of universities, where institutions belonging to one group have made similar strategic choices, leading to homogeneity within groups. The product differentiation model is capable of showing how universities in an environment capturing the stylized facts of German higher education make these strategic choices, i.e., set the strategic variables research quality and teaching quality, creating heterogeneity as an equilibrium outcome of their decisions. Both approaches are related to each other with the higher specificity of investments in research quality providing the crucial link.

Discussing teaching quality and research quality as the two prime strategic variables of universities, barriers to mobility in higher education are greater in research than in teaching which results in greater heterogeneity in research than in teaching. While offering interesting insights in itself, the positioning model developed in this study can also be considered a more formal theoretical basis for the concept of strategic groups.

Solving the three-stage model of two-dimensional differentiation leads to an equilibrium with universities showing distinctly different behavior. In a three-stage game two universities position themselves optimally by choosing the same quality level in one dimension and different quality levels in the other. They receive public funds on a per-student base and face a population of heterogeneous students who pay no tuition and expect support such as dormitories or subsidized public transportation. A demand effect pulls universities together in one dimension and a strategic effect forces them apart in the other dimension. It turns out that they choose minimum differentiation in one dimension – teaching – and maximum differentiation in the other – research. Seen from this angle, two strategic groups evolve. These groups are stabilized by barriers to mobility as pointed out in the concept of strategic groups. Taken together, the results suggest that teaching and research have to be analyzed simultaneously to capture the effects for positioning which is a more general insight applicable analogously to other sectors with multi-dimensional product characteristics. In this way, the insights gained in this study can be transferred to other environments with multiple product dimensions and without market prices.

Both the concept of strategic groups and the formal positioning model of universities predict heterogeneity across universities. More specifically, the hypotheses derived postulate that heterogeneity is greater in research than in teaching, that average teaching quality is higher than average research quality, that the impact of teaching quality and research quality is higher for the group of high-ranked universities, and that the probability of being a high-ranked university depends more on research quality than on teaching quality.

Data from various official sources serve to test these hypotheses of heterogeneity for German universities. The empirical analysis shows that teaching and research quality have a significant impact on productivity, suggesting that universities choose their positions based upon the expected impact. Differences in parameters of teaching quality and research quality support the notion of greater returns on investments in quality for high-ranked universities compared to low-ranked universities. Although both teaching quality and research quality influence performance positively, they have a significantly greater impact at high-ranked institutions. The concept of strategic groups implies that the relative specificity of investments in quality causes this result. Investments in research are more specific than in teaching, leading to higher barriers to mobility in the area of research. Therefore, changing positions is more difficult in research quality than in teaching quality. This suggests more differentiation in research than in teaching and is in line with the formal model of positioning that predicts an equilibrium with maximum differentiation in one dimension and minimum differentiation in the other.

There is, however, a second difference between the impact of teaching quality and of research quality: qualities differ empirically in their influence on the probability of being in the group of high-ranked universities. Research quality has a stronger positive influence on this probability. Again, this supports the positioning model which, based on differentiation via the strategic variables teaching quality and research quality, predicts that universities in equilibrium do not choose identical quality levels in both dimensions.

A number of alternative procedures supplementing each other ensures the robustness of the results in three ways: First, scores of four DEA models, indicating performance, correlate highly. Second, two mechanisms to generate groups of high-ranked and low-ranked universities which lead to very similar results are carried out. And, third, various estimation procedures explain the four performance indicators taking both grouping mechanisms into account. All three steps of the analysis yield very robust results as testing for robustness after each step indicates, thus providing confidence to the reliability of the entire empirical findings.

Data Envelopment Analysis (DEA) is used in this study to evaluate the performance of universities. It is a widely applied performance measure for environments with multiple inputs and multiple outputs and unavailable or nonexistent market prices for inputs, outputs or both. Running several separate DEA models for teaching and research delivers information about the heterogeneity of universities in these two dimensions. A closer look at the results then reveals low correlations over teaching scores from different model specifications and over time. This insight suggests low costs of changing positions in teaching. Reversely, correlations of scores from research models are greater, indicating greater barriers to mobility as implied by the concept of strategic groups and the specificity of investments in research quality. DEA models were also run to calculate a measure of overall performance of the universities. The results confirm the hypothesis of performance differences among German universities. As has become a standard practice during the last decade among researches working with DEA, the performance scores were then used in an econometric analysis aiming at an explanation of performance differences and a group structure in the sector. Based on the DEA productivity scores, groups can be identified by applying cluster analysis and the Zivot-Andrews test.

The results from the econometric analysis – focusing on the strategic variables of teaching quality and research quality – help explain performance differences between universities. However these two key variables are not the only ones to have a significant influence. University characteristics, competitive variables and environmental factors beyond the control of university administrations have significant effects on performance. There is evidence for the existence of groups based on performance, where positions of universities are determined by teaching and research quality. Briefly, there is heterogeneity among German universities caused by teaching quality and research quality, and these choices of different quality levels can be explained theoretically for a system of publicly funded universities.

Going beyond a mere evaluation of performance, this study explicitly focuses on positioning of universities by combining various approaches to explain empirically observed heterogeneity, taking into account competitive and regional variables that play an important role in university positioning. Both theoretical and empirical evidence on the structure of the German university system is provided. The results obtained are driven by taking teaching and research simultaneously into account, both in the theoretical and in the empirical analysis, as those attributes of a university are neither independent nor separable. Although German universities were designed to be homogenous, they show a considerable degree of heterogeneity across institutions as a consequence of the universities' positioning strategically in teaching and research. Thus this study reveals strategic choices and a competitive spirit at German universities.

In summary, this study sets out from the casual observation that universities in Germany are heterogeneous despite several decades of policy-making directed at creating and sustaining homogeneous conditions in German higher education. This observation motivated two research questions: Where does the heterogeneity come from? And how do universities actually differ? In offering answers to these questions, the study contributes to a better understanding of a publicly funded university system, both in theoretical and in empirical terms. It transfers and adapts two approaches previously used for the analysis of for-profit organizations to the specifics of the German university sector. The discussion of the concept of strategic groups and the solution of the three-stage positioning model point to the role of teaching quality and research quality together with mobility barriers as explanations for heterogeneity. Both theoretical approaches also imply testable hypotheses on heterogeneity and the empirical analysis fully supports the theory.

Interesting questions for future research concern the effects of very recent policy changes in Germany as the attitude towards heterogeneity in the university system seems to be changing. I will provide a brief sketch of these most recent developments in the final section, concluding that they further strengthen the relevance of the results of this study.

8.2 RECENT DEVELOPMENTS

Although the German higher education sector was designed to be homogenous, theory as well as empirical evidence suggest a certain degree of heterogeneity, i.e., universities choose different positions in teaching and research. Recently, quite a number of reforms have taken place in German higher education, some of which even point to deliberately encouraging heterogeneity by policy, thereby increasing the importance of positioning. Some of the changes were initiated by policy, some by higher education institutions themselves. Most of the reforms aim at more competition within the country, but improving the German universities' position in international competition has also become more important. The initiatives and reforms affect internal as well as external procedures. Changes within the university aim for performance-based allocation of resources among departments and professors. Policies focused on reforming compensation of professors intensify competition by offering incentives for excellent research.

The recent reforms that I will briefly outline below affect various areas of universities and the higher education sector in general, influencing the teaching as well as the research dimension. While admission procedures, the results of the Bologna Process leading to bachelor and master degrees, and the introduction of tuition and fees at public universities in several states point mainly to teaching, the Excellence Initiative concentrates primarily on research. Modifying compensation rules of professors may affect both teaching and research of universities, the precise the effects depending on criteria and their impacts.

In politics and in the general public, there has been a lively debate about the introduction of tuition for students at German universities and about the effects this would have on the decisions of students as buyers and universities as sellers of higher education services. While studying at public institutions of higher education in Germany has been costless until very recently, a number of states will start charging students tuition very soon. This new policy has been made possible by a ruling in 2005 of the Constitutional Court, rejecting the declaration of a federal law in 2002 that was to ensure studies for free to receive one first qualified degree. As a consequence of the federal structure of Germany decisions about introducing tuition and fees belong to the responsibilities of the states thus leading to different policies across states. At the same time, however, the Constitutional Court argued that states have to care for equal educational opportunities independent of the income of students and their parents.

Although states pursue different strategies in charging students tuition, the majority currently collects about €500 to 650 for those studying longer than a fixed number of semesters (differing over fields) and for those students aiming for a second degree. The states of Baden-Württemberg, Bavaria, Hamburg, Lower Saxony and North Rhine Westphalia are now planning to charge every student tuition up to €500 per semester starting in the winter term 2006/2007 or in summer 2007. Parallel to the introduction of tuition those states offer student loans that students have to repay after finishing their studies depending on their income. Compared to business firms, tuition is the analogue to the price of a product and thus serves as a major competition parameter, which is also a quality signal. The positioning model from Chapter 5 not only offers a framework for university systems where institutions provide support to students but also allows for the inclusion of recent changes. The introduction of tuition at universities in some states is such a change covered by the model since tuition can be interpreted as a negative component of the support level. Qualitative results remain the same considering this institutional modification.

Admission standards serve as another competition parameter of higher education institutions, especially as the idea of a customer-input technology is applicable to universities. After having played no rule in the selection of applicants for decades, since July 2004 the admission reform for institutions of higher education allows universities to participate actively in the selection process of students, especially in those fields facing a national capacity restriction (biology, dental medicine, medicine, pharmacy and veterinary medicine). Starting in winter term 2005/2006, 20 percent of university places are allocated to those applicants with the best average high school grades ('Abiturnote'). They are free to choose the university they want to enroll at. Another 20 percent of the capacity is distributed on the basis of waiting periods, i.e., high school graduates with low final grades get the opportunity for studying after waiting, where the time to get a study place depends on the grade. Finally, the majority of university places, i.e., the remaining 60 percent, are now filled by selection made at the higher education institution itself.

The new law specifies the selection procedure as follows: Universities have to consider a number of criteria in the application process to allocate 60 percent of the university places. It is obligatory to take final grades of school leaving certificates into account. Further criteria may be the weighted grades from certain subjects of the school leaving certificate which provide information on the subject-specific aptitude, results of an admission test, type of vocational training or work experience, if any, results of an interview which is to provide motivation for and identification with the study course and the desired occupation or a combination of these criteria. State law can define further criteria, but average high school grade must be given a major influence in the admission procedure. The number of applications per student can be limited to six universities. Given that universities select the majority of their students, customer-input technology, which has been irrelevant for a description of higher education in Germany, will become more important for German universities in the near future.

While the introduction of tuition and selectivity mainly affects students, the third of the recent reforms, the consequences of the Bologna Process brings mobility and potential employers into the game. In 1999 a large number of European countries agreed on building a common higher education area in Europe before 2010. The main issue of the Bologna Process is to establish a consecutive study structure where bachelor and master degrees are comparable across the participating countries in Europe. In 2005 there were 45 countries participating. German higher education institutions, scientific universities as well as universities of applied sciences, have to take a number of steps during this process, including the implementation of an undergraduate (bachelor) and graduate (master) degree and the establishment of a system of credit points to evaluate student performance (based on the ECTS, the European Credit Transfer System). Furthermore, quality assurance by evaluation and accreditation, improved opportunities to mobility and lifelong learning are to be implemented among others.

If these reforms lead to increased mobility of students, there may arise the need for international or European positioning, at least for some universities or departments. In summer 2005, there were about 2,934 master and bachelor programs at German higher education institutions which accounts for about 27 percent of the overall range available to study in Germany. Due to the same names of degrees from scientific universities and universities of applied sciences, employers cannot distinguish anymore between graduates from these two types of institutions which therefore induces additional competition not only within but also across these different types. This is especially novel as in the old system the degrees conferred from different institutions served as reliable signals for the characteristics of graduates to employers.

The major program to improve research in German higher education is the initiative for excellence competition ('Excellence Initiative by the German federal and state governments to promote science and research at German universities'). The German Research Foundation (DFG) and the Science Council ('Wissenschaftsrat') coordinate a contest for the title of an 'elite university' where the federal and state governments provide additional funds for the winning institutions. Starting in 2006 three main types of programs will receive about €1,900 million during a five-year-period to 2011. First, graduate schools are to support young researchers. Second, clusters of excellence are to extend excellent research. And finally, there are 'Institutional Strategies to Promote Top-Level Research' ('Zukunftskonzepte') that are to support the research profiles of up to ten leading universities. In a high-quality research environment, graduate schools are to promote young researchers and train doctoral students. About 40 such graduate schools are planned to be set up, receiving about one million Euros on average per year. Clusters of excellence are to conduct excellent and competitive research and offer such training facilities. They will support and establish outstanding research centers in specific fields. About 30 such clusters are to be instituted, also to enforce scientific networking and cooperation with nonuniversity institutions. The objectives of the 'Institutional Strategies to Promote Top-Level Research' include the improvement of top-level university research and competitiveness in an environment where at least one graduate school and one cluster of excellence pass the contest successfully.

The program of the Excellence Initiative will be carried out in two rounds, the first one started in summer 2006; funding for the second one starts in 2007. An international group of referees evaluates the proposals and the proceeding full applications based on scientific quality, interdisciplinary approach, international visibility and integration of regional research capacities. Participating universities had to submit a proposal until October 2005, from which the best ones were selected in January 2006. Out of 74 submitting universities 36 were invited to provide a full application.

There can be no doubt that policy wants to enhance competition among German universities at different levels. The major program to establish elite universities looks like a move to mimic the results of the UK or US system where some institutions perform excellently in international comparisons.

In 2002 the Federal Parliament enacted the 'Professorenbesoldungsreformgesetz', a law which alters the compensation of professors in Germany substantially. Starting in January 2005, the law incorporates performance-based compensation leading to a more flexible and competitive pay structure for professors. The seniority pay rule that raised compensation every two years no longer exists under the new law. The main idea of this reform is to reduce the fixed basic salary of professors and to add variable components at the same time in order to motivate tenured staff to improve performance both in quantitative and in qualitative terms. Which tasks of professors are addressed depends on the criteria that are negotiated when writing the contracts. The law offers three main and rather wide areas for variable components:[1] First, getting an offer from another university and renegotiation with the home institution may lead to a bonus payment. Second, professors may receive additional variable compensation for extraordinary performance in teaching, research, arts, further education and/or promoting young researchers. Third, engagement in academic self-administration may serve as a criterion for getting variable payments. It remains, however, open whether professors receive performance-based payments for a limited or an unlimited time period, whether these payments are considered for calculating the pension after retirement, and how performance is measured. States and universities have a wide scope to shape these new structures.

While the changes described before address teaching and research at the university-level or at the department-level, the reform of compensation for professors targets the individual level, thus contributing to install university positioning more efficiently. At the same time when compensation of tenured professors was reformed, in 2004 the federal government confirmed the introduction of the concept of the junior professorship (similar to an assistant professorship) to support careers of young researchers. Successful doctoral graduates holding such a position are enabled to teach and to conduct research independently and on their own, usually when they are around 30 years old. In this way the junior professorship replaces the habilitation as the formal qualification to get a full professorship. The majority of states have already established these positions, while some appealed against the amendment.

Taken together, these recent discussions and developments clearly indicate that the German university system is about to become more openly heterogeneous than it used to be and that explicit competition within the system will increase (The Science Council – Wissenschaftsrat (2006) – and the Federal Ministry of Education and Research – BMBF (2006) – provide information recent changes in German higher education). It would be premature, if not impossible, to examine these changes already with the theoretical and empirical tools used in this study. There is no doubt, however, that the impact of the policy changes will further increase the relevance of positioning and heterogeneity of German universities and will pose interesting research questions in about five years time when new data are available. Therefore, the ideas and arguments of this book will become even more relevant and the theoretical and empirical tools developed here can serve as a starting point for future research.

NOTES

1 Bundesgesetzblatt Jahrgang 2002 Teil I Nr. 11, ausgegeben zu Bonn am 22. Februar 2002, Gesetz zur Reform der Professorenbesoldung (Professorenbe-soldungsreformgesetz – ProfBesReformG).

Bibliography

Abbott, M. and C. Doucouliagos (2003), The efficiency of Australian universities: a data envelopment analysis, *Economics of Education Review*, 22, 89–97.

Ahn, T., Charnes, A. and W.W. Cooper (1988), Some statistical and DEA evaluations of relative efficiencies of public and private institutions of higher learning, *Socio-Economic Planning Sciences*, 22, 259–267.

Ahn, T., Arnold, V., Charnes, A. and W.W. Cooper (1989), DEA and ratio efficiency analyses for public institutions of higher learning in Texas, *Research in Governmental and Nonprofit Accounting*, 5, 165–185.

Aigner, D.J., Lovell, C.A.K. and P. Schmidt (1977), Formulation and estimation of stochastic frontier production models, *Journal of Econometrics*, 6, 21–36.

Alfonso, A. and M. Santos (2004), Public tertiary education expenditure in Portugal: a non-parametric efficiency analysis, *Discussion Paper*.

Ali, A.I. and D. Gstach (2000), The impact of deregulation during 1990–1997 on banking in Austria, *Empirica*, 27, 265–281.

Ansari, A., Economides, N. and J. Steckel (1998), The max-min-min principle of product differentiation, *Journal of Regional Science*, 38, 207–230.

Arcelus, F.J. and D.F. Coleman (1997), An efficiency review of university departments, *International Journal of Systems Science*, 28, 721–729.

Arts and Humanities Index (2003), 'Web of Science', date: November 2003.

Athanassopoulos, A.D. and E. Shale (1997), Assessing the comparative efficiency of higher education institutions in the UK by means of data envelopment analysis, *Education Economics*, 5, 117–134.

Avkiran, N.K. (2001), Investigating technical and scale efficiencies of Australian universities through data envelopment analysis, *Socio-Economic Planning Sciences*, 35, 57–80.

Backes-Gellner, U. (1992), Berufsethos und akademische Bürokratie – Zur Effizienz alternativer Motivations- und Kontrollmechanismen im Vergleich deutscher und US-amerikanischer Hochschulen, *Zeitschrift für Planung*, 4, 403–434.

Backes-Gellner, U. and D. Sadowski (1991), Zur Lage der deutschen Universität – Eine organisationsökonomische Zwischenbilanz, in Helberger, C. (ed.), *Ökonomie der Hochschule II*, Schriften des Vereins für Socialpolitik, Band 181/II, Duncker&Humblot, Berlin, 9–37.

Backes-Gellner, U. and E. Zanders (1989), Lehre und Forschung als Verbundproduktion. Data-Envelopment-Analysen und organisationsökonomische Interpretationen der Realität in wirtschaftswissenschaftlichen Fachbereichen, *Zeitschrift für Betriebswirtschaft*, 59, 271–290.

Banker, R.D., Charnes, A., and W.W. Cooper (1984), Some models for estimating technical and scale efficiencies in data envelopment analysis, *Management Science*, 30, 1078–1092.

Bayenet, B. and O. Debande (1999), Performance des activités d'education et de recherche des systèmes d'enseignement supérieur de l'ocde, *Annals of Public and Cooperative Economics*, 70, 659–686.

Beasley, J.E. (1990), Comparing university departments, *OMEGA International Journal of Management Science*, 18, 171–183.

Beasley, J.E. (1995), Determining teaching and research efficiencies, *Journal of the Operational Research Society*, 46, 441–452.

Berger, A.N. and D.B. Humphrey (1997), Efficiency of financial institutions: international survey and directions for duture research, *European Journal of Operational Research*, 98, 175–212.

Berghoff, S., Federkeil, G., Giebisch, P., Hachmeister, C.-D. and D. Müller-Böling (2005), Das CHE ForschungsRanking deutscher Universitäten 2005, working paper no. 70.

Bester, H. (1998), Quality uncertainty mitigates product differentiation, *RAND Journal of Economics*, 29, 828–844.

BMBF (2002), *Grund- und Strukturdaten 2001/2002*, Bundesministerium für Bildung und Forschung, Bonn.

BMBF (2006), Federal Ministry of Education and Research. www.bmbf.de/en

Bommer, R. and H.W. Ursprung (1998), Spieglein, Spieglein an der Wand. Eine publikationsanalytische Erfassung der Forschungsleistungen volkswirtschaftlicher Fachbereiche in Deutschland, Österreich und der Schweiz, *Zeitschrift für Wirtschafts- und Sozialwissenschaften*, 118, 1–28.

Bontems, P. and V. Réquillart (2001), Remarks on good vs. bad characteristcs in vertical differentiation, *Economics Letters*, 70, 427–429.

Braid, R.M. (1999), The price and the profit effects of horizontal mergers in two-dimensional spatial competition, *Economics Letters*, 62, 113–119.

Breu, T.M. and R.L. Raab (1994), Efficiency and perceived quality of the nation's 'Top 25' national universities and national liberal arts colleges: an application of data envelopment analysis to higher education, *Socio-Economic Planning Sciences*, 28, 33–45.

Canoy, M. and M. Peitz (1997), The differentiation triangle, *Journal of Industrial Economics*, 45, 305–328.

Caves, R. and M.E. Porter (1977), From entry barriers to mobility barriers: conjectural decisions and contrived deterrence to new competition, *Quarterly Journal of Economics*, 91, 241–261.

Chakraborty, K., Biswas, B. and W.C. Lewis (2001), Measurement of technical efficiency in public education: a stochastic and nonstochastic production function approach, *Southern Economic Journal*, 67, 889–905.

Charnes, A., Cooper, W.W. and E. Rhodes (1978), Measuring the efficiency of decision making units, *European Journal of Operational Research*, 2, 429–444.

Coelli, T.J., Prasada Rao, D.S. and G.E. Battese (1998), *An introduction to efficiency and productivity analysis*, Kluwer Academic Publishers, Boston.

Cohn, E., Rhine, S.L.W. and C. Santos (1989), Institutions of higher education as multi-product firms: economies of scale and scope, *Review of Economics and Statistics*, 71, 284–290.

Colbert, A., Levary, R.R. and M.C. Shaner (2000), Determining the relative efficiency of MBA programs using DEA, *European Journal of Operational Research*, 125, 656–669.

Combes, P.-P. and L. Linnemer (2003), Where are the economists who publish? Publication concentration and rankings in Europe based on cumulative publications, *Journal of the European Economic Association*, 1, 1250–1308.

Cooper, W.W., Seiford, L.M. Tone, K. (2000), *Data Envelopment Analysis, a comprehensive text with models, applications, references and DEA-solver software*, Kluwer Academic Publishers, Boston.

Coupé, T. (2003), Revealed performances: worldwide rankings of economists and economics departments, 1999–2000, *Journal of the European Economic Association*, 1, 1309–1345.

D'Aspremont, C., Thisse, J.-F. and J.J. Gabszewicz (1979), On Hotelling's stability in competition, *Econometrica*, 47, 1145–1150.

De Fraja, G. and E. Iossa (2001), Competition among universities and the emergence of the elite institution, *Bulletin of Economic Research*, 54, 275–293.

DeGroot, H., McMahon, W.W. and J.F. Volkwein (1991), The cost structure of American research universities, *Review of Economics and Statistics*, 73, 424–431.

Degryse, H. (1996), On the interaction between vertical and horizontal product differentiation: an application to banking, *The Journal of Industrial Economics*, 44, 169–186.

Degryse, H. and A. Irmen (2001), Attribute dependence and the provision of quality, *Regional Science and Urban Economics*, 31, 547–569.

Del Rey, E. (2001), Teaching versus research: a model of state university competition, *Journal of Urban Economics*, 49, 356–373.

Del Rey, E. (2003), Competition among universities: the role of preferences for research and government finance, *Revista de Economia Pública*, 164, 75–80.

Deutsche Bibliotheksstatistik (2003), www.bibliotheksstatistik.de, date: December 2003.

DFG (2000), *Bewilligungen an Hochschulen und ausseruniversitäre Forschungseinrichtungen – 1996 bis 1998*, Deutsche Forschungsgemeinschaft, Bonn.

DFG (2003), *Förder-Ranking 2003, Institutionen-Regionen-Netzwerke. DFG-Bewilligungen und weitere Basisdaten öffentlich geförderter Forschung*, Deutsche Forschungsgemeinschaft, Bonn.

Diez-Ticio, A. and M.-J. Mancebon (2002), The efficiency of the Spanish police service: an application of multiactivity DEA model, *Applied Economics*, 34, 351–365.

Doyle, J., Arthurs, A., Green, R., McAulay, L., Pitt, M.R., Bottomley, P.A. and W. Evans (1996), The judge, the model of the judge, and the model of the judged as judge: analyses of the UK 1992 Research Assessment Exercise data for business and management studies, *OMEGA International Journal of Management Science*, 24, 13–28.

Dundar, H. and R.D. Lewis (1995), Departmental productivity in American universities: economics of scale and scope, *Economics of Education Review*, 14, 119–144.

Dusansky, R. and C. Vernon (1998), Rankings of US economics departments, *Journal of Economic Perspectives*, 12, 157–170.

Economides, N. (1986), Nash equilibrium existence in duopoly with products defined by two characteristics, *Rand Journal of Economics*, 17, 431–439.

Economides, N. (1989), Symmetric equilibrium existence and optimality in differentiated product markets, *Journal of Economic Theory*, 47, 178–194.

Economides, N. (1993), Hotelling's 'main street' with more than two competitors, *Journal of Regional Science*, 33, 303–319.

Eisenkopf, G. (2004), The impact of university deregulation on curriculum choice, *Diskussionspapiere der Forschergruppe Heterogene Arbeit*, University of Konstanz, 04/17.

Fabel, O. and F. Heße (1999), Befragungsstudie versus Publikationsanalyse, *Die Betriebswirtschaft*, 59, 196–204.

Fabel, O., Lehmann, E. and S. Warning (2002), Der relative Vorteil deutscher wirtschaftswissenschaftlicher Fachbereiche im Wettbewerb um studentischen Zuspruch: Qualität des Studienganges oder des Studienortes?, *Zeitschrift für betriebswirtschaftliche Forschung*, 54, 509–526.

Facanha, L.O. and A. Marinho (1999), Instituicoes federais de ensino superior: modelos de financiamento e o incentivo a eficiencia, *Revista Brasileira de Economia*, 53, 357–386.

Fandel, G. and T. Gal (2001), Redistribution of funds for teaching and research among universities: the case of North Rhine-Westphalia, *European Journal of Operational Research*, 130, 111–120.

Federal Ministry of Education and Research (2002), *Basic and structural data 2001/2002*, Bonn.

Ferguson, T.D., Deephouse, D.L. and W.L. Ferguson (2000), Do strategic groups differ in reputation?, *Strategic Management Journal*, 21, 1195–1214.

Fiegenbaum, A. and H. Thomas (1995), Strategic groups as reference groups: theory, modeling, and empirical examination of industry and competitive strategy, *Strategic Management Journal*, 16, 461–476.

Forsund, F.R. and K.O. Kalhagen (1999), Efficiency and productivity of Norwegian colleges, in G. Westermann (ed.), *Data envelopment analysis in the public and private sector*, Gabler, Wiesbaden, 269–308.

Garella, P.G. and L. Lambertini (1999), Good vs. bad characteristics in vertical differentiation, *Economic Letters*, 65, 245–248.

Gary-Bobo, R.J. and A. Trannoy (2002), Public subsidies, tuition charges, and incentives in a normative economic analysis of universities, University of Cergy-Pontoise, mimeo.

Gary-Bobo, R.J. and A. Trannoy (2004), Efficient tuition fees, examinations, and subsidies, Discussion Paper, http://ssrn.com/abstract=551424.

Geiger, R.L. (2004), *Knowledge and money: research universities and the paradox of the marketplace*, Stanford University Press, Stanford, California.

Geiger, R.L. (2005), Ten generations of American higher education, in Altbach, P.G., Berdahl, R.O. and P.J. Gumport (eds), *American higher education in the twenty-first century, social, political, and economic challenges*, Second Edition, John Hopkins University Press, Baltimore and London, 38–70.

Getz, M. and J.J. Siegfried (2004), The sensitivity of capital use to price in higher education, *Review of Industrial Organization*, 24, 379–391.

Glass, C.J., McKillop, D.G. and G. O'Rourke (1997), Productivity growth in UK accountancy departments 1986–96, *Financial Accountability and Management*, 13, 313–330.

Glass, C.J., McKillop, D.G. and G. O'Rourke (1998), A cost indirect evaluation of productivity change in UK universities, *Journal of Productivity Analysis*, 10, 153–175.

Gonzales-Fidalgo, E. and J. Ventura-Victoria (2002), How much do strategic groups matter?, *Review of Industrial Organization*, 21, 55–71.

Greene, W.H. (2003), *Econometric analysis*, Fifth Edition, Prentice Hall.

Gumport, P.J. (2005), Graduate education and research: interdependence and strain, in Altbach, P.G, Berdahl, R.O. and P.J. Gumport (eds), *American higher education in the twenty-first century, social, political, and economic challenges*, Second Edition, John Hopkins University Press, Baltimore and London, 425–485.

Gupta, B., Lai, F.-C., Pal, D., Sarkar, J. and C.-M. Yu (2004), Where to locate in a circular city?, *International Journal of Industrial Organization*, 22, 759–782.

Haksever, C. and Y. Muragishi (1998), Measuring value in MBA programmes, *Education Economics*, 6, 11–26.

Hallock, K. and R. Koenker (2001), Quantile regression, *Journal of Economic Perspectives*, 51, 143–156.

Hashimoto, K. and E. Cohn (1997), Economies of scale and scope in Japanese private universities, *Education Economics*, 5, 107–116.

Hattie, J. and H.W. Marsh (1996), The relationship between research and teaching: a meta-analysis, *Review of Educational Research*, 66, 507–542.

Hinshaw, C.E. and J.J. Siegfried (1994), Who gets on the AEA program?, *Journal of Economic Perspectives*, 9, 153–163.

Heublein, U., Schmelzer, R. and D. Sommer (2005), Studienabbruchstudie 2005. Die Studienabbrecherquoten in den Fächergruppen und Studienbereichen der Universitäten und Fachhochschulen, Kurzinformation HIS.

Hotelling, H. (1929), Stability in competition, *Economic Journal*, 39, 41–57.

Houthoofd, N. and A. Heene (1997), Strategic groups as subsets of strategic scope groups in the Belgian brewing industry, *Strategic Management Journal*, 18, 653–666.

Irmen, A. and J.-F. Thisse (1998), Competition in multi-characteristic spaces: Hotelling was almost right, *Journal of Economic Theory*, 78, 76–102.

Izadi, H. and G. Johnes (1997), Stochastic frontier estimation of a CES cost function: the case of higher education, Centre for Research in the Economics of Education, Working Paper.

Johnes G. (1995), Scale and technical efficiency in the production of economic research, *Applied Economics Letters*, 2, 7–11.

Johnes, G. (1996), Multi-product cost functions and the funding of tuition in UK universities, *Applied Economics Letters*, 3, 557–561.

Johnes, G. (1997), Costs and industrial structure in contemporary British higher education, *Economic Journal*, 107, 727–737.

Johnes, G. (1999), The management of universities. President's lecture delivered at annual general meeting of the Scottish Economic Society 6–8th April 1999, *Scottish Journal of Political Economy*, 46, 505–522.

Johnes, G. and J. Johnes (1993), Measuring the research performance of UK economics departments: an application of data envelopment analysis, *Oxford Economic Papers*, 45, 332–347.

Johnes, J. and G. Johnes (1995), Research funding and performance in UK university departments of economics: a frontier analysis, *Economics of Education Review*, 14, 301–314.

Kalaitzidakis, P., Mamuneas, T.P. and T. Stengos (2003), Rankings of academic journals and institutions in economics, *Journal of the European Economic Association*, 1, 1346–1366.

Kao, C. (1994), Evaluation of junior colleges of technology: the Taiwan case, *European Journal of Operational Research*, 72, 43–51.

Kemnitz, A. (2006), Universities funding reform, competition and teaching quality, Discussion Paper University of Mannheim.

King, G., Tomz, M. and J. Wittenberg (2000), Making the most of statistical analyses: improving interpretation and presentation, *American Journal of Political Science*, 44, 347–361.

Kirman, A. and M. Dahl (1994), Economic research in Europe, *European Economic Review*, 38, 505–522.

Kling, J.A. and K.A. Smith (1995), Identifying strategic groups in the US airline industry: an application of the Porter model, *Transportation Journal*, 35, 26–34.

KMK (1998), Kultusministerkonferenz. Quantitative Entwicklungen im Schul- und Hochschulbereich bis 2015, *Statistische Veröffentlichungen der Kultusministerkonferenz*, Sonderheft 97, Bonn.

KMK (2002), Kultusministerkonferenz. Die Mobilität der Studienanfänger und Studierenden in Deutschlang von 1980–2000, *Statistische Veröffentlichungen der Kultusministerkonferenz*, Dokumentation Nr. 160, Bonn.

Kocher, M.G., Luptacik, M. and M. Sutter (2006), Measuring productivity of research in economics. A cross-country study using DEA, *Socio-Economic Planning Sciences*, 40, 314–332.

Korhonen, P., Tainio, R. and J. Wallenius (2001), Value efficiency analysis of academic research, *European Journal of Operational Research*, 130, 121–132.

Koshal, R.K. and M. Koshal (1999), Economics of scale and scope in higher education: a case of comprehensive universities, *Economics of Education Review*, 18, 270–277.

Koshal, R.K. and M. Koshal (2000), Do liberal arts colleges exhibit economies of scale and scope? *Education Economics*, 8, 209–211.

Koshal, R.K., Koshal, M. and A. Gupta (2001), Multi-product total cost function for higher education: a case of bible colleges, *Economics of Education Review*, 20, 297–303.

Kwoka, J.E., Jr. and C.M. Snyder (2004), Dynamic adjustment in the U.S. higher education industry, 1955–1997, *Review of Industrial Organization*, 24, 355–378.

Laband, D. (1985), An evaluation of 50 ranked economics departments by quantity and quality of faculty publications and graduate student placement and research success, *Southern Economic Journal*, 52, 216–240.

Lehmann, E.E. and S. Warning (2002), Teaching or Research? What affects the efficiency of universities?, Discussion Paper, http://ssrn.com/abstract=393780.

Leszczensky, M. and D. Orr (2004), Stattliche Hochschulfinanzierung durch indikatorgestützte Mittelverteilung. Dokumentation und Analyse der Verfahren in 11 Bundesländern. Kurzinformation HIS A2/2004.

Lewis, D.R. and H. Dundar (1995), Economics of scale and scope in Turkish universities, *Education Economics*, 3, 133–157.

Lovell, K.C.A. (1993), Production frontiers and productive efficiency, in Harold, O.F., Lovell, K.C.A. and S.S. Schmidt (eds), *The measurement of productive efficiency*, Oxford University Press, Oxford, 3–77.

Lubrano, M., Bauwens, L., Kirman, A. and C. Protopescu (2003), Ranking economics departments in Europe: a statistical approach, *Journal of the European Economic Association*, 1, 1367–1401.

Luptacik, M. (2003): Data Envelopment Analysis als Entscheidungshilfe für die Evaluierung von Forschungseinheiten in der Universität, *Zeitschrift für Betriebswirtschaft*, 3, 59–74.

MacMillan, M.L. and D. Datta (1998), The relative efficiencies of Canadian universities: a DEA perspective, *Canadian Public Policy*, 24, 485–511.

Madden, G., Savage, S. and S. Kemp (1997), Measuring public sector efficiency: a study of economics departments at Australian universities, *Education Economics*, 5, 153–168.

Mangani, A. and P. Patelli (2001), Experimental analysis of strategic product differentiation, Discussion Paper, http://ssrn.com/abstract=294139

Marinho, A., Resende, M. and L.O. Facanha (1997), Brazilian federal universities: relative efficiency evaluation and data envelopment analysis, *Revista Brasileira de Economia*, 51, 489–508.

Martin, S. (2002), *Advanced industrial economics*, Second Edition, Oxford: Blackwell Publishers.

Martinez Cabrera, M. (2000), Analisis de la eficiencia productiva de las instituciones de educacion superior, *Papeles De Economia Espanola*, 86, 179–191.

Más Ruís, F.J. (1998), Dynamic analysis of competition in marketing – strategic groups in Spanish banking, *European Journal of Marketing*, 32, 252–278.

McNamara, G.M., Luce, R.A. and G.H. Tompson (2002), Examining the effect of complexity in strategic group knowledge structures on firm performance, *Strategic Management Journal*, 23, 153–170.

Mehra, A. (1996), Resource and market based determinants of performance in the US banking industry, *Strategic Management Journal*, 17, 307–322.

Meussen, W. and J. van den Brock (1977), Efficiency estimation from Cobb-Douglas production functions with composed error, *International Economic Review*, 18, 435–444.

Meyer, M., Bürkle, B. and P. Prockl (1995), Die Effizienz von Lehrstühlen, in K.A. Schachtschneider (ed.), *Wirtschaft, Gesellschaft und Staat im Umbruch*, Duncker&Humblot, Berlin, 169–182.

Moreno, A.A. and R. Tadepalli (2002), Assessing academic department efficiency at a public university, *Managerial and Decision Economics*, 23, 385–397.

Morrison, A.J. and K. Roth (1992), A taxonomy of business-level strategies in global industries, *Strategic Management Journal*, 13, 399–418.

Mussa, M. and S. Rosen (1978), Monopoly and product quality, *Journal of Economic Theory*, 18, 301–317.

Nair, A. and S. Kotha (2001), Does group membership matter? Evidence from the Japanese steel industry, *Strategic Management Journal*, 22, 221–235.

Nath, D. and T.S. Gruca (1997), Convergence across alternative methods for forming strategic groups, *Strategic Management Journal*, 18, 745–760.

Nelson, R.A. and K. Hevert (1992), The effects of class size on economies of scale and marginal costs in higher education, *Applied Economics*, 24, 473–482.

Netz, J.S. and B.A. Taylor (2002), Maximum or minimum differentation? Location patterns of retail outlets, *The Review of Economics and Statistics*, 84, 162–175.

Neven, D. and J.-F. Thisse (1990), On quality and variety competition, in Gabszewitz, J.J., Richard, J.-F. and L.A. Wolsey (eds), *Economic Decision-Making: Games, Econometrics, and Optimisation. Contributions in Honour of Jacques H. Dreze*, North-Holland, Amsterdam, 175–199.

Ng, Y.C. and S.K. Li (2000), Measuring the research performance of Chinese higher education institutions: an application of data envelopment analysis, *Education Economics*, 8, 139–156.

OECD (2003), *Education at a glance*, OECD Indicators, Paris.

Oleson, O.B. and N.C. Petersen (1995), Chance constrained efficiency evaluation, *Management Science*, 41, 442–457.

Oleson, O.B. and N.C. Peterson (2002), The use of data envelopment analysis with probabilistic assurance regions for measuring hospital efficiency, *Journal of Productivity Analysis*, 17, 83–109.

Owen-Smith, J. (2003), From separate systems to a hybrid order: accumulative advantage across public and private science at research one universities, *Research Policy*, 32, 1081–1104.

Pesenti, R. and W. Ukovich (1996), *Evaluating academic activities using DEA*, Discussion Paper, University of Trieste.

Phlips, L. and J.-F. Thisse (1982), Spatial competition and the theory of differentiated markets: an introduction, *The Journal of Industrial Economics*, 31, 1–9.

Plümper, T. and C.J. Schneider (2006), Too much to die, too little to live: unemployment, higher education policies and university budgets in Germany, *Journal of European Public Policy*, forthcoming.

Porter, M.E. (1979), The structure within industries and companies performance, *The Review of Economics and Statistics*, 61, 214–227.

Porter, M.E. (1981), The contributions of industrial organization to strategic management, *The Academy of Management Review*, 6, 609–620.

Post, T. and J. Spronk (1999), Performance benchmarking using interactive data envelopment analysis, *European Journal of Operational Reserach*, 115, 472–487.

Ranking of World Universities (2004), *Ranking of World Universities 2004*, Institute of Higher Education, Shanghai Jiao Tong, http://ed.sjtu.edu.cn/rank/2004/top500list.htm (December 30, 2004).

Ralston, D., Wright, A. and K. Garden (2001), Can mergers ensure the survival of credit unions in the third millenium?, *Journal of Banking and Finance*, 25, 2277–2304.

Rhodes, E.L. and L. Southwick (1993), Variations in public and private university efficiency, applications of management science, *Public Policy Applications of Management Science*, 7, 145–170.

Rothschild, M. and L.J. White (1995), The analytics of the pricing of higher education and other services in which the customers are inputs, *The Journal of Political Economy*, 103, 573–586.

Salop, S. (1979), Monopolistic competition with outside goods, *Bell Journal of Economics*, 10, 141–156.

Sarrico, C.S. and R.G. Dyson (2000), Using DEA for planning in UK universities – an institutional perspective, *Journal of the Operational Research Society*, 51, 789–800.

Scherer, F.M. and D. Ross (1990), *Industrial Market Structure and Economic Performance*, Third Edition, Boston: Houghton Mifflin.

Science Citation Index (2003), 'Web of Science', date: november 2003.

Shaked, A. and J. Sutton (1982), Relaxing price competition through product differentiation, *Review of Economic Studies*, 49, 3–13.

Siegfried, J. (1972), The publishing of economics papers and its impact on graduate faculty ratings, 1960–1969, *Journal of Economic Literature*, 10, 31–49.

Sinuany-Stern, Z., Mehrez, A. and A. Barboy (1994), Academic departments efficiency via DEA, *Computers and Operations Research*, 21, 543–556.

Social Science Citation Index (2003), 'Web of Science', date: November 2003.

Statistisches Bundesamt (1998), *Prüfungen an Hochschulen*, Fachserie 11, R 4.2, Statistisches Bundesamt, Wiesbaden.

Statistisches Bundesamt (1999), *Prüfungen an Hochschulen*, Fachserie 11, R 4.2, Statistisches Bundesamt, Wiesbaden.

Statistisches Bundesamt (2000), *Prüfungen an Hochschulen*, Fachserie 11, R 4.2, Statistisches Bundesamt, Wiesbaden.

Statistisches Bundesamt (2001a), *Prüfungen an Hochschulen*, Fachserie 11, R 4.2, Statistisches Bundesamt, Wiesbaden.

Statistisches Bundesamt (2001b), *Hochschulstatistische Kennzahlen, Monetäre Kennzahlen 1998/1999*, Wiesbaden.

Statistisches Bundesamt (2001c), *Personal an Hochschulen*, Fachserie 11, R 4.4, Statistisches Bundesamt, Wiesbaden.

Statistisches Bundesamt (2002), *Hochschulstatistische Kennzahlen, Monetäre Kennzahlen 1999/2000*, Wiesbaden.

Statistisches Bundesamt (2003a), *Hochschulstandort Deutschland 2003*, Wiesbaden: Statistisches Bundesamt–Pressestelle.

Statistisches Bundesamt (2003b), *Hochschulstatistische Kennzahlen, Monetäre Kennzahlen 2000/2001*, Wiesbaden.

Statistisches Bundesamt (2003c), Bericht zur finanziellen Lage der Hochschulen, Wiebaden.

Statistisches Bundesamt (2004), Genesis-Online, www.regionalstatistik.de, date: February 2004.

Stern Magazin (1999), Start – Das Magazin für Ausbildung und Karriere, 205–247.

Stern Magazin (2000), Start – Der Studienführer. Erste Hilfe für das Studium, 138–182.

Stern Magazin (2001), Spezial – Campus und Karriere, Der Studienführer 2001, 148–193.

Tabuchi, T. (1994), Two-stage two-dimensional spatial competition between two firms, *Regional Science and Urban Economics*, 24, 207–227.

Tang, M.-J. and H. Thomas (1992), The concept of strategic groups: theoretical construct or analytical convenience, *Managerial and Decision Economics*, 13, 323–329.

Thanassoulis, E. (2001), *Introduction to the theory and application of data envelopment analysis: a foundation text with integrated software*, Kluwer Academic Publishers, Norwell Mass.

Thomas, H. and T. Pollock (1999), From I-O economics' S-C-P paradigm through strategic groups to competence-based competition: reflections on the puzzle of competetive strategy, *British Journal of Management*, 10, 127–140.

Thursby, J.G. (2000), What do we say about ourselves and what does it mean? Yet another look at economic department research, *Journal of Economic Literature*, 38, 383–404.

Thursby, J.G. and S. Kemp (2002), Growth and productive efficiency of university intellectual property licensing, *Research Policy*, 31, 109–124.

Tirole, J. (1988), *The Theory of Industrial Organization*, MIT Press.

Tomkins, C. and R. Green (1988), An experiment in the use of data envelopment analysis for evaluating the efficiency of UK university departments of accounting, *Financial Accountability and Management*, 4, 147–164.

Tomz, M., Wittenberg, J. and G. King (2003), *CLARIFY: Software for interpreting and presenting statistical results*, Version 2.1, Stanford University, University of Wisconsin, and Harvard University, January 5. Available at http://gking.harvard.edu

Ursprung, H.W. (2003), Schneewittchen im Land der Klapperschlangen: Evaluation eines Evaluators, *Perspektiven der Wirtschaftspolitik*, 2, 177–189.

Vandenbosch, M.B. and C.B. Weinberg (1995), Product and price competition in a two-dimensional vertical differentiation model, *Marketing Science*, 14(2), 224–248.

Warning, S. (2004), Performance differences in German higher education: empirical analysis of strategic groups, *Review of Industrial Organization*, 24, 393–408.

Warning, S. (2006), A model of strategic university positioning, Discussion Paper, Institute for Labour Law and Industrial Relations, University of Trier, Trier.

Welsch, H. and V. Ehrenheim (1999), Ausbildung des wissenschaftlichen Nachwuchses. Zur Produktivität volkswirtschaftlicher Fachbereiche in Deutschland, Österreich und der Schweiz, *Zeitschrift für Wirtschafts- und Sozialwissenschaften*, 119, 455–473.

Wernerfeldt, B. (1984), A resource based view of the firm, *Strategic Management Journal*, 5, 171–180.

Wilson, J.D. (2002), Tiebout competition versus political competition on a university campus, in R. Ehrenberg (ed.), *Governing academia*, New York: Cornell University Press.

Winston, G.C. (1999), Subsidies, hierarchy and peers: the awkward economics of higher education, *Journal of Economic Perspectives*, 13, 13–36.

Wissenschaftsrat (1993), Empfehlungen zum 23. Rahmenplan für den Hochschulbau, 1994–1997, 2–5, Köln.

Wissenschaftsrat (1994), Empfehlungen zum 24. Rahmenplan für den Hochschulbau, 1995–1998, 2–5, Köln.

Wissenschaftsrat (1995), Empfehlungen zum 25. Rahmenplan für den Hochschulbau, 1996–1999, 2–5, Köln.

Wissenschaftsrat (1996), Empfehlungen zum 26. Rahmenplan für den Hochschulbau, 1997–2000, 2–5, Köln.

Wissenschaftsrat (1997), Empfehlungen zum 27. Rahmenplan für den Hochschulbau, 1998–2001, 2–5, Köln.

Wissenschaftsrat (1998), Empfehlungen zum 28. Rahmenplan für den Hochschulbau, 1999–2002, 2–5, Köln.

Wissenschaftsrat (1999), Empfehlungen zum 29. Rahmenplan für den Hochschulbau, 2000–2003, 2–5, Köln.

Wissenschaftsrat (2000a), Drittmittel und Grundmittel der Hochschulen 1993 bis 1998, Dokument 4717-00.

Wissenschaftsrat (2000b), Empfehlungen zum 30. Rahmenplan für den Hochschulbau, 2001–2004, 2–5, Köln.

Wissenschaftsrat (2001), Empfehlungen zum 31. Rahmenplan für den Hochschulbau, 2002–2005, 2–5, Köln.

Wissenschaftsrat (2002a), Empfehlungen zur Stärkung wirtschaftswissenschaftlicher Forschung an den Hochschulen, Document 55455-02.

Wissenschaftsrat (2002b), Empfehlungen zum 32. Rahmenplan für den Hochschulbau, 2003–2006, 2–5, Köln.

Wissenschaftsrat (2005), Entwicklung der Fachstudiendauer an Universitäten von 1999 bis 2003, Document 6825/05.

Wissenschaftsrat (2006), Wissenschaftsrat: www.wissenschaftsrat.de

Zivot, E. and D.W.K. Andrews (1992), Further evidence on the great crash, the oil price shock and the unit root hypothesis, *Journal of Business and Economic Statistics*, 10, 251–70.

Appendix A: DEA Models in Higher Education

The tables in this appendix display results and modeling of DEA in the higher education literature. Tables A.1 and A.2 present DEA scores of the separate models for teaching and research and indicate heterogeneity in the results. Studies in the first three tables are listed alphabetically. Then, Table A.3 highlights an overall measure of efficiency.

Finally, Table A.4 gives an overview of the ingredients for a DEA model in higher education. The focus of the analysis as well as the underlying input and output factors are in the center. The tables starts with studies focusing on teaching followed by those focusing on research and those concentrating on both teaching and research simultaneously.

Table A.1 Results of Teaching Efficiency with DEA

Author(s) (year)	Country, Institution Type, Year of Data	Efficient Units	Min Efficiency	Std. Dev. Efficiency
Alfonso and Santos (2004)	Portugal: 45 universities, faculties and institutes, 36 faculties and institutes, faculties and institutes without medical faculties, 7 medical faculties, 2001	3; 4; 3; 3; 5; 5; 1; 4; 4; 1; 1; 1; 1; 2; 2; 1; 2; 2; 1	0.04; 0.03; 0.04; 0.03; 0.02; 0.02; 0.02; 0.02; 0.00; 0.00; 0.00; 0.00; 0.04; 0.03; 0.00; 0.30; 0.14; 0.05	0.33; 0.32; 0.32; 0.31; 0.32; 0.32; 0.31; 0.23; 0.23; 0.24; 0.24; 0.31; 0.31; 0.20; 0.31; 0.31; 0.25; 0.36
Arcelus and Coleman (1997)	Canada: 32 units of a university, na	16; 17; 18	0.42; 0.43; 0.71	0.19; 0.17; 0.06
Avkiran (2001)	Australia 36 universities, 1995	12; 10	0.91; 0.15	0.03; 0.29
Beasley (1995)	UK: 52 chemistry departments, 50 physics departments, 1986/1987	3; 1	0.34; 0.32	0.15; 0.16
Breu and Raab (1994)	US: 25 top ranked universities, 1990	7	0.87	0.04
Colbert et al. (2000)	US: 24 top ranked MBA programs, 1997	16; 11; 8; 15; 13	0.95; 0.93; 0.91; 0.95; 0.94	0.01; 0.03; 0.03; 0.01; 0.02
Facanha and Marinho (1999)	Brazilia: 52 universites, 1994	5	0.00	0.25
Haksever and Muragishi (1998)	US: 40 MBA programs, 1987/1991	18; na	0.88; 0.77	0.03; 0.05
Kao (1994)	Taiwan: 11 colleges of technology, na	2; 1; 2; 3	0.82; 0.51; 0.64; 0.42	0.05; 0.13; 0.11; 0.20
Lehmann and Warning (2002)	UK: 112 universities, 1998/1999	21; 17; 11	0.48; 0.75; 0.68	0.13; 0.04; 0.09
Marinho et al. (1997)	Brazilia: 52 federal institutions of higher learning, na	16	0.77	0.08
Meyer et al. (1995)	Germany: 11 business departments of one university, na	5	0.72	0.10
Warning (2004)	Germany: 73 universities, 1999	4	0.01	0.30

Table A.2 Results of Research Efficiency with DEA

Author(s) (year)	Country, Institution Type, Year of Data	Efficient Units	Min Efficiency	Std. Dev. Efficiency
Backes-Gellner (1992)	Germany: 22 economics departments, US: 40 business departments, na	na	na	0.06; 0.10
Beasley (1995)	UK: 52 chemistry departments, 50 physics departments, 1986/1987	9; 8	0.61; 0.54	0.11; 0.12
Doyle et al. (1996)	UK: 30 business and management departments, 1988/1992	1	0.44	0.14
Johnes (1995)	UK: 60 economics departments, 1992	1; 5; 1; 3; 6; 3; 7; 4; 6	0.00; 0.17; 0.00; 0.00; 0.17; 0.00; 0.05; 0.18; 0.02	0.22; 0.22; 0.18; 0.22; 0.23; 0.22; 0.19; 0.25; 0.23
Johnes and Johnes (1993)	UK: 36 economics departments, 1984–1988	2; 6; 4	0.24; 0.15; 0.28	0.20; 0.27; 0.22
Johnes and Johnes (1995)	UK: 36 economics departments, 1989	2; 9; 7	0.18; 0.24; 0.19	0.24; 0.24; 0.27
Kocher et al. (2006)	21 OECD countries, 1990–1998	1; 3; 1; 2; 2; 3; 1; 1	0.04; 0.04; 0.04; 0.04; 0.03; 0.06; 0.03; 0.03	0.23; 0.32; 0.23; 0.31; 0.31; 0.34; 0.29; 0.34
Korhonen et al. (2001)	Finland: 18 economics departments, 1996	4; 3	0.17; 0.06	0.26; 0.31
Lehmann and Warning (2002)	UK: 112 universities, 1998/1999	15; 22; 10	0.06; 0.01; 0.01	0.18; 0.28; 0.29
Martinez Cabrera (2000)	Spain: 23 economics departments, 1994/1995	5; 5; 5; 5; 5; 6; 3	0.13; 0.13; 0.08; 0.10; 0.12; 0.25; 0.12	0.28; 0.28; 0.31; 0.29; 0.29; 0.28; 0.30
Ng and Li (2000)	China: 84 universities, 1993–1995	16; 18; 6; 16; 9; 10; 10; 4; 6	0.40; 0.45; 0.38; 0.10; 0.52; 0.38; 0.55; 0.40; 0.46	0.19; 0.17; 0.20; 0.22; 0.16; 0.19; 0.16; 0.21; 0.18

Table A.2 (continued)

Author(s)(year)	Country, Institution Type, Year of Data	Efficient Units	Min Efficiency	Std. Dev. Efficiency
Olesen and Petersen (1995)	Denmark: 18 business administration and economics departments, 1975–1986	11	0.27	0.21
Thursby (2000)	USA: 104 universities with a PhD program in economics, 1986–1993	69	0.55	0.10
Thursby and Kemp (2002)	USA: 112 universities, 1991–1996	54	0.35	0.19
Warning (2004)	Germany: 73 universities, 1999	5	0.12	0.23

172

Table A.3   Results of Overall Performance (DEA) in Higher Education

Author(s) (year)	Country, Institution Type, Year of Data	Efficient Units	Min Efficiency	Std. Dev. Efficiency
Abbott and Doucouliagos(2003)	Australia: 36 government universities, 1995	25; 13; 28; 16	0.39; 0.70; 0.74; 0.72	0.11; 0.05; 0.06; 0.05
Ahn et al. (1988)	USA: 161 doctoral granting universities, 1984/1985	13; 5; 11; 12	na	0.02; 0.03; 0.02; 0.02
Ahn et al. (1989)	USA (Texas): 33 public universities, 1981–1985	17	0.61	0.10
Athanassopoulos and Shale (1997)	UK: 45 universities, 1992/1993	3; 7; 6; 13; 4; 15; 11; 27	0.67; 0.71; 0.43; 0.54; 0.37; 0.49; 0.45; 0.49	0.10; 0.09; 0.14; 0.14; 0.18; 0.16; 0.13; 0.12
Avkiran (2001)	Australia: 36 universities, 1995	23; 13	0.40; 0.45;	0.10; 0.13
Backes-Gellner and Zanders (1989)	Germany: 17 economics departments, na	9	0.42	0.23
Bayenet and Debande (1999)	17 OECD countries, 1991	4; 6; 5; 3; 3; 7	0.33; 0.41; 0.52; 0.34; 0.23; 0.10	0.28; 0.21; 0.18; 0.23; 0.26; 0.32
Beasley (1990)	UK: 52 chemistry departments, 50 physics departments, 1986/1987	3; 1	0.81; 0.80	0.16; 0.14
Forsund and Kalhagen (1999)	Norway: 99 departments, 1994–1996	47	na	na
Johnes (1999)	UK: 99 universities, na	12	0.65	0.10
Lehmann and Warning (2002)	UK: 112 universities, 1998/1999	18	0.25; 0.28	0.22; 0.22
MacMillan and Datta (1998)	Canada: 45 universities, 1992/1993	18; 22; 27; 31; 36; 34; 15; 18; 29	0.58; 0.59; 0.51; 0.65; 0.65; 0.63; 0.54; 0.55; 0.54	0.10; 0.10; 0.10; 0.08; 0.07; 0.09; 0.12; 0.11; 0.10

Table A.3 (continued)

Author(s)(year)	Country, Institution Type, Year of Data	Efficient Units	Min Efficiency	Std. Dev. Efficiency
Madden et al. (1997)	Australia: 24 economics departments, 1987, 1991	7; 11	0.01; 0.26	0.33; 0.26
Moreno and Tadepalli (2002)	USA: 42 departments at one public university, na	23	0.30	0.17
Pesenti and Ukovich (1996)	Italy: 37 departments of one university, na	18; 36	0.48; 0.93	0.17; 0.01
Post and Spronk (1999)	UK: 50 physics departments, 1986/1987	na	na	na
Rhodes and Southwick (1993)	USA: 96 public and 54 private universities, 1979/1980	na	na	na
Sarrico and Dyson (2000)	UK: 10 departments of a university and universities, na	na	0.73	0.07
Sinuany-Stern et al. (1994)	Israel: 21 departments at one university, 1988	5; 5; 3	0.35; 0.50; 0.33	0.22; 0.19; 0.20
Tomkins and Green (1988)	UK: 20 accounting departments, na	4; 6; 10; 9; 9; 5	0.41; 0.48; 0.48; 0.56; 0.61; 0.51	0.72; 0.79; 0.90; 0.89; 0.89; 0.76
Warning (2004)	Germany: 73 universities, 1999	3; 5; 13	0.01; 0.01; 0.17	0.30; 0.27; 0.24

Table A.4   Overview of DEA Models in Higher Education

Author	Model	Focus	Input Factors	Output Factors
Alfonso and Santos (2004)	CRS, VRS, I-O, O-O	T Univ., Dep.	o Annual spending o Teachers	o Undergraduate students o Graduate students
Arcelus and Coleman (1997)	CRS, VRS, I-O	T Dep.	o FTE teachers o Support staff o Operating expenses o Library expenses	o Average enrollment per class o Average no. classes taught per department o FTE of undergraduate students in each department's program o Undergraduate students in each department's program receiving their degree in a given year o FTE of graduate students in each department's program o Graduate students in each department's program receiving their degree in a given year
Breu and Raab (1994)	CRS, I-O	T Univ.	o SAT average o Percentage of faculty with doctorates o Faculty to student ratio o Educational and general expenditures per student o Tuition charges per student	o Graduation rate o Freshmen rentention rate
Colbert et al. (2000)	VRS, I-O	T Dep.	o Faculty to student ratio o Average GMAT store of students in the program o Electives offered	*Model A:* o Average salary of graduates o Percentage of alumni who donate the money to the program o Student satisfaction with teaching,

175

Table A.4 (continued)

Author	Model	Focus	Input Factors	Output Factors
Colbert et al. (2000) (cont.)				curriculum and placement ○ Recruiter satisfaction with analytical skills, team work and global view *Model B:* ○ Percentage of alumni who donate the money to the program ○ Student satisfaction with teaching, curriculum and placement *Model C:* ○ Average salary of graduates ○ Recruiter satisfaction with analytical skills, team work and graduates' global view *Model D:* ○ Percentage of alumni who donate the money to the program ○ Student satisfaction with teaching, curriculum and placement *Model E:* ○ Average salary of graduates ○ Recruiter satisfaction with analytical skills, team work and graduates' global view
Haksever and Muragishi (1995)	CRS, I-O	T Dep.	○ Average GMAT score of entering students ○ Average grade points average of entering students ○ Average age of entering students ○ Acceptance rate ○ Tuition cost for the program ○ Publications by the academic staff (index) ○ Percentage of students with work experience ○ Percentage of academic staff with PhD degree or equivalent	○ Average starting salary ○ Percentage of students who have a job by graduation ○ Gourman score, an index indicating program quality

Table A.4 (continued)

Author	Model	Focus	Input Factors	Output Factors
Marinho et al. (1997)	VRS, I-O	T Univ.	o Area of buildings o Area of hospitals o Area of laboratories o Total number of students o Academic staff with doctoral degree o Academic staff with master degree o Academic staff with specialization degree o Academic staff with undergraduate degree o Academic staff of second and first degree teaching o Administrative personnel at support level o Administrative personnel with high school background o Administrative personnel with undergraduate degree or higher o Budget for current expenses o Incoming students at undergraduate level o Incoming medical residents	o Undergraduate courses o Graduate courses (master degree level) o Graduate courses (doctoral degree level) o Undergraduate degree certificates o Medical school certificates o Masters' thesis approved o Weighted average of evaluation of master degree courses o Weighted average of evaluation of doctoral degree courses
Meyer et al. (1995)	CRS, I-O	T Dep.	o Hours taught o Secretaries	o Lecture rating o Tutorial rating o Rating for service at the chair o Exams in 93/94 o Oral exams in 93/94 o Diploma theses in 93/94
Backes-Gellner (1992)	CRS, O-O	R Dep.	o Senior faculty members o Junior faculty members and lectures	o Monographies o Edited books o Articles in edited books o Journal articles, quality weighted

Table A.4 (continued)

Author	Model	Focus	Input Factors	Output Factors
Doyle et al. (1996)	CRS, O-O	R Dep.	na	na
Johnes (1995)	CRS, VRS, I-I	R Dep.	o Academic staff on the institution's payroll o Academic staff, externally funded o Short works	o Articles in academic journals o Income from research council grants o Authored books
Johnes (1999)	CRS, I-O	R Univ.	na	na
Johnes and Johnes (1993)	CRS, I-O, O-O	R Dep.	o Research and teaching staff o Teaching staff o Grants per capita	o Papers in academic journals o Letters in academic journals o Authored books o Contributions to edited works o Papers or communications in 'core' journals o Grants
Johnes and Johnes (1995)	CRS, I-O, O-O	R Dep.	o Research and teaching faculty o Per capita value of external research grants o Time available for research o Research faculties	o Papers and letters in core economic journals o Papers in academic journals o Letters in academic journals o Articles in professional journals o Authored books o Edited books o Published official reports o Contributions to edited works
Kocher et al. (2006)	CRS, VRS, O-O	R Coun.	o Population o R&D expenditures o Number of universities	o Papers in top-journals 1990–1998
Korhonen et al. (2001)	VRS, O-O	R Dep.	o 1000 Fmk per month	o Articles in referred journals o Scientific books o Citations

Table A.4 (continued)

Author	Model	Focus	Input Factors	Output Factors
Korhonen et al. (2000) (cont.)				o Papers in conference proceedings o Conference presentations o Citations by other researchers o Foreign coauthors o Doctoral degrees produced o Doctoral students supervised o Memberships in editorial books o Edited books and journals o Service as an expert o Conferences organized (groups)
Martinez and Cabrera (2000)	CRS, O-O	R Dep.	o Professors o Non-academic staff o Books o Thesis	o International articles o National articles
Olesen and Petersen (1995)	CRS, I-O	R Dep.	o Full professors o Associate and assistant professors o Research fellows	o Books o Articles published in Danish o Articles published in foreign languages o Working papers
Thursby (2000)	VRS, O-O	R Dep.	o Private or public university o Faculty size o Federal grant years o Library expenditure o Ratio of the number of economics faculty per 100 undergraduate students at the university o Median time to complete the PhD over the period 1986–1992	o Recent publications o Citation data (1988–1992) o PhDs awarded (1986–1992)

179

Table A.4 (continued)

Author	Model	Focus	Input Factors	Output Factors
Thursby and Kemp (2002)	VRS, O-O	R Univ.	o Professionals employed o Federal support o Total faculty (biological sciences, engineering, physical sciences) o Quality rating in the PhD granting departments of program area (biological sciences, engineering, physical sciences) o Ratio of the number of economics faculty per 100 undergraduate students at the university	o Licenses executed o Amount of industry sponsored research o New patent applications o Invention disclosures o Amount of royalties received
Abbott and Doucouliagos (2003)	CRS, VRS, I-O	T&R Univ.	o Academic staff (FTE) o Non-academic staff (FTE) degrees enrolled o Expenditure on all other inputs other than labor o Value of non-current assets	o FTE students o Graduate and undergraduate o Graduate degrees conferred o Undergraduate degrees conferred o Research quantum allocation o Research grant o Research spending
Ahn et al. (1988)	CRS, I-O	T&R Univ.	o Instructional expenditures o Physical expenditures o Overhead expenditures	o Undergraduates o Graduates o Federal research grants and contracts
Ahn et al. (1989)	VRS, I-O	T&R Univ.	o Total faculty salaries o State funds appropriated for research o Overhead expenditures o Total investment in physical plants	o Undergraduate enrollments o Graduate enrollments o Total semester credit hours generated o Amount of federal government and private research funds
Athanassopoulos and Shale (1997)	CRS, VRS,	T&R Univ.	o General academic expenditure o Research income	o Successful leavers o Higher degrees awarded

Table A.4 (continued)

Author	Model	Focus	Input Factors	Output Factors
Athanassopoulos and Shale (1997) (cont.)	I-O, O-O		○ Research income ○ FTE graduates ○ FTE undergraduates ○ FTE academic staff ○ Mean A-level entry score over the last three years ○ Tuition charges per student	○ Weighed research rating
Backes-Gellner and Zanders (1989)	CRS, O-O	T&R Dep.	○ Full professors ○ Academic staff ○ Non-academic staff ○ Students ○ Average study duration	○ Exams ○ Dissertations ○ Publication index
Bayenet and Debande (1999)	I-O	T&R Coun.	○ Permanent expenditure on education ○ Research expenditure on teaching ○ Diplomas	○ Students ○ Diplomas ○ Percentage of academics in the labor market ○ Weighed number of publications ○ Expenditure of research for secondary education
Beasley (1995)	CRS, I-O	T&R Dep.	○ General expenditure (salaries) ○ Equipment expenditure ○ Research income	○ Undergraduates ○ Graduates taught ○ Graduates doing research ○ Research income ○ Research rating dummy (star, A+, A, A−)
Beasley (1990)	AR, CRS, I-O	T&R Dep.	○ General expenditure (salaries) ○ Equipment expenditure ○ Research income	○ Undergraduates ○ Graduates taught ○ Graduates doing research ○ Research income ○ Research rating dummy (star, A+, A, A−)

181

Table A.4 (continued)

Author	Model	Focus	Input Factors	Output Factors
Forsund and Kalhagen (1999)	VRS, I-O	T&R Dep.	○ Academic staff ○ Administrative staff ○ Net operating expenses ○ Building size ○ FTE undergraduates	○ Short studies leavers ○ Long studies ○ Research publications
Kao (1994)	CRS, I-O	T&R Dep.	no inputs	○ Instructors degree, publication, position ○ Curriculum (companies, instructor-student ratio) ○ Equipment(expenditures past score) ○ Administration (more or less than one workshop)
MacMillan and Datta (1998)	CRS O-O	T&R Univ.	○ Full time faculty ○ Full time faculty eligible for grants ○ Full time faculty eligible for Canadian grants ○ Total expenditure less faculty salaries and benefits ○ Total operating expenditure and sponsored research expenditure	○ FTE undergraduates ○ FTE undergrad sciences ○ FTE undergrad other than science ○ Graduates ○ FTE graduate in master program ○ FTE graduate in doctoral steam program ○ Total sponsored research expenditure ○ Active grants Canada council ○ Active MRC grants
Madden et al. (1997)	CRS, I-O	T&R Dep.	○ Staff	○ Publications in core journals ○ Publications in other journals ○ Books ○ Edited books ○ Undergraduates ○ Graduates
Moreno and Tadepalli (2002)	CRS, O-O	T&R Dep.	○ Faculty salaries ○ Staff salaries	○ Graduate majors ○ Ungraduate majors

Table A.4 (continued)

Author	Model	Focus	Input Factors	Output Factors
Moreno and Tadepalli (2002) (cont.)			o Operational budget o Equipment budget o Building space allocated to each academic unit	o FTE produced o Student credit hours generated o Amount of grants awarded
Ng and Li (2000)	CRS, O-O	T&R Univ.	o Researchers o Research supporting staff o In-budget funds o Out-budget funds	o Manuscripts o Articles o Recognized research output o Contracts o Prices
Pesenti and Ukovich (1996)	CRS, VRS, I-O, O-O FDH,	T&R Dep.	o Salaries o Ordinary funds	o Exams o Courses o International papers o Other papers o Research funds
Post and Spronk (1999)	VRS, I-O	T&R Dep.	o Amount of general expenditure o Amount of equipment expenditure	o Amount of research income o Undergraduate students o Graduate students on taught courses o Graduate students doing research o University Grant Committee research rating
Rhodes and Southwick (1993)	na	T&R Univ.	o Full professors o Associate professors o Assistant professors and other teachers o Dollars spent annually on maintenance o Dollars spent annually on library activities	o Undergraduate enrollment o Graduate enrollment o Bachelors degrees awarded o Masters degrees awarded o Doctoral degrees awarded o Research funds secured
Sarrico and Dyson (2000)	CRS, O-O,	T&R Dep.	o 10 nominal variables for each department	o Teaching rating o Proportion of students from the department

Table A.4 (continued)

Author	Model	Focus	Input Factors	Output Factors
Sarrico and Dyson (2000) (cont.)	AR			taking employment of further study o Proportion of students in residential accommodation o Library spending o 'Cheapness' of living
Sinuany-Stern et al. (1994)	CRS, O-O	T&R Dep.	o Operational expenditures o Faculty salaries o Direct departmental operational costs o Departments share in its school's operational costs o Teaching services given by other departments	o Grant money o Publications o Graduate students (head count) o Credit hours given by the department (hours) o Income from tuition fees o Overhead from external grants o Teaching services given to other departments o Other incomes
Tomkins and Green (1988)	CRS, I-O	T&R Dep.	o Staff numbers o Non-staff expenditure o Academic salaries	o Undergraduates o Research graduates o Taught graduates o Total research income (research council income, other, research income, other income) o Publications
Avkiran (2001)	CRS, VRS, I-O	T, T&R Univ.	o Academic staff o Non-academic staff	o Overall enrollment o Undergraduate enrollment o Graduate enrollment o Research quantum o Educational services o Student retention rate o Student progress rate

Table A.4 (continued)

Author	Model	Focus	Input Factors	Output Factors
Avkiran (2001) (cont.)				o Graduate full-time employment rate o Fee-paying enrollment o Overseas fee-paying enrollment o Non-overseas fee-paying graduate enrollments
Lehmann and Warning (2002)	VRS, O-O	T, R, T&R Univ.	o Researchers o Teachers o Library spending o Research grants (1997 and 98)	o SCI papers o SSCI papers o Research grants (1998 and 99) o Undergraduates o Graduates o Graduation rate o Employment rate o 2:1 First (%) o A-level points
Warning (2004)	CRS, O-O	T, R, T&R Univ.	o Expenditure on personal o Academic salaries	o Graduates taught o Total research income (research council income, other, research income, other income) o Publications

CRS: Constant Returns to Scale, VRS: Variable Returns to Scale, T: Teaching, R: Research, T&R: Teaching&Research, FTE: Full Time Equivalents, na: not available, no.: number of, I-O: input-orientation, O-O: output-orientation, Dep.: Department, Univ.: University, Coun.: Country

Appendix B: Individual DEA Scores of Universities

This table shows the DEA scores for all models (*TR1*, *TR2*, *TR3*, *TR4*) for the single universities. The last column shows the mean over the four models and can be interpreted as an overall value.

Table B.1 Individual DEA-Scores of Universities

Name of the University	*TR1*	*TR2*	*TR3*	*TR4*	Overall
Brandenburgische TU Cottbus	57.57	44.89	62.62	54.05	54.78
Europa-U Viadrina Frankfurt (Oder)	96.94	100.00	96.78	97.60	97.83
FU Berlin	78.89	92.71	91.27	92.23	88.77
GH Kassel	76.95	77.27	83.00	87.74	81.24
Humboldt-Universität Berlin	63.55	56.86	60.25	58.23	59.72
TH Aachen	97.95	89.17	89.93	85.96	90.75
TU Bergakademie Freiberg	62.70	50.92	27.49	26.21	41.83
TU Berlin	83.62	83.92	87.08	87.05	85.42
TU Braunschweig	68.85	67.77	70.31	67.07	68.50
TU Chemnitz	47.48	33.29	30.58	31.16	35.63
TU Clausthal	100.00	100.00	100.00	99.98	100.00
TU Darmstadt	91.24	89.45	89.64	88.89	89.81
TU Dresden	60.24	56.07	58.86	60.49	58.91
TU Hamburg-Harburg	70.86	65.10	97.53	82.38	78.97
TU Ilmenau	44.18	55.20	47.48	47.44	48.58
TU München	98.29	98.31	98.75	99.20	98.63
U Augsburg	90.83	90.35	91.19	91.19	90.89
U Bamberg	96.85	96.90	96.97	97.43	97.03
U Bayreuth	98.79	96.95	98.61	98.56	98.23
U Bielefeld	98.02	97.81	99.29	98.05	98.29
U Bochum	97.24	94.93	99.49	95.85	96.87
U Bonn	84.37	88.64	97.86	97.89	92.19
U Bremen	92.94	77.92	75.24	74.52	80.16
U des Saarlandes Saarbrücken	72.92	76.50	74.12	74.32	74.46
U Dortmund	85.40	85.40	92.06	98.24	90.27
U Düsseldorf	77.80	80.29	87.40	85.70	82.80
U Erlangen-Nürnberg	78.06	77.42	76.93	76.76	77.29
U Frankfurt a.M.	72.75	73.12	75.40	72.88	73.54
U Freiburg i.Br.	78.57	84.79	89.92	86.91	85.04
U Gießen	78.97	79.32	90.27	85.36	83.48
U Göttingen	75.88	79.69	80.12	78.29	78.49
U Greifswald	28.18	31.95	34.96	33.43	32.13

Table B.1 *(continued)*

Name of the University	*TR1*	*TR2*	*TR3*	*TR4*	Overall
U Halle	36.91	36.83	35.88	36.06	36.42
U Hamburg	73.42	75.60	75.25	72.91	74.30
U Hannover	95.79	94.74	98.05	94.21	95.70
U Heidelberg	86.97	96.52	96.44	88.47	92.10
U Hildesheim	85.97	89.05	94.92	93.57	90.88
U Jena	42.99	44.16	49.37	49.10	46.40
U Kaiserslautern	93.42	93.18	94.48	92.50	93.39
U Karlsruhe	96.14	94.83	95.49	94.93	95.35
U Kiel	72.57	77.39	77.65	78.20	76.45
U Koblenz-Landau	90.89	92.06	91.57	93.23	91.94
U Köln	98.31	98.31	100.00	100.00	99.16
U Konstanz	99.78	99.02	99.65	100.00	99.61
U Leipzig	49.16	50.55	57.26	56.82	53.45
U Lüneburg	97.21	97.04	100.00	100.00	98.56
U Magdeburg	25.78	29.85	37.48	40.62	33.43
U Mainz	75.80	78.53	76.52	79.97	77.70
U Mannheim	91.15	96.18	98.68	96.81	95.71
U Marburg	70.48	79.84	89.34	88.71	82.09
U München	100.00	100.00	100.00	100.00	100.00
U Münster	93.32	93.54	93.50	97.38	94.43
U Oldenburg	77.14	88.44	84.25	78.20	82.01
U Osnabrück	93.05	94.99	97.49	97.75	95.82
U Passau	83.32	84.80	84.88	82.88	83.97
U Potsdam	71.57	71.57	74.16	94.51	77.95
U Regensburg	75.22	76.59	77.18	76.05	76.26
U Rostock	36.24	36.67	38.16	35.57	36.66
U Stuttgart	96.97	86.82	92.57	85.94	90.58
U Trier	98.04	87.85	95.57	96.19	94.41
U Tübingen	80.18	86.26	90.00	88.26	86.17
U Ulm	99.10	98.67	100.00	100.00	99.44
U Würzburg	85.24	89.27	90.70	93.32	89.63
U-GH Duisburg	56.81	59.14	56.88	57.91	57.68
U-GH Essen	65.99	67.22	68.25	66.59	67.01
U-GH Paderborn	95.35	94.93	95.94	76.01	90.55
U-GH Siegen	62.85	64.79	66.29	59.97	63.48
U-GH Wuppertal	64.87	66.65	66.16	61.66	64.83

Appendix C: Coefficients for Teaching and Research Quality

These figures display the coefficients of several quantile regressions for teaching quality and research quality with inefficiency from the different models (*TR2*, *TR3*, *TR4*) being the endogenous variable. The left-hand side graph shows the coefficients for research quality while the right-hand side graphs the coefficients of the teaching quality.

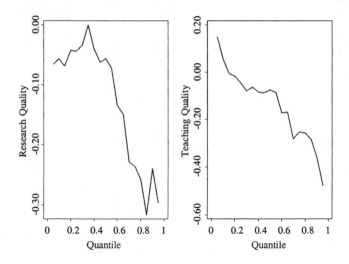

Figure C.1   Coefficients for Teaching and Research Quality in TR2 *Model*

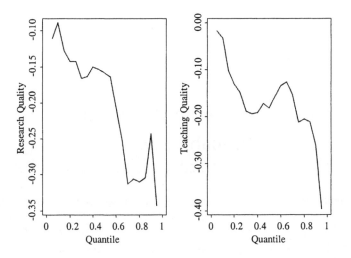

Figure C.2 Coefficients for Teaching and Research Quality in TR3 Model

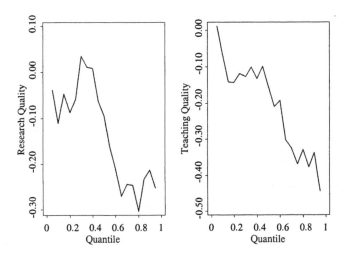

Figure C.3 Coefficients for Teaching and Research Quality in TR4 Model

Appendix D: Graph of Predicted Probabilities

These figures show the conditional effects of teaching quality and research quality using different grouping mechanisms. The left-hand graph shows the conditional predicted probabilities for the different models (*TR2*, *TR3*, *TR4*) under the Zivot-Andrews test. The right-hand side graph shows the predicted probabilities when when all variables, except for teaching quality, are set to their mean. Bold lines show predicted probabilities when all variables except for research quality are set to their mean.

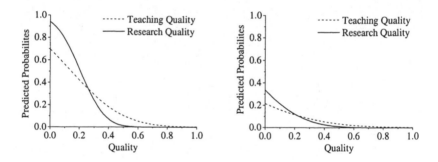

Figure D.1   Graph of Predicted Probabilities for Model TR2

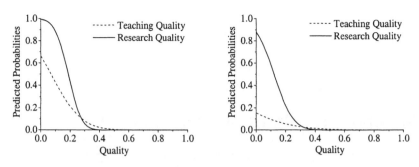

Figure D.2   Graph of Predicted Probabilities for Model TR3

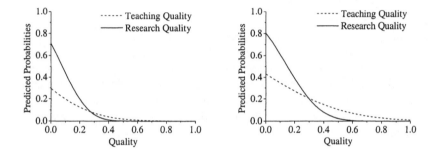

Figure D.3   Graph of Predicted Probabilities for Model TR4

Appendix E: Proof of Proposition 1

Proof.
The proof of Proposition 1 proceeds in three steps. After proving (1.1) and (1.2) the third part (1.3) follows immediately. Different cases of research dominance and teaching dominance are discussed.

Research Dominance

Comparative research dominance. The best response of university 1 is $r_1 = \underline{r}$ and $t_1 = \bar{t}$. According to Table 5.2 the performance of university 1 increases, when r_1 becomes smaller and when t_1 becomes larger. The conditions for region A are checked by inserting the optimal values into the conditions summarized in Table 5.2 presenting the unilateral incentives for the universities. It always holds that $(\bar{t} - \underline{t}) \leq (\bar{r} - \underline{r})$ as $(\bar{r} - \underline{r}) > 0$, is always true under comparative research dominance. This leads to a performance of university 1 of

$$P_1^* \left(\underline{r}, \bar{t}; \bar{r}, \bar{t} \right) = \frac{1}{9} \left(\bar{r} - \underline{r} \right). \tag{E.1}$$

Absolute research dominance, region A. In region A university 1's best response is the same as under comparative research dominance, i.e., $r_1 = \underline{r}$ and $t_1 = \bar{t}$. The condition $(\bar{t} - \underline{t}) \geq -1/2(\bar{r} - \underline{r})$ holds as $(\bar{r} - \underline{r}) > 0$ is always true. It thus results in the same performance

$$P_1^{**} \left(\underline{r}, \bar{t}; \bar{r}, \bar{t} \right) = \frac{1}{9} \left(\bar{r} - \underline{r} \right). \tag{E.2}$$

Absolute research dominance, region B. In region B under absolute research dominance the best response for university 1 is $r_1 = \underline{r}$ and $t_1 = \underline{t}$ as long as $(\bar{t} - \underline{t}) \in [1/2(\bar{r} - \underline{r}), (\bar{r} - \underline{r})]$. Then performance of university 1 is

$$P_1^{***} \left(\underline{r}, \underline{t}; \bar{r}, \bar{t} \right) = \frac{1}{16} \sqrt{-2 \left(\bar{r} - \underline{r} \right) \left(\underline{t} - \bar{t} \right)} \tag{E.3}$$

if $1/2 \left(\bar{r} - \underline{r} \right) \leq \left(\bar{t} - \underline{t} \right) \leq \left(\bar{r} - \underline{r} \right)$. If $(\bar{t} - \underline{t}) < 1/2(\bar{r} - \underline{r})$ university 1 chooses $r_1 = \underline{r}$ and $t_1 = \bar{t} - 1/2(\bar{r} - \underline{r})$. This combination results in a performance of

$$P_1^{***} \left(\underline{r}, \bar{t} - \frac{1}{2} \left(\bar{r} - \underline{r} \right); \bar{r}, \bar{t} \right) = \frac{1}{16} \left(\bar{r} - \underline{r} \right), \text{ if } \left(\bar{t} - \underline{t} \right) \leq \frac{1}{2} \left(\bar{r} - \underline{r} \right). \tag{E.4}$$

Teaching Dominance

Comparative teaching dominance. The best response for university 1 is $r_1 = \bar{r}$ and $t_1 = \bar{t}$. By inserting the optimal replies, the strongest condition of Table 5.2 always holds as $(\bar{t} - \underline{t}) \geq (\bar{r} - \underline{r})$. This leads to a performance of university 1 of

$$P_1^\dagger\left(\bar{r}, \bar{t}; \bar{r}, \bar{t}\right) = \lim_{(t_1 - t_2) \to 0} \left[\frac{1}{(t_1 - t_2)} \left(-\frac{1}{6}(\bar{r} - \bar{r}) + \frac{2}{3}(t_1 - t_2) \right)^2 \right] \quad \text{(E.5)}$$

$$= 0.$$

Absolute teaching dominance, region A. In region A the best response for university 1 is $r_1 = \bar{r}$ and $t_1 = \underline{t}$. The condition from region A is fulfilled because $(\underline{t} - \bar{t}) \leq -2(\bar{r} - \underline{r})$ is always true as $(\underline{t} - \bar{t}) < 0$ under absolute teaching dominance. Performance is then given by

$$P_1^{\dagger\dagger}\left(\bar{r}, \underline{t}; \bar{r}, \bar{t}\right) = \frac{1}{9}\left(\bar{t} - \underline{t}\right). \quad \text{(E.6)}$$

Absolute teaching dominance, region B. In region B under absolute teaching dominance the best response for university 1 is $r_1 = \bar{r} - (\bar{t} - \underline{t})$ and $t_1 = \underline{t}$ as long as $(\bar{t} - \underline{t}) \leq (\bar{r} - \underline{r})$. Inserting the best response values into the strongest condition from Table 5.2, it turns out that $-(\bar{t} - \underline{t}) \leq (\underline{t} - \bar{t}) \leq -1/2(\bar{t} - \underline{t})$ which is always true. As $(\underline{t} \leq \bar{t})$, this inequality always holds which leads to a performance for university 1 of

$$P_1^{\dagger\dagger\dagger}\left(\bar{r} - (\bar{t} - \underline{t}), \underline{t}; \bar{r}, \bar{t}\right) = \frac{1}{16}\sqrt{2}\left(\bar{t} - \underline{t}\right), \text{ if } (\bar{t} - \underline{t}) \leq (\bar{r} - \underline{r}). \quad \text{(E.7)}$$

Comparison of the Performance Levels

This paragraph identifies the best of the best responses of university 1, where the criterion for the 'best best reply' is performance. Comparing performance levels of the best responses in this way leads to the best best reply of university 1. Under research dominance, it turns out that

$$P_1^*\left(\underline{r}, \bar{t}; \bar{r}, \bar{t}\right) = P_1^{**}\left(\underline{r}, \bar{t}; \bar{r}, \bar{t}\right) = \frac{1}{9}\left(\bar{r} - \underline{r}\right)$$

$$> \frac{1}{16}\left(\bar{r} - \underline{r}\right)$$

$$= P_1^{***}\left(\underline{r}, \bar{t} - \frac{1}{2}(\bar{r} - \underline{r}); \bar{r}, \bar{t}\right), \text{ if } (\bar{t} - \underline{t}) \leq \frac{1}{2}(\bar{r} - \underline{r}).$$

$$\text{(E.8)}$$

Comparing performance levels of the best responses leads to the best best reply and identifies the valid region.

$$P_1^* \left(\underline{r}, \overline{t}; \overline{r}, \overline{t} \right) = P_1^{**} \left(\underline{r}, \overline{t}; \overline{r}, \overline{t} \right) = \frac{1}{9} \left(\overline{r} - \underline{r} \right)$$

$$> \frac{1}{16} \sqrt{-2 \left(\overline{r} - \underline{r} \right) \left(\underline{t} - \overline{t} \right)} = P_1^{***} \left(\underline{r}, \underline{t}; \overline{r}, \overline{t} \right)$$

$$\Leftrightarrow \left(\overline{t} - \underline{t} \right) \leq \frac{128}{81} \left(\overline{r} - \underline{r} \right), \tag{E.9}$$

$$\text{if } \frac{1}{2} \left(\overline{r} - \underline{r} \right) \leq \left(\overline{t} - \underline{t} \right) \leq \left(\overline{r} - \underline{r} \right)$$

Consequently, under the assumption $\left(\overline{t} - \underline{t} \right) \leq \left(\overline{r} - \underline{r} \right)$ the maximum performance is achieved with $P_1^* \left(\underline{r}, \overline{t}; \overline{r}, \overline{t} \right) = P_1^{**} \left(\underline{r}, \overline{t}; \overline{r}, \overline{t} \right) = 1/9 \left(\overline{r} - \underline{r} \right)$. Furthermore, for the ordering of performance levels under teaching dominance, it can be stated that

$$P_1^{\dagger\dagger} \left(\overline{r}, \underline{t}; \overline{r}, \overline{t} \right) = \frac{1}{9} \left(\overline{t} - \underline{t} \right)$$

$$> \frac{1}{16} \sqrt{2} \left(\overline{t} - \underline{t} \right) = P_1^{\dagger\dagger\dagger} \left(\overline{r} - \left(\overline{t} - \underline{t} \right); \overline{r}, \overline{t} \right)$$

$$> P_1^{\dagger} \left(\overline{r}, \overline{t}; \overline{r}, \overline{t} \right) = 0.$$

To identify the maximum performance level, conditions need to be found which reveal the relation between $P_1^* \left(\underline{r}, \overline{t}; \overline{r}, \overline{t} \right) = P_1^{**} \left(\underline{r}, \overline{t}; \overline{r}, \overline{t} \right)$ and $P_1^{\dagger\dagger} \left(\overline{r}, \underline{t}; \overline{r}, \overline{t} \right)$. The maximum performance level is at $P_1^* \left(\underline{r}, \overline{t}; \overline{r}, \overline{t} \right) = P_1^{**} \left(\underline{r}, \overline{t}; \overline{r}, \overline{t} \right)$ under the following condition:

$$P_1^* \left(\underline{r}, \overline{t}; \overline{r}, \overline{t} \right) = P_1^{**} \left(\underline{r}, \overline{t}; \overline{r}, \overline{t} \right) = \frac{1}{9} \left(\overline{r} - \underline{r} \right)$$

$$> \frac{1}{9} \left(\overline{t} - \underline{t} \right) = P_1^{\dagger\dagger} \left(\overline{r}, \underline{t}; \overline{r}, \overline{t} \right)$$

$$\Leftrightarrow \left(\overline{r} - \underline{r} \right) > \left(\overline{t} - \underline{t} \right) \tag{E.10}$$

$P_1^{**} \left(\underline{r}, \overline{t}; \overline{r}, \overline{t} \right) = P_1^* \left(\underline{r}, \overline{t}; \overline{r}, \overline{t} \right)$, the performance under absolute research dominance in region A and under comparative research dominance, is highest if the condition $\left(\overline{t} - \underline{t} \right) < \left(\overline{r} - \underline{r} \right)$ holds. If university 2 chooses $r_2 = \overline{r}$ and $t_2 = \overline{t}$, then the best reply of university 1 is to choose $r_1 = \underline{r}$ and $t_1 = \overline{t}$ if $\left(\overline{t} - \underline{t} \right) < \left(\overline{r} - \underline{r} \right)$. This proves (1.1) from proposition 1.

To find the best reply of university 2, assume now that university 1 chooses $r_1 = \underline{r}$ and $t_1 = \overline{t}$. We then identify the best best response of university 2, given the choice of university 1. Additionally, we examine, whether $(r_1, t_1; r_2, t_2) = \left(\underline{r}, \overline{t}; \overline{r}, \overline{t} \right)$ is a Nash equilibrium.

Research Dominance

Comparative research dominance. The best response of university 2 is $r_2 = \overline{r}$ and $t_2 = \overline{t}$. The condition from Table 5.2 always holds after inserting the optimal values for teaching and research quality because $\left(\overline{t} - \overline{t} \right) \leq \left(\overline{r} - \overline{r} \right)$.

This leads to a performance of university 2 of

$$P_2^* \left(\underline{r}, \bar{t}; \bar{r}, \bar{t} \right) = \frac{4}{9} \left(\bar{r} - \underline{r} \right). \tag{E.11}$$

Absolute research dominance, region A. In region A the best response for university 2 is $r_2 = \bar{r}$ and $t_2 = \bar{t}$. The condition always holds as $\left(\bar{t} - \bar{t} \right) \leq -2 \left(\bar{r} - \bar{r} \right)$ is always true. This optimal response thus results in the same performance as under comparative research dominance

$$P_2^{**} \left(\underline{r}, \bar{t}; \bar{r}, \bar{t} \right) = P_2^* \left(\underline{r}, \bar{t}; \bar{r}, \bar{t} \right) = \frac{4}{9} \left(\bar{r} - \underline{r} \right). \tag{E.12}$$

Absolute research dominance, region B. In region A under absolute research dominance the best response for university 2 is $r_2 = \underline{r}$ and $t_2 = \bar{t}$ as a result of the inequality conditions from Table 5.2. These conditions always hold as $- \left(\underline{r} - \underline{r} \right) \leq \left(\bar{t} - \bar{t} \right) \leq -1/2 \left(\underline{r} - \underline{r} \right)$ is true. Then performance of university 2 is

$$P_2^{***} \left(\underline{r}, \bar{t}; \underline{r}, \bar{t} \right) = 0. \tag{E.13}$$

Teaching Dominance

Comparative teaching dominance. The best response for university 2 is $r_2 = \bar{r}$ and $t_2 = \underline{t}$ as long as $(t_1 - t_2) \geq (r_2 - r_1)$. This condition always holds because of comparative teaching dominance. Performance is maximized, when the relation holds with equality. This leads to a performance of university 2 of

$$P_2^{\dagger} \left(\underline{r}, \bar{t}; \bar{r}, \underline{t} \right) = \frac{1}{\left(\bar{t} - \underline{t} \right)} \left(\frac{1}{6} \left(\bar{r} - \underline{r} \right) + \frac{1}{3} \left(\bar{t} - \underline{t} \right) \right)^2$$

$$= \frac{1}{4} \left(\bar{t} - \underline{t} \right) = \frac{1}{4} \left(\bar{r} - \underline{r} \right). \tag{E.14}$$

Absolute teaching dominance, region A. In region A the best response for university 2 is $r_2 = \underline{r}$ and $t_2 = \bar{t}$, as the condition from Table 5.2 must be fulfilled. It always holds because $\left(\bar{t} - \bar{t} \right) \leq -2 \left(\underline{r} - \underline{r} \right)$. This results in the limit in zero performance

$$P_2^{\dagger\dagger} \left(\underline{r}, \bar{t}; \underline{r}, \bar{t} \right) = 0. \tag{E.15}$$

Absolute teaching dominance, region B. In region B under absolute teaching dominance the best response for university 2 is $r_2 = \underline{r}$ and $t_2 = \bar{t}$ under the condition $\left(\bar{t} - \underline{t} \right) \leq \left(\bar{r} - \underline{r} \right)$. Again, the optimal response of university 2 is driven by the inequalities from Table 5.2. Performance then is

$$P_2^{\dagger\dagger\dagger} \left(\underline{r}, \bar{t}; \underline{r}, \bar{t} \right) = 0. \tag{E.16}$$

Comparison of the Performance Levels

Now, the best of the best replies of university 2 are identified by comparing the performance levels of the best responses. Under research dominance, it turns out that

$$P_2^* \left(\underline{r}, \bar{t}; \bar{r}, \bar{t} \right) = P_2^{**} \left(\underline{r}, \bar{t}; \bar{r}, \bar{t} \right) = \frac{4}{9} \left(\bar{r} - \underline{r} \right) > P_2^{***} \left(\underline{r}, \bar{t}; \underline{r}, \bar{t} \right) = 0. \quad \text{(E.17)}$$

Consequently, the maximum performance is achieved with

$$P_2^* \left(\underline{r}, \bar{t}; \bar{r}, \bar{t} \right) = P_2^{**} \left(\underline{r}, \bar{t}; \bar{r}, \bar{t} \right) = \frac{4}{9} \left(\bar{r} - \underline{r} \right).$$

Furthermore, for the ordering of performance levels under teaching dominance we find

$$P_2^{\dagger\dagger} \left(\underline{r}, \bar{t}; \underline{r}, \bar{t} \right) = \frac{1}{4} \left(\bar{r} - \underline{r} \right) > P_2^{\dagger\dagger\dagger} \left(\underline{r}, \bar{t}; \underline{r}, \bar{t} \right) = P_2^{\dagger} \left(\underline{r}, \bar{t}; \bar{r}, \underline{t} \right) = 0. \quad \text{(E.18)}$$

The maximum performance under absolute teaching dominance is in region A.

To identify the maximum performance level, conditions must be found which reveal the relation between $P_2^* \left(\underline{r}, \bar{t}; \bar{r}, \bar{t} \right) = P_2^{**} \left(\underline{r}, \bar{t}; \bar{r}, \bar{t} \right)$ and $P_2^{\dagger\dagger} \left(\underline{r}, \bar{t}; \underline{r}, \bar{t} \right)$. For $P_2^* \left(\underline{r}, \bar{t}; \bar{r}, \bar{t} \right) = P_2^{**} \left(\underline{r}, \bar{t}; \bar{r}, \bar{t} \right)$, the maximum performance level, we need:

$$P_2^* \left(\underline{r}, \bar{t}; \bar{r}, \bar{t} \right) = P_2^{**} \left(\underline{r}, \bar{t}; \bar{r}, \bar{t} \right) = \frac{4}{9} \left(\bar{r} - \underline{r} \right) > \frac{1}{4} \left(\bar{r} - \underline{r} \right) = P_2^{\dagger\dagger} \left(\underline{r}, \bar{t}; \underline{r}, \bar{t} \right)$$

Consequently, $P_2^* \left(\underline{r}, \bar{t}; \bar{r}, \bar{t} \right) = P_2^{**} \left(\underline{r}, \bar{t}; \bar{r}, \bar{t} \right)$, performance under absolute research dominance in region A and under comparative research dominance, is the maximum performance. University 2 chooses $r_2 = \bar{r}$ and $t_2 = \bar{t}$ as best reply with the highest performance, if university 1 chooses $r_1 = \underline{r}$ and $t_1 = \bar{t}$ under the condition $\left(\bar{t} - \underline{t} \right) < \left(\bar{r} - \underline{r} \right)$. Under these conditions, $r_2 = \bar{r}$ and $t_2 = \bar{t}$ is the best best response of university 2. This proves (1.2) of proposition 1.

To sum up, after selection of the best response based on performance, if university 2 chooses $r_2 = \bar{r}$ and $t_2 = \bar{t}$, then university 1 locates at $r_1 = \underline{r}$ and $t_1 = \bar{t}$ as long as $\left(\bar{t} - \underline{t} \right) < \left(\bar{r} - \underline{r} \right)$ holds.

If university 1 chooses $r_1 = \underline{r}$ and $t_1 = \bar{t}$, then university 2 chooses $r_2 = \bar{r}$ and $t_2 = \bar{t}$ as long as $\left(\bar{t} - \underline{t} \right) < \left(\bar{r} - \underline{r} \right)$ holds. Consequently, $(r_1, t_1; r_2, t_2) = \left(\underline{r}, \bar{t}; \bar{r}, \bar{t} \right)$ is a subgame perfect Nash equilibrium which is stated in (1.3) of Proposition 1. This concludes the proof of Proposition 1. ∎

Index